TEACHING FOR CHANGE

Addressing Issues of Difference
in the College Classroom

Edited by

KATHRYN GEISMAR AND GUITELE NICOLEAU

REPRINT SERIES NO. 25 • HARVARD EDUCATIONAL REVIEW

Contents

Introduction

Anger, prejudice, and discrimination have been endemic on college campuses for many years. As the differences that divide students seem to overshadow the commonalities that join them, professors and college administrators have tried to grapple with the real and painful issues of difference that underlie the anger and hatred. Classes, courses, and workshops have sprung up on college campuses throughout the United States and Canada in which educators are attempting to articulate, understand, and respect difference while working and living together.

In this book, we have brought together a collection of writings by college professors who are actively struggling to address issues of difference in the college classroom. In these chapters, which originally appeared as articles in the pages of the *Harvard Educational Review*, the authors describe how they address such topics as race, gender, and social class in their courses, and focus on methods they use to ensure that their curricula and class discussions represent the perspectives of all students. This collection illuminates the myriad philosophical, pedagogical, and educational concerns that underlie discussions about diversity and difference in higher education. Our intention in bringing these articles together is to generate a greater dialogue of perspectives among educators about the pedagogical complexities inherent in altering the ways in which we acknowledge, frame, and talk about differences among human beings.

We begin with a theoretical "conversation" among three authors who discuss the conditions and possibilities for communication across the various differences contained in the human experience — in this case, ideology, race, gender, class, culture, and sexual orientation. In "Dialogue across Differences: Continuing the Conversation," coauthors Nicholas Burbules and Suzanne Rice argue that a dialogue that challenges conventional and progressive educational theory and practice *is* possible. They draw on fundamental insights of the postmodern tradition to propose specific conditions under which people can communicate while still maintaining the heterogeneity of their experiences, ideas, and ethnicities. Burbules and Rice maintain that, although "public schools and universities are certainly no more free from social and political conflict and patterns of domination" (p. 15), these institutions nevertheless potentially provide a forum for tackling the challenges of talking across what often seem to be insurmountable differences. The authors call for a "multiplicity of as many voices and perspectives as possible, without seeking to reconcile them or combine them into a single, consistent, unified account" (p. 2). As a way to promote this multiplicity of voices, Burbules and Rice describe what they call "communicative virtues" — dispositions created in relation to communicative partners that are necessary for the success of dialogues both across differences and over time.

In "Can We Talk?" Mary Leach responds to Burbules and Rice by arguing that the conditions they propose "[gloss] over complex ethical and political issues, erasing the very politics of knowledge involved in teaching and learning about difference" (p. 31). As a feminist educator using postmodern insights, Leach proposes a disruption of the current definitions of difference that tend to promote homogeneous identities along racial, ethnic, and gender lines. She instead seeks a context in which the goal for "talk" is not synthesis, but an "ongoing state of metamorphosis" wherein a space is created for "heterogeneity within personal identities" (p. 32). Continuing the dialogue in "Can We Be Heard?" Burbules and Rice draw from Leach's feminist reading of their work to refine the lines of their argument, further clarifying the specific contexts and conditions under which communicative virtues can be practiced. This lively discussion between Burbules and Rice and Leach raises theoretical concerns that inform the educational theory/praxis-based arguments of the three following chapters, as well as the practice-focused deliberations of the final five chapters included in this book.

In "Why Doesn't This Feel Empowering? Working through the Repressive Myths of Critical Pedagogy," Elizabeth Ellsworth challenges the often abstract and utopian lines of the theoretical literature that touts "dialogue," "empowerment," and "student voice." Motivated to act by a racist incident on the University of Wisconsin-Madison campus, Ellsworth created a course on media and anti-racist pedagogies in which she explored the tenets and practical applications of "critical" and "liberatory" educational theory. Her experience in the classroom that year revealed that "dialogue in its conventional sense is impossible in the culture at large because at this historical moment, power relations between raced, classed, and gendered students and teachers are unjust" (p. 59). Furthermore, the practice of the "prescriptions" offered in the theoretical literature not only produced results that were "unhelpful"; Ellsworth writes that they actually "exacerbated the very conditions we were trying to work against, including Eurocentrism, racism, sexism, classism, and 'banking education'" (p. 44).

Kathleen Weiler, like Ellsworth, challenges the abstract and utopian lines of a theoretical literature and focuses on the practical applications of liberatory pedagogical theory as articulated by Paulo Freire. In "Freire and a Feminist Pedagogy of Difference," Weiler traces the evolution of feminist educational discourse and practice and raises questions about Freire's unitary definition of oppression and his abstract pedagogical goals of liberation and "humanization." Like Leach, Weiler recognizes in emergent feminist educational theory and practice the possibilities for locating and negotiating the meanings of complex lives, experiences, and internal conflicts that oppressed groups bring to any dialogue or discourse "within" and "between" their differences. For her, feminist pedagogy, enhanced by the voices of women of color and lesbians, enriches Freire's vision of collective conscientization and struggle against oppression because it acknowledges difference and conflict and, as in Freire's view, it "rests on a belief in the human capacity to feel, to know, and to change" (p. 93).

In "Interrupting Patriarchy: Politics, Resistance, and Transformation in the Feminist Classroom," Magda Lewis joins Leach, Ellsworth, and Weiler in her espousal of feminist educational theory and practice as a way to disrupt male-dominated discourse boundaries around difference. For Lewis, the impetus for the creation of her course on social class, gender, and race in education was a series of misogynous acts on campuses across Canada that culminated in the massacre of fourteen women at the Université de Montréal in 1989. She builds her course on a pivotal pedagogical question:

> How might I create a feminist pedagogy that supports women's desire to wish well for ourselves when for many women the "good news" of the transformative powers of feminist consciousness turns into the "bad news" of social inequality and, therefore, a perspective and politics they want to resist? (p. 100)

Drawing on student resistance and a fusion of political perspectives and educational practice, Lewis reflects on her teaching in an effort to form a viable feminist pedagogy of transformation — a pedagogy that is "forged from the contradictions [students] perceive between the dominant discourse of school knowledge on the one hand and their own lived experiences of subordination and violation on the other" (p. 100). The story she tells is one that probes theoretical, psychological, social, and sexual dynamics engendered in her "feminist classroom" between her own voice as a feminist educator and those of her male and female students — dynamics that, when considered against the very real backdrop of violence perpetrated against women, bear increased significance in pedagogical efforts that seek to explore "the space between the public and theoretical agenda of the course and the privacy of [students'] everyday lives, where complex negotiations across gender often take their most salient form" (p. 103). The strong link between theory and praxis that Lewis discovers through her course is emphasized by the remaining authors as they attempt to find ways to promote personal, social, and pedagogical transformations through curricular innovations.

In "Nobody Mean More to Me Than You and the Future Life of Willie Jordan," June Jordan illustrates the power of language as a means of including or excluding a range of human experiences and perspectives. Shocked by the initial resistance of her predominantly African-American students to the language of Alice Walker's *The Color Purple*, Jordan uses her classroom as a forum for students to investigate the epistemological and linguistic differences between Black English and (White) Standard English when articulating Black experiences of life. In doing so, she invites her students to challenge the hegemonic position given to Standard English — a position that often forces African Americans either to "hide [their] original word habits" or to "completely surrender [their] own voice, hoping to please those who will never respect anyone different from themselves" (p. 123). When a Black classmember's unarmed brother is killed by White police officers, Jordan's students decide to use Black English to write a collective personal statement voicing their outrage to the police and the newspapers, despite the painful realization that the use of "Black English had doomed our writings, even as the distinctive reality of our Black lives always has doomed our efforts to 'be who we been' in this country" (p. 133).

Some of Jordan's students' emotional responses to the effects of racist institutions that deny them authentic representations of their lives, views, and thoughts are echoed in Beverly Daniel Tatum's chapter, "Talking about Race, Learning about Racism: The Application of Racial Identity Development Theory in the Classroom." During ten years of teaching a course on the psychology of racism at a large public university, a small state college, and an elite private women's college, Tatum has found that, for both White students and students of color, "the introduction of these issues of oppression often generates powerful emotional responses in students that range from guilt and shame to anger and despair" (p. 137). Carefully laying out the working assumptions of her pedagogy and students' sources of resistance to discussing and learning about racism, Tatum proceeds to describe a curriculum that uses racial identity development theory as a framework for building pedagogical strategies that enable students to articulate and process their confusing range of emotions. In this way, Tatum has created a curricular tool with which "to facilitate positive student development, as well as to improve interracial dialogue within the classroom" (p. 153).

The effort to create such interracial dialogues within college classrooms is at the heart of "Basic Writing: Moving the Voices on the Margin to the Center" by Anne Herrington and Marcia Curtis. Much like previous authors in this volume, Herrington and Curtis use their classroom to respond to racially motivated unrest on the campus of a large state university. They altered the existing curriculum and formed a reading list for their basic writing course that focused on Latino/a, African-American, and other non-White authors in an effort to reflect more accurately the ethnicities represented in their classrooms. Recognizing their own complicity in marginalizing the experiences of people of color by excluding them from the "required" reading list of their basic writing course, the authors changed the entire focus and function of the course so that "rather than having [their] curriculum be an image of the university, [they] decided to construct it in the image of [their] students" (p. 162). Thus, Herrington and Curtis try to take up the plea of the students demonstrating on their campus, who demanded that their voices be included not just when racial tension explodes, but through systemic change within the university. Their chapter offers a reflective description of the shifts they made in their practice, and includes samples of the students' written interactions with the texts included in the revised reading list.

Kimberly Christensen's "Teaching Undergraduates about AIDS: An Action-Oriented Approach" ushers us into yet another exploration of curricular innovation. She, too, is moved to integrate her growing awareness of AIDS as a societal problem into the university curriculum as a form of political and pedagogical action. Besides providing information about HIV transmission and prevention, Christensen explores with her students the deeper causes of the AIDS epidemic in an effort to foster a "sense of empowerment and commitment" and to "create an atmosphere in the classroom in which students would not only feel free to confront and change their own risk behaviors, but would also become actively involved in the fight against AIDS" (p. 171). Over the course of the semester, Christensen proves with her students the ways that

> the rapid spread of AIDS in the United States is symptomatic of many deeper problems in our society, including the persistence of racism and heterosexism, an economy that does not provide jobs or adequate income for many of its citizens, an increasingly inadequate health care delivery and finance system, and a "war on drugs" that does little to address the real roots of the drug crisis. (p. 171)

Christensen describes, critiques, and evaluates the content and pedagogy of her course based on her own experience with AIDS activism and the responses of her students. She maintains that "students need supportive spaces in which they can freely discuss their fears and confusions about AIDS, as well as avenues to put their energies to constructive use. It is up to us as educators to create such spaces for them" (p. 186).

The idea of "taking a stand as both educators and activists" (p. 192) is taken up by Marilyn Cochran-Smith in "Learning to Teach against the Grain." In this chapter, Cochran-Smith analyzes two approaches to preparing pre-service teachers to reform teaching; that is, to "teach against the grain." She argues that university-based programs that aim to help student teachers develop critical perspectives that confront issues of race, class, power, labor, and gender have had limited success. She believes that a powerful way for student teachers to become agents of change is for them to learn the practice of teaching alongside experienced teachers who are themselves struggling to "alter curricula, raise questions about common practices, and resist inappropriate decisions" (p. 192). Through an analysis of teachers' and student teachers' discourse during weekly school-site meetings in four urban schools, Cochran-Smith shows how power is shared among participants in the community of learning at the schools, how "knowledge about teaching is fluid and socially constructed; . . . and, in the end, [how] the power to liberalize and reinvent notions of teaching, learning, and schooling is located in neither the university nor the school, but in the collaborative work of the two" (p. 195). Within such supportive collaborations, the possibility for educational reform is magnified and the education of pre-service teachers incorporates exposure to new perspectives, "alternative ways of documenting and measuring learning, transforming and constructing curriculum, and thinking through issues of race, class, and culture" (p. 217).

As the authors in this book have demonstrated, new visions of educational theory and practice must be articulated, supported, and enriched in order to bring about changes in the way we address differences that separate and join us. Their reflections about the theories and practices that underlie the struggle to hear and be heard across boundaries of race, class, gender, sexual orientation, and physical challenges, have the potential to change forever the ways in which we teach and learn about ourselves as educators and students. Their work indeed furthers this struggle for change in constructive and challenging ways.

KATHRYN GEISMAR • GUITELE NICOLEAU
Harvard Graduate School of Education

Dialogue
across Differences:
Continuing the Conversation

NICHOLAS C. BURBULES
SUZANNE RICE

In this chapter, Nicholas Burbules and Suzanne Rice address head-on the question of whether it is possible to have true understanding across differences that stem from race, class, gender, sexual orientation, and the subjective positions people bring into dialogical relations. They begin by discussing postmodernism, and in particular the "antimodernist" concepts of difference that impede true understanding across differences. Building on postmodern insights into the essential nature of differences, they provide a carefully reasoned argument for and description of a form of dialogue across differences that involves the development of communicative virtues, tolerance, and respect that they feel is critical to furthering the fundamental educational goals of personal, moral, and social development.

Postmodernism has had a growing influence on critical educational studies. Leftist theoretical approaches that argue for a specific method of analysis and assume the explanatory primacy of some particular social factor — including Marxism and some versions of feminism — are being challenged by an outlook that stresses the constructed and essentially arbitrary character of any explanatory framework. By situating all claims of knowledge and value within a web of discursive and nondiscursive practices, Postmodernism[1] seeks to disclose the partiality and contentiousness of any purportedly universal social theory:

> The study of language itself and of the way it is used in discursive practices to constitute the social structure answered many of the problems created by earlier models. Individuals were no longer lost in the overpowering, controlling social structure — they were, rather, constituting those social structures through the discursive practices in which they were engaged. Class and gender were no longer imposed unitary structures but shifting sets of possibilities, of subject positionings made available in the texts, the narrative structures, the discursive practices in which each person participates.[2]

For these authors, the active processes by which we construct and interpret systems of belief or value are infinitely variable and highly contingent. This contingency is thought to undercut any purely intellectual, internal justification for epistemic, moral, or political claims. Any such justification is rejected as simply the special pleading of a particular group seeking to promote a discursive order

Harvard Educational Review Vol. 61 No. 4 November 1991, 393–416

that legitimates their own advantages and privileges by promoting a specific basis of justification as the best one; any ultimate claim to "rightness" is a ploy to discourage further investigation or to allow investigation only on one's terms, and thus is seen as restrictive. Postmodernism regards itself as a challenge to these restrictions, often by directly and purposely flouting them:

> [Postmodern writers] want to "interrupt" academic norms by writing inside of another logic, a logic that displaces expectations of linearity, clear authorial voice, and closure. . . . The deconstructive text is a point of interrogation where binary notions of "clarity" are displaced as the speaking voice uses its authority to displace authority.[3]

In such a view, the only possible nonhierarchical, nondominating, nonmonolithic discursive approach is one that decenters all claims to transcendental justification (even its own). The very aims of developing general theories or universalizable moral claims are dismissed as anachronistic, and frequently totalitarian, like the styles of epic architecture. Hence one frequently encounters terms in Postmodern writing such as "fracturing," "breaking," and — of course — "deconstruction." This outlook embraces incommensurability across worldviews, not as an unfortunate failure to establish common meanings and values, but as a desired state:

> Postmodernism . . . is completely indifferent to the questions of consistency and continuity. It self-consciously slices genres, attitudes, styles. It relishes the blurring or juxtaposition of forms . . . stances . . . moods . . . cultural levels. . . . It neither embraces nor criticizes, but beholds the world blankly, with a knowingness that dissolves feeling and commitment into irony. It pulls the rug out from under itself, displaying an acute self-consciousness about the work's constructed nature. It takes pleasure in the play of surfaces, and derides the search for depth as mere nostalgia.[4]

Accordingly, we should encourage the multiplicity of as many voices and perspectives as possible, without seeking to reconcile them or combine them into a single, consistent, unified account: Bakhtin terms this a state of "Heteroglossia."[5] In the context of social and political theories, this outlook has often been expressed as a celebration of "difference." While particular Postmodern theorists might implicitly favor a factor such as race, gender, class, ethnic identity, or sexual preference as a primary theoretical/political category, they undercut this claim by arguing at the same time that all these factors (and others as well) must also be accommodated within a broader theoretical/political analysis. This theoretical pluralism is not justified by any particular value placed on complexity or comprehensiveness; rather, Postmodernists argue that, from the standpoint of the subjective construction of identity, such factors cannot be regarded separately: a person is, for example, Black, and female, and poor. Any external attempt to isolate or prioritize such factors is simply another dimension of an "essentialism" that is dominating.[6]

These ideas have made rapid headway into critical studies of education. One reason for their popularity has been the widespread rejection of the "economism," "determinism," or "pessimism" of Marxian analyses of education, such as that of Samuel Bowles and Herbert Gintis's *Schooling in Capitalist America*.[7] The language of Postmodernism has served well in articulating the limits of such accounts by stressing the ideological, cultural, and discursive elements that they fail to illuminate. In this, Postmodernism seeks to broaden the terrain of struggle available to pedagogues at a time when traditional Left struggles over work, resources, and political access seem sharply limited.[8]

In this chapter, we focus on the Postmodern elevation of *difference* as a value that is in opposition to such traditional values as consensus and intersubjectivity, and examine whether a sympathetic response to the Postmodern critique can be made consistent with positive educational goals — in this case, the pedagogical value of *dialogue*. We will consider whether dialogue can be maintained across differences, whether it is desirable to try, and what conditions might make it possible.

POSTMODERNISM, BY AND LARGE

Because the term Postmodernism has been used to refer to so many different views, it is difficult to attribute essential themes to the Postmodern trend.[9] But at least three ideas recur in the literature generally, and specifically in Postmodern work in educational studies.

First is the rejection of absolutes. Postmodernists usually insist that there can be no single rationality, no single morality, and no ruling theoretical framework for the analysis of social and political events. The conventional language here, deriving from Jean-François Lyotard, is that there are no "metanarratives" that are not themselves the partial expressions of a particular point of view.[10] As Zygmunt Bauman puts it:

> The philosophers' search for the ultimate system, for the complete order, for the extirpation of everything unknown and unruly, stems from the dream of having a firm soil and a secure home, and leads to closing down the obstinately infinite human potential. Such search for the universal cannot but degenerate into a ruthless clamp-down on human possibilities.[11]

Second is the perceived saturation of all social and political discourses with power or dominance.[12] Any metanarrative is taken to be synonymous with the hegemony of a social and political order:

> To learn to see not only what we do but also what structures what we do, to deconstruct how ideological and institutional power play in our own practices, to recognize the partiality and open-endedness of our own efforts, all of this is to examine the discourses within which we are caught up. Imploding canons and foregrounding the power/knowledge nexus by deconstructing "natural" hierarchies demonstrate that what had seemed transparent and unquestionable is neither. All of this is to participate in the radical unsettling that is postmodernism in ways that have profound implications for pedagogy and curriculum. . . . In this context of ferment, educational inquiry is increasingly viewed as no more outside the power/knowledge nexus than any other human enterprise.[13]

If, as many Postmodernists argue, there are no sustainable norms of rationality and value, then all educational discourse is political discourse; it exists, in this view, only for the purpose of enfranchising certain group interests over others. If this is true, then the burden of responsibility is placed on any progressive educator to consider the political consequences of the vocabulary, structures of argument, and substantive conclusions of his or her teaching and writing. While teachers and scholars are inclined to see themselves as answerable only to their disciplinary standards of truth, evidence, accuracy, and so on, this critique challenges them to consider also the way in which their statements and actions exist within a system of power and privilege, and to reflect critically on their practices in light of the effects their speaking and writing are likely to have.

For example, this critical vantage point enjoins teachers to consider when classroom relations, even the most apparently benign, might instantiate and help perpetuate broader patterns of social and political dominance. The Postmodern critique argues that teacher authority, even if it is adopted with beneficial intent, takes significance against a pervasive background of relations of domination; some authors argue that the only alternative is to abandon all relations of classroom authority and disinterested claims to knowledge.[14] Obviously, such a criticism poses a direct challenge to our standard models of teaching.

A third idea that recurs in the Postmodern literature is the celebration of "difference." Rather than attempting to judge or prioritize the explanatory or political significance of given elements in a social situation, the Postmodern trend is to argue that, because all signifiers are mere constructions, there is no clear reason to grant any one special significance or value over others:

> What the inherently polysemous and controversial idea of *postmodernity* most often refers to . . . is first and foremost an acceptance of the ineradicable plurality of the world — not a temporary state on the road to the not-yet-attained perfection, sooner or later to be left behind, but the constitutive quality of existence. By the same token, postmodernity means a resolute emancipation from the characteristically modern urge to overcome difference and promote sameness. . . . In the plural and pluralistic world of postmodernity, every form of life is *permitted on principle;* or, rather, no agreed principles are evident which may render any form of life impermissible.[15]

Thus, previous theoretical efforts, even from the Left, have been blamed with neglecting, or even suppressing, the perspectives and experiences of marginalized groups:

> We and you do not talk the same language. When we talk to you we use your language: the language of your experience and your theories. We try to use it to communicate our world of experience. But since your language and theories are inadequate in expressing our experiences, we only succeed in communicating our experience of exclusion. We cannot talk to you in our language because you do not understand it. So the brute facts that we understand your language and that the place where most theorizing . . . is taking place is your place, both combine to require us either to distort our experience not just in the speaking of it, but in the living of it, or that we remain silent.[16]

An increased sensitivity to such difference clearly urges a more inclusive approach to pedagogy. It is crucial to recognize that for the Postmodernist, this responsibility goes beyond mere "pluralism," or an invitation for all to participate. It is not enough merely to create the conditions of a forum in which all parties present have the right to speak. In a society structured by power, not all differences reside at the same level. Therefore, further questions must be posed:

Who may feel unable to speak without explicit or implicit retribution? Who may want to speak, but feel so demoralized, or intimidated, by the circumstances that they are effectively "silenced"? What tacit rules of communication may be operating in schools and classrooms that rule certain areas of concern or modes of speech out of bounds by the very procedures that the discussion takes for granted? All of these constitute forms of exclusion. In each of these cases, the Postmodernist will argue, the promulgation of many voices and the representation of the concerns of different groups extend beyond mere tolerance or the creation of an "open forum" that may be less open than it appears, when judged from the perspective of marginalized persons or groups.

TWO VARIETIES OF POSTMODERNISM

Postmodernism provides a set of critical categories that pose a serious challenge, not only to conventional educational activities, but to many previous efforts by Leftist scholars to develop a progressive educational theory and practice. However, because the Postmodern tradition avoids committing itself to a political/moral metanarrative of its own, it often discloses and rejects the shortcomings of other views without positing clear alternatives to them. Instead, it relies on an implicitly normative vocabulary of liberation, empowerment, and issue-specific critique that is much clearer in specifying what it is against than what it is for and why.[17]

Part of the difficulty in identifying and justifying positive aims in the Postmodern tradition is that there seem to be two distinct trends within Postmodernism, which adopt fundamentally different positions relative to modernism itself. We call these two trends postmodernism and antimodernism, the first of which we see as fundamentally continuous with the modernist tradition, although it seeks to challenge and redefine it, the second of which regards itself as making a complete break from modernism.[18] These are not, however, discrete or self-contained schools of thought; we will show how postmodern and antimodern elements coexist in numerous authors, although some clearly tend toward one position rather than the other. Complicating this analysis further is the tendency of certain authors to slide back and forth between these positions — authors for whom rejection and reformulation are not clearly distinguished.

First, then, is what we have called *postmodernism* per se. The "post" implies a moving beyond, of course, but also a continuity; any tradition identifying itself as post-something is also accepting the basic significance of the tradition it proposes to go beyond — if it did not accept this, there would be no reason to define itself in relation to that earlier tradition. In this sense, postmodernism is not entirely alien to modernism; it frequently invokes modernist categories, such as reason or equality, but seeks to reappropriate, redefine, and reground them. In this, postmodernism does identify a potential basis for defining a positive social and political agenda, although it faces a difficulty in defending this agenda, since it has forsworn the modernist "metanarratives" that had previously underlaid it.

Within the educational literature, this approach is best exemplified by the work of Henry Giroux and Peter McLaren.[19] Their arguments often take the form of invoking modernist categories, which they seek to reappropriate and expand in significance. For example:

> Postmodernism must extend and broaden the most democratic claims of modernism. . . . [It must be] linked with the modernist language of public life . . . as part of a public philosophy that broadens and deepens individual liberties and rights. . . . [Postmodern pedagogy] is informed by a political project that links the creation of citizens to the development of a critical democracy; that is, a political project that links education to the struggle for public life in which discourse, vision, and compassion are attentive to the rights and conditions that organize public life as a democratic social form.[20]

Here we see a clear attempt to reappropriate and expand modernist concepts such as democracy, liberty, rights, citizenship, and so forth. Giroux and McLaren explicitly and repeatedly challenge other views that fail to offer a positive educational and political agenda.[21] We believe they are quite justified in this criticism. Yet, we also see reflected in their work the difficulty postmodernism encounters in providing principled arguments to support positive positions; in place of such arguments we often find a highly charged rhetorical style that *asserts* the primacy of certain values or *condemns* their suppression without articulating why anyone not already sympathetic with their position ought to be so. This endeavor is made even more difficult when postmodern skepticism about modernist values and metanarratives blurs into an antimodern rejection of them.

This *antimodernist* position is characterized by a strong antipathy to the language, issues, and values of modernism, and seeks to formulate an entirely different problematic. It defines itself in opposition to modernism, not as a position growing out of and moving beyond modernist concerns. Hence it is not concerned with recapturing and reformulating modern values, such as reason or equality, but with deconstruction them and rejecting them. Not surprisingly, this tradition in particular has been more convincing in pointing out the limitations and contradictions of modernism than in reformulating positive alternatives. Having deconstructed all metanarratives and radically relativized all possible values, antimodernism is left with no clear way of justifying *any* alternatives. For example, Elizabeth Ellsworth, a strong critic of Giroux and McLaren, writes:

> By prescribing moral deliberation, engagement in the full range of views present, and critical reflection, the literature on critical pedagogy implies that students and teachers can and should engage each other in the classroom as fully rational subjects. . . . In schools, rational deliberation, reflection, and consideration of all viewpoints has become a vehicle for regulating conflict and the power to speak. . . . In a racist society and its institutions, such debate has not and cannot be "public" or "democratic" in the sense of including the views of all affected parties and affording them equal weight and legitimacy.[22]

It is one thing to note society's failure in practice to fulfill such values as "public" or "democratic" debate and the consideration of all viewpoints, and to disclose the ways in which rhetorical aspirations to such values have frequently masked practices that actually undermine them. But it is very difficult to see what could follow, educationally, from their wholesale rejection.

We do not question for a moment the relations of dominance, or histories of conflict and hostility, or gulfs of nonunderstanding or misunderstanding across differences, that undercut conventional educational aims and practices. Indeed, identifying and criticizing these is the necessary starting point for any new thinking on the problems of education. But unless one conceives freedom only negatively (as the mere avoidance or removal of such impediments), it is not clear what follows from this critique for educational or political practice. Antimodernism lacks a clear conception of a "positive freedom" that identifies social conditions in which freer thought and action are possible; lacking this, antimodernism has not been able to articulate a clear and defensible educational theory.

As we have noted, many writers exhibit both postmodern and antimodern tendencies, and their positions tend to slide back and forth between the two views. The argument that traditional modernist principles are inadequate or ineffective, and so need to be reformulated and regrounded on less absolutistic premises, is frequently conflated with the position that these principles are inherently illegitimate and ought to be abandoned entirely. We will further develop this point later.

These two critical vantage points pose strong challenges to educational thought and practice: the deconstruction of conventional claims to knowledge and authority; the analysis and critique of the power relations underlying traditional educational aims and practices; and the insistence that we abandon presumptions of homogeneity and acknowledge the real and possibly unbridgeable gulfs of diversity among people. The view we have termed postmodernism has sought to turn these critiques toward an alternative conception of education based partly on the reformulation of selected modernist principles such as democracy or self-determination, but without sharing modernist assumptions, such as a belief in progress or the rational rule of law. The view we have termed antimodernism has, on the other hand, been largely content with emphasizing points of critique. The educational practices that are generated from the antimodern perspective seem largely dependent upon the preferences of those who advance them. This is not necessarily to denigrate such practices, but merely to stress, again, that antimodernism cannot justify them by reference to generalizable values. As a result, value assumptions that actually do underlie these practices are frequently left implicit and unexamined.

As noted, one concern shared by both postmodern and antimodern writers has been the question of *difference*. The rejection of metanarratives has often been taken to imply what Bauman calls an "ineradicable plurality" of languages and worldviews, a conclusion especially prominent in antimodern arguments. At this point we want to turn to a detailed discussion of "difference" and dialogue. In the process, we hope to show how certain postmodern conceptions of difference yield more fruitful educational implications than do antimodern conceptions.

DIFFERENCE AND *DIFFÉRANCE*

The notion of "difference" appealed to in this literature derives primarily from Jacques Derrida, although originating in Saussurian linguistics. For Ferdinand de Saussure, it was the *difference* between two signifiers that allowed them to serve as such; this difference is, typically, arbitrary and meaningless in and of itself —

but there must be some difference between signifiers for them to work. To pick a very simple instance, O and Q are quite similar shapes, distinguished only by a small mark that is present in one, absent in the other; yet they are distinct letters (in English). But precisely the same mark added, say, as a flourish at the end of a word written in cursive, may not constitute a significant difference. Which differences mean something is entirely a consequence of how those differences exist in the context of a system of differences; a point of difference only *makes* a difference under specific circumstances. While often intrinsically arbitrary, the overall significance of a mark of difference, for Saussure, can be analyzed objectively.

Derrida coined the term *différance* to identify a different sort of difference. For Derrida, what constitutes a significant difference (*différance*) is a changing determination; a differentiating factor is not merely an arbitrary and "passive" element in a sign system, but also an "active," context-sensitive variant:

> [*Différance*] is a structure and a movement no longer conceivable on the basis of the opposition presence/absence. *Différance* is the systematic play of difference, of the traces of difference, of the *spacing* by means of which elements are related to each other. This spacing is the simultaneously active and passive . . . production of the intervals without which the "full" terms would not signify, would not function.[23]

Derrida's analysis constitutes a rejection of formalism, and an assertion of the dynamic character of all signification. In place of Saussure's abstract analysis of relational structures, Derrida and other poststructuralists insist that the *relations* that bind and the *spaces* that distinguish cultural elements are themselves in constant interaction, so that — as for Werner Karl Heisenberg's measures of motion and position for subatomic particles — each changes as one attempts to fix the other. For Derrida, this simultaneity of passive and active elements in signification is tied to a larger rejection of the Saussurian dichotomy of *langue* (formal language) and *parole* (discourse, or practical speech).[24] Formal analysis is insufficient to describe the practical elements of interpretation and judgment that give language its meaning in use; furthermore, any particular formalization is for Derrida nothing more than the momentary crystallization and institutionalization of one particular set of rules and norms — others are always possible.

Extended now into the domain of social or political theories, this concept of *différance* denies the purely external and formal assignment of persons to membership in a sociological category or position in the social structure by virtue of some characteristic they possess; it pertains as well to the active, subjective process of identification with a group, and all that signifies to the subject. Any overall theory that seeks to identify from the outside the differences that classify people must fail, on this view, because it excludes these active processes of group identification and the formation of subjectivity. To put it simply, there are differences we choose, and differences we do not choose. However, the active/passive tension in Derrida's original term has been lost in certain recent appropriations of *différance*; often, as in the earlier quote from Bronwyn Davies, *all* differences are regarded as mere constructions, as expressions of the subjective process of identity-formation — there are no differences that we don't choose. Christine Di Stefano terms this the "dilemma of difference": how to identify a basis for specifying which differences matter, whether we choose them or not. She asks, "Are some differences more basic than others?"[25]

The postmodern/antimodern distinction is helpful here. On the one hand, postmodernism provides strong reasons for valuing diversity, for not assuming homogeneity when it does not exist, and for avoiding modes of discursive and nondiscursive practice that implicitly or explicitly exclude subjects who do not participate in dominant modes of thought, speech, and action. This position might even be pushed a step further, to insist that, given occasions of conflict and misunderstanding, we ought to err on the side of respecting the self-iden-tification and worldview of others, especially for members of groups who have been traditionally *told* who they are, what is true, and what is good for them.

However, at some points in the literature, this position lapses over into claims that are much more problematic. Specifically, the celebration of difference be-comes a presumption of incommensurability, a denial of the possibility of inter-subjective understanding, and an exaggerated critique that *any* attempt to estab-lish reasonable and consensual discourse across difference inevitably involves the imposition of dominant groups' values, beliefs, and modes of discourse upon others. These views are antimodern in their rejection of such goals as dialogue, reasonableness, and fair treatment of alternative points of view; such legacies of the modernist tradition are not only regarded as difficult and sometimes impos-sible to attain — which they are — but as actually undesirable ends.

In our view, this antimodernist position is unsustainable either intellectually or practically. It derives from a deep misunderstanding of the nature of differ-ence and has counter-educational implications for pedagogy. The literature that espouses this view is often internally contradictory, suggesting that such a severe critique is difficult to sustain consistently; many authors who advocate strong antimodern critiques later find themselves reversing direction when the time comes to offer positive recommendations. We want to analyze these inconsisten-cies in antimodern treatments of difference, and show how a more defensible postmodern understanding of difference can support and inform a broadened conception of education.

The difficulty of sustaining a consistent antimodern analysis of difference can be seen in Ellsworth's essay. At one point, she argues a strong antimodern thesis:

> Dialogue . . . consists of ground rules for classroom interaction using language. These rules include the assumptions that all members have equal opportunity to speak, all members respect other members' right to speak and feel safe to speak, and all ideas are tolerated and subjected to rational critical assessment against fundamental judgement and moral principles. . . . Dialogue in its conventional sense is impossible in the culture at large because at this historical moment, power relations between raced, classed, and gendered students and teachers are unjust.[26]

For Ellsworth, modernist aims such as pluralism and open discussion are con-sidered fond illusions — or worse, actual instruments of control and dominance. Yet elsewhere in the same essay she says:

> If you can talk to me in ways that show you understand that your knowledge of me, the world, and the "Right thing to do" will always be partial, interested, and poten-tially oppressive to others, and if I can do the same, then we can work together on

shaping and reshaping alliances for constructing circumstances in which students of difference can thrive.[27]

Thus at times it seems that dialogue across differences is *not* possible in a nonoppressive way, and at other time that it *is* possible, but only if we conceive of dialogue differently. We agree with Ellsworth that a reconstructed conception of dialogue is achievable only when we recognize the barriers to dialogue "in its conventional [modernist] sense." But Ellsworth appears not to recognize that her latter position is a *reaffirmation* of such modernist values as "all members have equal opportunity to speak, all members respect other members' right to speak and feel safe to speak, and all ideas are tolerated. . . ." Indeed, it is not clear what "dialogue" could mean without them. This example shows how antimodern and postmodern positions are often intermingled, and how "rejected" modern concepts or principles often reappear in a new guise.[28]

The antimodern view of difference is also unsustainable practically. We can see this problem clearly in a recent essay by Iris Young. Young rejects the ideal of community, which she argues "privileges unity over difference, immediacy over mediation, sympathy over recognition of the limits of one's understanding of others from their point of view."[29] She vigorously rejects the goal of intersubjective understanding, in which "persons will cease to be opaque, other, not understood, and instead become fused, mutually sympathetic, understanding one another as they understand themselves. . . . Political theorists and activists should distrust this desire for reciprocal recognition and identification with others."[30] Instead she calls for a "politics of difference," based on the positive experiences of "modern urban life." Having criticized previous models of community as "wildly utopian and undesirable," she then posits "a vision of the good society. Our political ideal is the unoppressive city":[31]

> City life is the "being together" of strangers. Strangers encounter one another, either face to face or through media, often remaining strangers and yet acknowledging their contiguity in living and the contributions each makes to the others. In such encounters people are not "internally" related, as the community theorists would have it, and do not understand one another from within their own perspective. They are externally related, they experience each other as other, different, from different groups, histories, professions, cultures, which they do not understand.[32]

We believe that this position is fundamentally inconsistent. We do not disagree at all with "celebrating the distinctive cultures and characteristics of different groups,"[33] but merely point out that the very reason for celebrating such differences is based on the ability of different groups to a) coexist nonviolently and b) interact in a way that enriches and invigorates each other's lives. These values *assume* some ability to communicate and coordinate actions across differences. *There is no reason to assume that dialogue across differences involves either eliminating those differences or imposing one group's views on others; dialogue that leads to understanding, cooperation, and accommodation can sustain differences within a broader compact of toleration and respect.* Thus what we need is not an antimodern denial of community, but a postmodern grounding of community on more flexible and less homogeneous assumptions.[34]

Does the lack of a single master metanarrative lead automatically to the conclusion that any attempt at consensus or common understanding depends on the imposition of one particularistic view over another (as Bauman, Ellsworth, and Young fear), or can a dialogical relation be established and maintained even across significant cultural or political differences?

Three important conceptual points about difference help to address these questions. First, any concrete discussion of difference also implies *sameness*: two objects, two people, two points of view, and so on, can be contrasted usefully only when there are at least some respects in which they are similar. To paraphrase Lewis Carroll, no one seriously asks the difference between a raven and a writing-desk. Two different political outlooks, or two racial groups, or two sexual orientations often have as many common elements as they do differences, although the differences are perhaps more salient to the people concerned — indeed, it is often their points of similarity that make the members all the more aware of their differences. Second, and following from this, "difference" is a relative term, depending on one's frame of reference. An essential point of difference that divides two groups or persons from each other, however crucial it may seem to them, might seem marginal, even arbitrary, seen from a third point of view; from this point of view, the similarities between the two will be much more striking than the differences. Highlighting criteria of difference across subgroups of difference is the same, conceptually, as identifying similarities among each subgroup's members. Thus, an exclusive focus on difference is logically inconsistent — again, difference *implies* sameness. In general, then, we recommend a framework that regards difference and sameness as being in constant interaction with one another; whether one sees a particular cultural element as a signifier of difference or sameness is a highly dynamic and contextual judgment.

None of this is meant to deny or minimize the fact of difference, or the barriers of conflict and misunderstanding difference can create; but these observations should make us cautious about reifying difference or elevating it to the primary position in our analysis of social and political relations. It is understandable why postmodern and antimodern writers have generally emphasized points of difference as a corrective to monolithic and dominating presumptions of homogeneity, and to the imposition of one subgroup's worldview as the "neutral" or "universal" one, which forces other subgroups either to accept the imposed view as their own or to remain silent. But having stressed certain valid criticisms as a corrective, it is important not to exaggerate them to the point that they become implausible and counterproductive.

Of course, much of this analysis will sound familiar to readers of John Dewey. Dewey argued that democracy was marked by two kinds of communicative diversity. While he fully understood that the existence of cultural subcommunities was a necessary, and desirable, feature of any large society, he believed that a society could be democratic only to the extent that a) these subcommunities defined themselves over a range of common concerns, not only over single-issue identifications, and b) these subcommunities maintained some degree of communication among them, where broader social concerns affect them all.[35]

Clearly, these subcommunities are not all equal partners in the social commonwealth; there are dimensions of power and privilege that divide them and set their interests in conflict.[36] Furthermore, communication across such subcommunities is not simply a matter of good will and persistent effort, and it is unrealistic and unfair to ask groups already put upon also to take on the burden of trying to understand, and make themselves understood by, those who harm them or benefit from their deprivation. Modernism has tended to emphasize universality over particularity and concreteness, and to overlook the ways in which power operates in dialogic relations; it has therefore been overly secure in assuming that fair and equitable consensus can be reached. By taking seriously precisely those matters glossed over in much of modernism, postmodernism makes us more sensitive to the possibility of incommensurability and radical misunderstanding. Public forums are not as open as they may appear from the modern perspective, and it would be naive to think that everyone feels (or *is*) free to speak in such contexts.

Nevertheless, there must be *some* forums in which such discussions are seriously undertaken, and there must be *some* individuals from each group who are prepared to take on the burden (and risk) of attempting some degree of communication and translation across the gulf that divides them. Our concern here is with what the benefits of such an effort might be and with how an attempt at dialogue across differences might proceed, even as we acknowledge the difficulties and the prospects for both failure and success inherent in the endeavor. The tendency to judge the outcome of dialogical encounters prior to their actual occurrence, whether optimistically or pessimistically, are the twin errors of modernism and antimodernism; neither consensus nor incommensurability can be assumed in advance.

IS DIALOGUE ACROSS DIFFERENCES WORTHWHILE? IS IT POSSIBLE?

Three prospective kinds of benefit can be derived from dialogue across differences: those related to the construction of identity along lines that are more flexible without becoming arbitrary; those related to broadening our understanding of others and, through this, our understanding of ourselves; and those related to fostering more reasonable and sustainable communicative practices. We would like to elaborate these areas of potential benefit in this section.

The first benefit derives from Dewey's conception of democracy. To the extent that group identification is an element in the formation of personal identity, one's identity will be more flexible, autonomous, and stable to the degree that one recognizes one's self as a member of various different subcommunities simultaneously. Such simultaneous identification can, at its extremes, produce internal conflict and a feeling of "cultural schizophrenia," but more frequently it has a beneficial effect in fostering a broader and more inclusive sense of one's self and one's relations to others. From a societal standpoint, such multiple group identifications also make possible the establishment of relations of negotiation, cooperation, and pursuit of common interests (where they exist), which tends to promote mutual tolerance and the nonviolent resolution of conflicts.

Admittedly, such communicative efforts may often fail, and in some instances they may heighten rather than resolve tensions: understanding across differences does not necessarily entail agreement, and in some cases greater communication will make conflicts between groups all the more apparent. There is no reason, however, to *presume* this outcome, and weighed against this outcome are the many instances in which commonalities of interest can be, at least provisionally, identified.

Second, the anthropological categories of "emic" and "etic" perspectives (or similar categories) have often been exaggerated in discussion of dialogue across differences. Like the categories of sameness and difference, they have been too sharply dichotomized, and one perspective has been falsely prioritized over the other. The emic perspective is a group's own; the etic perspective is that of the outsider.[37] In the literature, the emic perspective has frequently been elevated to the "correct" or only legitimate interpretation of the meaning and significance of a group's beliefs and practices.[38] This view has been beneficial in some respects. It highlights the ways in which cultural meanings are internally constructed, situated in webs of signification that fully make sense only to initiates within that system. It heightens our sensitivity to the diversity of human cultures, and to how the "same" thing might look and feel quite different to members of different cultural groups. It prepares us for the possibility of radical misunderstanding, and should make us extremely modest and cautious about *imposing* an interpretive frame from one group onto another. Finally, it should make us err, it we are going to err, on the side of crediting and respecting a group's self-understanding when it seriously conflicts with our own — especially when dealing with a group already at a disadvantage in the communicative relation.[39]

Yet at the same time, these benefits should not be taken to mean that all etic perspectives are illegitimate. Sometimes an external perspective is helpful *precisely because* it is different from that of the group itself. This point has often been ignored in the literature. While it is a problem that certain privileged external groups' perspectives have tended to override other groups' internal ones so that the credibility of internal perspectives may need to be valorized as a corrective, this corrective has often been extended to the unhelpful extreme that external perspectives are inherently taken to be coercive and imperialistic. Both as individuals and groups, we can broaden and enrich our self-understanding by considering our beliefs, values, and actions from a fresh standpoint. This endeavor can yield what Walter Feinberg calls "reflective moments," opportunities for deeper self-understanding and a release from the commonsense assumptions that typically frame our daily existence.[40] This does not require embracing the other standpoint or letting it supersede our own, but it does stress the value of incorporating that perspective into a more complex and multifaceted framework of understanding.

Moreover, given the relativity of what constitutes a "difference" in the first place, the scope and limits of what we consider significant differences may change when dialogue is sustained over time; we may find a convergence of certain interests, and discover additional points of similarity or differences. All of this is to the better, if we value breadth and complexity in human understanding. Such considerations provide a second incentive for pursuing dialogue across differences.

Third, the very activity of pursuing and maintaining dialogue across differences can foster in us more general dispositions and practices of communication that help support more successful communicative relations with a variety of people over time. Attempting dialogue across difference, and persisting in the attempt even when it becomes difficult, develops such "communicative virtues" as tolerance, patience, and a willingness to listen. As a process, dialogue requires us to re-examine our own presuppositions and to compare them against quite different ones; to make us less dogmatic about the belief that the way the world appears to us is necessarily the way the world is.

However, effort and good will alone are not guarantees; dialogue is fallible. Yet even failed attempts at dialogue across differences can teach us something — that persistence does not resolve all conflicts, that some problems are not solvable but only manageable, and that a level of mystery and perplexity accompanies all attempts at human understanding. Such realizations foster in us a healthy modesty about the possibilities and limits of our communicative efforts.[41]

We have argued here for the benefits of establishing dialogue across differences where possible, and the value of pursuing it even when it turns out not to be possible. But is it ever possible?

A fascinating account of the pursuit of dialogue across differences has been offered by the Feminist Alliance Project in the Netherlands.[42] The goal of this project was to "nurture personal change, political strength, and theoretical understanding of divisions between women."[43] Parallel "alliance groups" were formed among one hundred women differing in terms of race, sexual orientation, and whether or not they were Jewish. Each group originally was internally differentiated across one of these three dimensions, in order to identify "multiple interlocking identities and oppressions."[44] For example, one group emphasized Black versus White relations, although within each racial group there was diversity along other dimensions. Their paper describes the processes by which these groups attempted to develop understanding and solidarity across such similarities and differences. These efforts were not entirely successful: "In every group past experiences with oppression and domination distorted the participants' perceptions of the present and blocked their identification with people in common political situations who did not share their history."[45] Various clusters of women opted for meeting in more homogeneous subgroups: for example, some Black women chose to meet only with other Black women; then Black lesbians wanted to meet separately from *that* group in a more homogeneous subgroup of their own. (The extreme extension of this logic, which is virtually mandated by strong theories of difference, would, of course, be absurd.) Overall, however, the project was successful in improving dialogue and understanding across differences: participants concluded the project with assessments such as, "I have less of a chip on my shoulder. I used to feel 'poor me, or lucky me, nobody knows what it feels like to be me' and now I'm better able to communicate naturally about my life and to expect respect from others."[46]

This example illustrates several important points about the possibilities, limits, and potential benefits of dialogue across differences. The first is that success is a partial and provisional human achievement; it is neither guaranteed by the existence of good intentions, nor precluded by the existence of serious differences. Second, the activities we might pursue to promote dialogue, such as encouraging the formation of subgroups to provide greater confidence and self-awareness when participants go back into large groups, may actually impede that goal by promoting greater separatism. Third, though, is that the greater our awareness of and sensitivity to dimensions of difference, the *stronger* the imperative to pursue means of understanding across them. The participants in the alliance groups, for example, repeatedly noted that it was through encountering women experiencing other dimensions of oppression that they gained a fuller appreciation of their own situation.

Thus the problem of "difference" poses a challenge, but not an insurmountable challenge, to the possibilities of dialogue. Antimodern arguments that rhetorically write off the very possibility of dialogue run the danger of being true, but in a self-confirming way, since if the effort to engage others across difference is never seriously made, it certainly can never succeed. And, as Nancy Hartsock has pointed out, it is exceedingly ironic that at the very time that traditionally disadvantaged groups are beginning to find their voice, an epistemological view has gained currency that legitimates relativizing their claims to credibility and respect.[47]

Earlier, we argued that there must be some forums in which such dialogue across differences is valued, and in which it is pursued by participants in good faith, even in the face of difficulty and initial misunderstanding. We believe that educational contexts potentially provide one such forum. Public schools and universities are certainly no more free from social and political conflict and patterns of domination than are any other institutions, but they do generally espouse and frequently enact a commitment — particularly at the university level — to the value of communication across difference and the benefits of encountering new and challenging points of view. All of the barriers and difficulties cited by postmodern and antimodern critics remain, but the wholesale abandonment of the possibility of overcoming them is tantamount to an abandonment of the goal of education itself. The practical questions that should concern educators are: What positive conditions make dialogue across differences possible? What can educators do to promote those conditions? What is realistic to expect from such communicative encounters? We would like to conclude by discussing several of these practical matters. Such questions are not unique to education, but they are crucial to the determination of whether education is worth the effort.[48]

EDUCATIONAL AIMS AND HOPES

The Varieties of Difference

If dialogue across difference is to succeed, sensitivity is required to the various kinds of diversity one may encounter. Differences that may not be apparent to, or salient for, others may be paramount in the minds of the individuals at hand. Difference is not simply a matter of sociological group membership, but also of the constructed worldview and subjectivity of the persons who enter a dialogical relation; thus "difference" (or its absence) cannot always be inferred or assumed from the outside. As Lisa Delpit argued, we should try to consider the elements

15

of difference that might affect the communicative possibilities in a particular encounter from the point of view of the parties involved. We should elicit and respect their self-identifications, and admit to ourselves the limits of our ability to identify with, or make inferences about, the subjectivity of others.

Playing what Peter Elbow calls "the believing game" is one way to begin this effort. The believing game involves taking the attitude that we stand to learn from what another has to say, and that we should grant the other's claims a provisional plausibility simply based on the fact that those claims are sincerely held. This attitude does not preclude questioning the other's self-expression at some later point, but it places the priority on establishing a communicative relation of trust and openness, and of trying to err on the side of sympathy and respectfulness when discussions first begin. Mary Belenky and her coauthors term this a "connected" form of knowing, because it places the interest inform-ing a particular type of relation ahead of purely intellectual interests.[49]

Such efforts are necessary, but not sufficient, to insure communicative suc-cess. The situation we face might be "inherently polysemous," to use Bauman's phrase, and jumping to the conclusion that one has understood the concerns and outlooks of another may simply constitute another form of presumptuous-ness and arrogance. But, as we have said repeatedly, this valuable insight has sometimes been exaggerated to *assume* the impossibility of such understanding. Admittedly, there are contexts of hostility, resentment, or domination in which only further harm can be done by attempts to communicate across conflicts and gulfs of misunderstanding. We do not wish for a moment to deny that more harm can and often does occur, or to posit the naive hope that if we just keep speaking with one another, all conflicts can be resolved. But neither do we want to posit, on theoretical grounds, a society of Babel that no one can seriously desire.

Incommensurability and Translation

As noted, dialogue across differences can run up against deep linguistic, cultural, or paradigmatic incommensurabilities. The frustrating experience of radical mis-understanding or nonunderstanding is familiar to us all. In certain cases, the gulf of misunderstanding might be so deep and wide that on specific points no meeting of the minds is possible, even at the level of mutual comprehension, let alone agreement.

But in addressing this problem, we need to keep in mind that dialogue across differences has two different aspects. On one hand, dialogue aims at the recon-ciliation of differences or the formation of new common meanings in pursuit of intersubjective understanding. Antimodern writers often deny the possibility of attaining intersubjectivity across differences, and regard the pursuit of such an end as threatening the elimination of differences or the domination of one particular perspective over others. This concern is supported by social and his-torical experiences in which the language of commonality, community, and con-sensus has simply masked the presumption or imposition of homogeneity, de-spite real diversity. But it is possible to acknowledge that threat, and work to avoid it, without giving up the hope of achieving some degree of intersubjectivity and common understanding. As Paulo Freire, Hans-Georg Gadamer, Jurgen

Habermas, and numerous others have argued, dialogue can proceed in a manner that aims toward careful, respectful, nondominating agreement.[50]

The ordinary experience of translation across natural languages tells us that the usual case is that effective common meanings *can* be established, and that sufficient equivalencies can be built over time so that speakers of any two languages can achieve a significant degree of mutual understanding and effective coordination of action. Translation does not need to be complete or perfect for this to occur. This point about natural languages can be extended to other cultural and paradigmatic systems as well. [51] The occasional experience of radical incommensurability should not obscure the much more important point that, despite enormous diversity, our ways of thinking and speaking about our world also exhibit striking commonalities. These commonalities give us some reason to pursue attempts at overcoming misunderstandings or nonunderstandings when they do occur, rather than abandoning the fort because it is assumed to be futile. Moreover, even where the goal of common understanding or consensus may not be achievable, a second aspect of dialogue across differences must be kept in mind.

Creating or establishing common meanings is not the only possible goal. In this second aspect, dialogue is nonconvergent, directed not toward conformity and agreement but toward understanding, tolerance, and respect across difference. Even if one rejects dialogue in the first sense described above, there still remains dialogue in this second sense — and, indeed, as we have stressed, the possibility and desirability of dialogue in at least this latter sense is *assumed,* not denied by positions that "celebrate difference." Moreover, the conflicts and tensions that exist in a complex society require more than the mere "acknowledgement of contiguity" that Young recommends. We need some way of coping with our differences and, if we are committed to a democratic form of life, a means of making discussions about such matters *more* inclusive, not less so.

Rethinking Dialogue

Dialogue, therefore, offers paths both to establishing intersubjectivity and consensus, and to creating a degree of understanding across (unresolved) differences. Recognizing this carries us beyond the conception of dialogue as a single, convergent method aimed toward Truth. Dialogue can also serve the purpose of creating partial understandings, if not agreement, across differences. Complete understanding and total incomprehensibility are not the only two alternatives — indeed, both of these are quite rare. At a deeper level, we need to realize that *understanding and misunderstanding always occur together.* No communication process is perfect; no intersubjective understanding, even among members who occupy the same category of difference, is ever complete. Moreover, it is by the very process of "misunderstanding" others — that is, interpreting their claims and beliefs in slightly different terms than they do themselves — that the process of communication actually moves forward to new understandings. This is partly why we engage in conversation. We need to be similar enough to make dialogue possible, but we also need to be different enough to make it worthwhile.

Thus, dialogue can take the form of *maintaining* difference, not trying to eliminate it. Once one embarks in a dialogical exchange, various degrees of convergent or divergent understandings might result. These can be seen along a spectrum comprising:

a) agreement and consensus, identifying beliefs or values all parties can agree to;

b) not agreement, but a common understanding in which the parties do not agree, but establish common meanings in which to discuss their differences;

c) not a common understanding, but an understanding of differences in which the parties do not entirely bridge these differences, but through analogies of experience or other indirect translations can understand, at least in part, each other's positions;

d) little understanding, but a respect across differences, in which the parties do not fully understand one another, but by each seeing that the other has a thoughtful, conscientious position, they can come to appreciate and respect even positions they disagree with;

e) irreconcilable and incommensurable difference.

Some antimodern writers argue as if denying the possibility of "a" leaves one only with "e" as an alternative. We have argued that a range of possibilities, of degrees of understanding and misunderstanding, can result, and that the sorts of understandings that will or will not result cannot be prejudged. We must be prepared to deal with the possibility of "e," but there is no reason to assume it.

This discussion of dialogue across difference assumes a pragmatic, contextual, fallibilistic approach that is in our view a helpful corrective to some of the excesses of antimodern discussions. We should not allow our theoretical abstractions to obscure or override the ordinary experiences of our daily lives. It will not be evident, a priori and at a purely intellectual level, whether dialogue in a particular circumstance will or will not be possible, or *how much* understanding will be necessary for our purposes. We may remember vividly the frustrations and pains caused by previous breakdowns of understanding, but it is in attempting to communicate across differences that we discover whether it is possible or not. As noted earlier, the presumption that incommensurability is inevitable threatens to be self-confirming, since when efforts at understanding are not made, are made half-heartedly, or are abandoned when they become difficult or discouraging, then incommensurability does indeed result — but it results as a psychological/social consequence, not because of any inherent necessity.

Context and Personal History

When possible, communicative situations of difference also need to be entered with a sense of the context and personal histories that inform the various parties' outlooks on the situation. Stereotypes about the other parties to a discussion, or degrees of skepticism that might be based on failures experienced in previous attempts, cannot be wished away. Prior experiences may have created feelings of intimidation, resentment, and hurt; an imposition of silence, or the self-imposed habit of silence, may be ingrained in some of the participants. Conversely, prior experiences may also have created feelings of superiority and a tendency to silence others.

Such factors, especially when they become self-perpetuating, can be serious barriers to successful communication. One starting point in overcoming such barriers is eliciting and honoring the self-expressions of previously silenced partners. This effort can be self-generating: attaining some degree of successful self-expression and mutual understanding creates, in part, the conditions of confidence and trust in which future attempts might be carried further (just as failures can reinforce skepticism about the possibility of success, or the value of even trying).

Another aspect of the effects of context and personal history among the participants in a discussion is the prejudgments they might have formed about one another. Successful communication, and understanding across differences, does not in itself reconcile all differences and conflicts — indeed it may draw them all the more sharply. But it can help draw them in terms that are more accurate, and make us more cognizant of the factors and rationales that have given rise to them.

The university setting, while based on certain broad norms of tolerance and open communication, is not by any means exempt from these constraints. We see a strong contemporary illustration of these issues in recent arguments over the possibilities and limits of "free speech" on college campuses.[52] While clearly dependent on tolerance of controversial and even inflammatory points of view, universities have begun struggling with the problem of how, given the conflicts and prejudices of the broader society, the exercise of certain kinds of speech (for example, racial epithets) might actually *restrict* the freedom of others to feel secure enough to participate in the broader educational conversation. Such tensions illustrate the real social and political context in which specific educational choices need to be made; they set competing values and interests against one another, and there is no guarantee that the compromises made to further dialogue will or can serve all points of view equally. The practical choices here are rarely clear-cut, and more talking is not always the best thing.

Communicative Virtues

Such external, institutional factors, and the presumptions that the participants to a dialogical situation bring with them, provide a context that often limits the kinds and degrees of understanding that can be achieved in the discussion. But the success of dialogue across differences also depends on what we have called "communicative virtues" that help make dialogue possible and help sustain the dialogical relation over time. These virtues include tolerance, patience, respect for differences, a willingness to listen, the inclination to admit that one may be mistaken, the ability to reinterpret or translate one's own concerns in a way that makes them comprehensible to others, the self-imposition of restraint in order that others may "have a turn" to speak, and the disposition to express one's self honestly and sincerely. The possession of these virtues influences one's capacities both to express one's own beliefs, values, and feelings accurately, and to listen to and hear those of others.[53]

These virtues do not reflect a preferred linguistic style per se, but rather express an affective and intellectual stance toward partners in conversation; they promote a generous and sympathetic regard for the perspectives and self-expression of others. The point of stressing the communicative virtues is not to advance a particular educational or political agenda over others, but rather to suggest the dispositions that seem necessary for promoting any open and serious discussion about such matters. If a tentative agreement about how we ought to proceed educationally is to be inclusive in any meaningful sense, then it will require dialogue expressive of the communicative virtues. This is not to say that the communicative virtues provide a "solution" to the difficulties and inequalities that exist in many communicative situations, or that making our dialogical relations more expressive of the communicative virtues is only a matter of good will and personal effort. We wish merely to suggest that if dialogue across differences is equitable, it must be animated by such virtues.

A central question for education, then, is how such communicative virtues are developed and how they can be sustained over time. In our view, these dispositions are created, reflexively, in the kinds of communicative relations in which we are engaged, as children and into adult life. The nature of these virtues is that they are only acquired in relation to communicative partners, and improved by practice. Thus, to develop these virtues is to be drawn into certain kinds of communicative relations: one becomes tolerant, patient, and respecting of others through association with people who are similarly disposed.

Virtues require close attention to the particulars of the communicative situation at hand, and how any of them are expressed will vary according to what these situations require. Listening, for example, although generally regarded as a virtue in situations where one's partner is struggling with ideas that he or she wants to articulate, might not be so regarded in situations where urgently needed directions or information are asked for, or where silence signals acquiescence to views one does not actually hold. Similarly, tolerance and patience may be virtues when practiced by a teacher striving to understand and appreciate a student's perspective, but not so when invoked to protect racist or sexist speech that intimidates, harms or silences others. Hence, these communicative qualities are best thought of as virtues or dispositions rather than rules, precisely because they need to be interpreted and applied thoughtfully to different situations.

Educational contexts foster some communicative virtues, but also foster habits and dispositions that interfere with effective communicative relations. The academic culture often rewards acquiring an aggressive style of communication, epitomized by an "adversary method" that assumes that the best way to evaluate another's ideas or arguments is to subject them to rigorous and severe questioning.[54] This communicative style impedes dialogue in many situations, especially given contexts of previous frustration, insecurity, or silencing. Nurturing communicative virtues in ourselves and in our students requires that we acknowledge these and other habits of speech that may work against our best intentions. While owning up to what we bring to a dialogic encounter does not ensure that we will actually practice the communicative virtues appropriate to that encounter, certainly such critical self-awareness is a step toward changing our practices.

The value of developing and sustaining the communicative virtues in ourselves and in others provides another justification for why dialogue across differences is worthwhile, even when it is difficult. Indeed, it is precisely because of the difficulty of such situations that we stand to learn from them. There are

benefits to be derived from conversations with those like us, but there are benefits also to be gained from persisting in discussions with those not like us. The
communicative virtues can be enhanced by pursuing and persisting in a variety
of conversations, even with reluctant partners. Yet it is also important to accept,
in some contexts at least, that chosen silence can be a mode of self-expression,
and that it may constitute a necessary phase of self-protection before future
communication can occur.[55]

CONCLUSION

One of the essential communicative virtues, we believe, is a tolerance and respect
across differences. There is no doubt that one of the essential personal characteristics that pre-exists and predetermines educational possibilities within a given
setting is the attitude of the participants, not only to the particular differences
that may divide them, but also toward the very fact of difference itself. Sometimes
there are tendencies to approach opposing points of view with suspicion, fear,
or scorn; these attitudes may arise from intolerance and prejudice, or from
previous painful encounters with such points of view. There may be a tendency
to infer from certain differences the likeliness of other kinds of conflict; to
prejudge, for example, that a person will be unreasonable or insensitive to one's
concerns because that person is a member of a particular group. We have discussed already how these sorts of prejudgments can prevent discussion by assuming that dialogue across differences cannot occur, or will have little benefit if it
does occur.

Such attitudes place a serious constraint on the possibilities of dialogue, and
education generally. In this article, we have tried to present a more pragmatic
view of dialogue, stressing the ways in which dialogical relations need to be
formed, protected, and developed over time; specifically, in education, we often
need to focus more on the formation and development of particular communicative relations, devoted to inquiry and understanding, than on specific predetermined learning outcomes. A central feature of these sorts of relations is coming to regard differences as providing educational opportunities, not as
intimidating barriers. We learn by making connections between what we know
and what is new to us: this cognitive process is paralleled, and fostered develop-
mentally, by the communicative relations in which we are engaged from a very
early age.

Our point in this article is that certain postmodern, and particularly antimodern, tendencies in educational theory have worked against the goal of trying to
achieve understanding across differences. There is a fundamental shift in worldview between regarding difference as a problem, a threat, a nuisance, or an
insurmountable barrier, and viewing difference — any difference — as an opportunity, as a challenge to our abilities to communicate and understand. In this
latter view, such differences, while difficult to overcome, can benefit our understanding of ourselves and others, to say nothing of its broader social benefits in
terms of promoting social concord and cooperation. If we "celebrate difference,"
then we also need clear positive insights into how to maintain discussion across
differences; such an endeavor is crucial socially, and especially educationally.

We cannot stress this final point too strongly: pursuing dialogue across differences is essential to important aims of personal development and moral conduct. We ought to help foster the disposition to work toward understanding across differences, and the communicative virtues and skills that make this possible. Yet antimodern conceptions of difference often have the effect of discouraging the exercise of such virtues.

In contrast, we have argued for the need to maintain a pragmatic stance toward framing educational problems and our methods of coping with them. Some antimodern writing has fostered an "all or nothing" attitude on these matters. If complete intersubjectivity is not possible, then it is not possible at all. If some frustrating and painful experiences have been borne in the past, this justifies future avoidance of such difficulties. If some relations have been tainted by elements of domination and inequity, they cannot be reestablished on more humane and decent grounds. If misunderstanding or nonunderstanding are encountered, a deep and irresolvable incommensurability is inferred. These sorts of exaggerations unnecessarily prejudge the prospects of success or failure in communicative relations, which is usually counterproductive, sometimes self-fulfilling, and nearly always oversimplifies the problem and the best way to cope with it.

As we have said, we do not wish to minimize the deep suffering, intimidation, and sense of anger that experiences of domination create. Nor do we deny the frequent failures of dialogue across differences. But our educational goal must be to learn from these, to try to avoid them in future efforts, and to move beyond them; the last thing educational theorists should be doing is exaggerating them, reifying them, and, in the process, exacerbating them. Learning and developing as a person involves incorporating painful lessons, failures, and frustrations, without being paralyzed by them; it involves living with tensions, rather than striving to mask them with oversimplifications that might make the world seem more palatable.[56] And it may be this willingness to continue the conversation without certainty of success that constitutes the basis for a fruitful postmodern outlook on education: "This is the 'postmodern' task of the critical educator — to live with courage and conviction with the understanding that knowledge is always partial and incomplete."[57]

NOTES

1. We capitalize the term here and elsewhere in the paper for a reason, to be explained.
2. Bronwyn Davies, "Education for Sexism: A Theoretical Analysis of the Sex/Gender Bias in Education," *Educational Philosophy and Theory, 21,* No. 1 (1989), 8.
3. Patti Lather, "Postmodernism and the Politics of Enlightenment," *Educational Foundations, 3,* No. 3 (1989), 8–9.
4. Todd Gitlin, "Postmodernism Defined, At Last," *Utne Reader,* July-August 1989, p. 52.
5. See M. M. Bakhtin, "Discourse in the Novel," in *The Dialogic Imagination: Four Essays* (Austin: University of Texas Press, 1981), pp. 272–282. See also Richard A. Quantz and Terence O'Connor, "Writing Critical Ethnography: Dialogue, Multivoicedness, and Carnival in Cultural Texts," *Educational Theory, 38,* No. 1 (1988), 95–109.
6. See, for example, Angela P. Harris, "Race and Essentialism in Feminist Legal Theory," *Stanford Law Review, 48* (1990), 581–616.

7. Samuel Bowles and Herbert Gintis, *Schooling in Capitalist America: Educational Reform and the Contradictions of Economic Life* (New York: Basic Books, 1977).

8. It is increasingly problematic, in fact, even to identify a coherent "Left" any longer; titles such as "What's Left?" recur in progressive publications. But two general trends are clear. One is a shift away from Marxian-flavored Leftism, which emphasized the objectivity of class, race, and gender positions as the basis for political organization and action, to a more culturalist notion of political identity, in which ethnicity, sexual orientation, body type, etc., are given at least co-equal significance with class, race, and gender — and in which even those traditional groupings are regarded more as cultural constructions than as objective "givens." The second shift, correspondingly, is a de-emphasis on the traditional stakes of Left struggle, vis-à-vis capitalist industry and the state, toward "new social movements" that elevate what previously might have been considered "personal" or "lifestyle" issues to the new terrain of politico-cultural struggle. Postmodernism, generally speaking, is the ideology of this new conception of political identity and activism.

9. For an extremely useful overview of the tradition, see David Harvey, *The Condition of Postmodernity: An Inquiry into the Origins of Cultural Change* (Cambridge, MA: Basil Blackwell, 1989).

10. Jean-François Lyotard, *The Postmodern Condition: A Report on Knowledge* (Minneapolis: University of Minnesota Press, 1984). For clear summaries of Lyotard's view, see Nancy Fraser and Linda Nicholson, "Social Criticism Without Philosophy: An Encounter Between Feminism and Postmodernism," in *Universal Abandon? The Politics of Postmodernism*, ed. Andrew Ross (Minneapolis: University of Minnesota Press, 1989), pp. 83–104; Carol Nicholson, "Postmodernism, Feminism, and Education: The Need for Solidarity," *Educational Theory*, *39*, No. 3 (1989), 197–205; and Michael Peters, "Techno-Science, Rationality, and the University: Lyotard on the 'Postmodern Condition,'" *Educational Theory*, *39*, No. 2 (1989), 93–105.

11. Zygmunt Bauman, "Strangers: The Social Construction of University and Particularity," *Telos*, *28* (1988–1989), 23.

12. The main source for these ideas, of course, is Michel Foucault. See *Power/Knowledge: Selected Interviews and Other Writings, 1972–1977* (New York: Pantheon Books, 1980), and "On Power" in *Politics, Philosophy, Culture: Selected Interviews and Other Writings, 1977–1984* (New York: Routledge, 1988), pp. 96–109. In the educational literature, a very good overview and analysis of these issues is offered by Cleo Cherryholmes, *Power and Criticism: Poststructural Investigations in Education* (New York: Teachers College Press, 1988). See also Nicholas C. Burbules, "A Theory of Power in Education," *Educational Theory*, *36*, No. 2 (1986), 95–114.

13. Lather, "Postmodernism and the Politics of Enlightenment," pp. 20–21.

14. Such a strong challenge to authority in all of its forms can be found in Elizabeth Ellsworth, "Why Doesn't This Feel Empowering? Working through the Repressive Myths of Critical Pedagogy," *Harvard Educational Review, 59* (1989), 297–324.

15. Bauman, "Strangers," pp. 39–40.

16. Maria C. Lugones and Elizabeth V. Spelman, "Have We Got a Theory for You! Feminist Theory, Cultural Imperialism, and the Demand for 'The Women's Voice,'" *Women's Studies International Forum, 6*, No. 6 (1983), 575.

17. This criticism is posed by a number of authors, including Fraser and Nicholson, "Social Criticism Without Philosophy"; Nicholson, "Postmodernism, Feminism, and Education"; Jane Flax, "Postmodernism and Gender Relations in Feminist Theory," and Christine Di Stefano, "Dilemmas of Difference: Feminism, Modernity, and Postmodernism," in *Feminism/Postmodernism*, ed. Linda J. Nicholson (New York: Routledge, 1990), pp. 39–62, 63–82; see also Peter McLaren, "Postmodernity and the Death of Politics: A Brazilian Reprieve," *Educational Theory, 36*, No. 4 (1986), 389–401.

18. To clarify our discussion, and avoid confusion, we will from now on identify postmodernism — lower case — as one particular tendency within Postmodern thought, and

cease to use the global — upper case — term. We do not think that "Postmodernism" is an accurate term for describing antimodern views.

19. For a range of postmodern views, see Linda Brodkey, "Postmodern Pedagogy for Progressive Educators," *Journal of Education, 169,* No. 3 (1987), 138–143; Henry A. Giroux, "Border Pedagogy in the Age of Postmodernism," *Journal of Education, 170,* No. 3 (1988), 162–181; Douglas Kellner, "Reading Images Critically: Toward a Postmodern Pedagogy," *Journal of Education, 170,* No. 3 (1988), 231–252; Peter McLaren, "Schooling the Postmodern Body: Critical Pedagogy and the Politics of Enfleshment," *Journal of Education, 170,* No. 3 (1988), 53–99; and Peter McLaren and Rhonda Hammer, "Critical Pedagogy and the Postmodern Challenge: Toward a Critical Postmodernist Pedagogy of Liberation," *Educational Foundations, 3,* No. 3 (1989), 29–62.

20. Henry A. Giroux, "Postmodernism and the Discourse of Educational Criticism," *Journal of Education, 170,* No. 3 (1988), 26–27, and republished in his book with Stanley Aronowitz, *Postmodern Education* (Minneapolis: University of Minnesota Press, 1991).

21. For example, see McLaren, "Postmodernity and the Death of Politics," pp. 393–394.

22. Ellsworth, "Why Doesn't This Feel Empowering?" pp. 301–302.

23. Jacques Derrida, *Positions* (Chicago: University of Chicago Press, 1981), p. 27.

24. Jacques Derrida, "Difference," in *Margins of Philosophy* (Chicago: University of Chicago Press, 1982), pp. 1–27.

25. Di Stefano, "Dilemmas of Difference," pp. 77–78.

26. Ellsworth, "Why Doesn't This Feel Empowering?" pp. 314, 316.

27. Ellsworth, "Why Doesn't This Feel Empowering?" p. 324. An airing of some of the issues raised by these comments can be found in an update to that article: "Correspondence," *Harvard Educational Review, 60* (1990), 388–405.

28. Similarly, Di Stefano identifies this tendency to slide between these two theoretical perspectives in the work of Sandra Harding, who asserts: "I argue for the primacy of fragmented identities but only for those *healthy* ones constructed on a *solid and non-defensive core identity,* and only within a *unified* opposition, a solidarity against the culturally dominant forces for unitarianism" (Di Stefano's emphases). As Di Stefano points out, criteria such as "healthy," "solid," and "core," all appeal implicitly to a thoroughly modern ontology (Di Stefano, "Dilemmas of Difference," pp. 76–77).

29. Iris Marion Young, "The Ideal of Community and the Politics of Difference," in Nicholson, *Feminism/Postmodernism,* p. 300.

30. Young, "The Ideal of Community," pp. 309, 311.

31. Young, "The Ideal of Community," pp. 316–317.

32. Young, "The Ideal of Community," p. 318.

33. Young, "The Ideal of Community," p. 319.

34. Indeed, like other antimodern writers, Young exhibits postmodern elements as well; returning later in the very same essay to the topic of "community," she admits that a communitarian ideal *can* be established that respects difference (p. 320). Hence, again, having vigorously "rejected" the ideal of community, it turns out that she actually only wants to reformulate it around certain values, such as tolerance for diversity, that are every bit as much *modern* as other values she wants to deny.

35. John Dewey, *Democracy and Education* (New York: Macmillan, 1916), pp. 95–97.

36. Burbules, "A Theory of Power in Education," pp. 97–99.

37. Pertti J. Pelto, *Anthropologist Research: The Structure of Inquiry* (New York: Harper & Row, 1970), pp. 67–88.

38. See, for example, Peter Winch, *The Meaning of a Social Science and Its Relation to Philosophy* (London: Routledge & Kegan Paul, 1958), pp. 107–108.

39. Lisa Delpit, "The Silenced Dialogue: Power and Pedagogy in Educating Other People's Children," *Harvard Educational Review, 58* (1988), 280–298; Ellsworth, "Why Doesn't This Feel Empowering?"

40. Walter Feinberg, "A Role for Philosophy of Education in Intercultural Research," in *Philosophy of Education 1989: Proceedings of the Forty-fifth Annual Meeting of the Philosophy*

of Education Society, ed. Ralph Page (Normal, IL: Philosophy of Education Society, 1990), pp. 2–19.

41. Nicholas C. Burbules, "The Tragic Sense of Education," *Teachers College Record, 91,* No. 4 (1990), 468–479.

42. Gail Pheterson, "Alliances between Women: Overcoming Internalized Oppression and Internalized Domination," *Signs: Journal of Women in Culture and Society, 12,* No. 11 (1986), 146–160.

43. Pheterson, "Alliances between Women," p. 146.

44. Pheterson, "Alliances between Women," p. 157.

45. Pheterson, "Alliances between Women," p. 151.

46. Pheterson, "Alliances between Women," p. 158.

47. Nancy Hartsock, "Rethinking Modernism: Minority and Majority Theories," *Cultural Critique, 7* (1987), 187–206; see also Frances E. Mascia-Lees, Patricia Sharpe, and Colleen Ballerino Cohen, "The Postmodernist Turn in Anthropology: Cautions from a Feminist Perspective," *Journal of the Steward Anthropological Society, 17,* Nos. 1, 2 (1987–1988), 251–282.

48. Peter Elbow, *Embracing Contraries: Explorations in Learning and Teaching* (New York: Oxford University Press, 1986), chap. 12.

49. Mary Field Belenky, Blythe McVicker Clinchy, Nancy Rule Goldberger, and Jill Mattuck Tarule, *Women's Ways of Knowing: The Development of Self, Voice, and Mind* (New York: Basic Books, 1986), chap. 6.

50. Paulo Freire, *Pedagogy of the Oppressed* (New York: Seabury, 1970); Ira Shor and Paulo Freire, "What Is the Dialogical Method of Teaching?" *Journal of Education, 169* (1987), 11–31; Hans-Georg Gadamer, *Truth and Method* (New York: Crossroads, 1982), pp. 273–274, 337; and Jurgen Habermas, *Communication and the Evolution of Society* (Oxford: Polity, 1990), chap. 1, and *Theory of Communicative Action: Vol. 1. Reason and the Rationalization of Society* (Boston: Beacon Press, 1984), pp. 8–42, 286–337.

51. Nicholas C. Burbules, "Education as Translation," Paper presented at meeting of the California Association for Philosophy of Education, Davis, CA, April 1988.

52. For a good summary of these issues, see Jon Weiner, "Free Speech for Campus Bigots?" *The Nation,* February 26, 1990, pp. 272–276.

53. We are completing a separate manuscript that develops the idea of "communicative virtues" in detail.

54. Janice Moulton, "A Paradigm of Philosophy: The Adversary Method," in *Discovering Reality: Feminist Perspectives on Epistemology, Metaphysics, Methodology, and Philosophy of Science,* ed. Sandra Harding and Merrill B. Hintikka (Dordrecht, Holland: Reidel, 1984), pp. 149–164.

55. Magda Lewis, "Framing Women and Silence: Disrupting the Hierarchy of Discursive Practices," Paper presented at the annual meeting of the American Educational Research Association, Boston, April 1990.

56. See Burbules, "The Tragic Sense of Education."

57. McLaren and Hammer, "Critical Pedagogy and the Postmodern Challenge," p. 32.

The authors wish to credit the helpful suggestions and criticisms of Walter Feinberg, Ralph Page, and Audrey Thompson.

Can We Talk?
A Response to Burbules and Rice

MARY S. LEACH

In recent years, questions of voice have been raised by feminists who have been working against the use of traditional analytic categories and political positionings within critical theories that discursively present women as a homogeneous group.[1] Women in the developing world have argued against a hastily derived notion of "universal sisterhood" and have emphasized the need for creating new analytical space for understanding women as individuals experiencing their own various struggles in their own particular histories.[2] Other scholars have begun to make similar arguments, and now the question of "voices" that embody and transcribe race and gender in the classroom is being addressed seriously in feminist educational scholarship.[3]

A central problem of this work is that it seeks to deal with and make room for the interaction of potentially antagonistic voices, but it does not attempt to absorb the differences into any universalizing discourse. Using selected aspects of postmodern thought as tools, some feminist educators are exploring pedagogical strategies capable of both making sense of and doing work within contexts of unassimilated difference. To do this they must, even as they problematize, engage in a "politics of difference." Their goal is to work toward building coalitions across recognized and respected deep divides of socially constructed and historically embedded differences among individuals and groups.[4]

Now this would seem a worthy effort for radical educators, especially at a time when the academy and the classroom are coming to be viewed even by the popular press as "contested terrains" — that is, as political and cultural sites that represent struggle over what constitutes "proper" knowledge by differently empowered social constituencies. If emancipatory educators can show that theoretical discourses, which ostensibly articulate goals of emancipatory education for everyone, actually *re*inscribe unequal power relations by unwittingly eliding voices of difference, then that would seem to be a major revelation worthy of serious consideration. Indeed, a fierce debate has now been generated within the educational arena over the effort to problematize presently constituted leftist educational discourses that presume a politics of commonality and unity for advancing the fight toward liberation. Work that proposes the idea of using educational practice as a tool for creating and sustaining viable cultural identities as communities of difference that make a difference has animated a flurry of new activity among educational theorists and practitioners.[5]

Harvard Educational Review   Vol. 62   No. 2   Summer 1992, 257–271.

While the debate has been articulated in a number of different ways, the majority of responses have simply reasserted, albeit in a variety of forms, a politics of commonality that answers the question "can we talk?" with "of course, and we must do so, lest we further endanger our political goals." However, one more carefully prepared response advances the idea that we can talk in a dialogue *across* differences, one that will not reproduce relations of domination and inequality but will allow us to communicate even across radical cultural and political diversity.[6] This dialogue, it is argued, is not only imminently possible, but also necessary, in order to take advantage of "the opportunity to challenge our abilities to communicate and understand one another."[7]

Let me begin by describing part of the effort made by Nicholas Burbules and Suzanne Rice to set out what a dialogue across differences would entail. My purpose is to raise what I see as problems in their view that I think warrant serious attention. In particular, while I do not think it is intended on their part, I believe there is a very real possibility that their entire project works to help reinscribe an individualist picture of social relations, and consequently to promote all the attendant problems that that position has historically brought to educational theory and practice. What follows here, then, is meant to be read as a warning against turning toward a well-worn path that we've been led down before — with disastrous consequences for all but a privileged few.

Individual Differences

In an interesting attempt to set out a view that promotes dialogue across differences, Burbules and Rice argue not only that the notion of dialogue has pedagogical value, but also that to spend our time working toward such a process would be a clear positive educational goal. Claiming that "there is no reason to assume (a priori) that dialogue across differences involves either eliminating those differences or imposing one group's view on others," and that it is both possible and worthwhile to work for a process that will promote understanding, cooperation, and accommodation, the authors attempt to articulate what must be present to establish and maintain the possibility of a "successful" dialogue.[8] The argument recognizes, and then proceeds to clearly set out, the important, indeed necessary, conditions for establishing such a dialogue. It is particularly vital, it is claimed, that these conditions be in place within educational contexts.

One key condition involves all parties at least attempting to adopt certain attitudes; for example, "playing the believing game." In this exercise, all participants need to adopt an attitudinal position that begins with the acknowledgment that we can learn from what each other has to say. It is important that all recognize and grant at least initial plausibility to others' sincerely held positions. As the authors explain, "This attitude does not preclude questioning the other's self-expression at some later point, but it places the priority on establishing a communicative relation of trust and openness, and of trying to err on the side of sympathy and respectfulness when discussions first begin."[9]

Playing the believing game can lead everyone participating to acquire a better sense of the context and personal histories of the "players," a second key condition for establishing successful communications. Whenever possible, prior experiences that serve to "inform" the various participants' outlooks on the present process should be taken into account. Also important to recognize are the institutional constraints that parties may believe have previously worked to promote certain points of view, legitimating certain discourse while devaluing others. The context in which the process is situated must be understood by all as affecting the judgments of those involved and, as often as not, limiting "the kinds and degrees of understanding that can be achieved in the discussion."[10]

A third and most important condition set out for effecting a successful dialogue across differences is seen to be dependent upon a set of personal "communicative" virtues. These are "dispositions" that participating individuals must "possess" and "enact" in order to foster and maintain a nurturing environment for successful conversation. These virtues, "essential personal characteristics" as they are called, are "tolerance, patience, respect for differences, a willingness to listen, the inclination to admit that one may be mistaken, the ability to reinterpret or translate one's own concerns in a way that makes them comprehensible to others, the self-imposition of restraint in order that others may have a turn to speak, and the disposition to express oneself honestly and sincerely."[11] These dispositions are believed to be created "reflexively *within* the individual in the communicative relations in which we *are* engaged, *as children and into adult life.*" (The emphasis is mine: note here that the claim is one of the present and past, not of some future time when equitable relations are effected.) Care is taken to point out that these virtues are general dispositions developed "in" us only "through association with people who are similarly disposed," and that their expression will necessarily depend upon interpretation and judgment made by each individual.

It is clear that these virtues are not easily developed or enacted in all situations: I think few would dispute this claim. In fact, despite the difficulties of living up to these personal ideals, difficulties expressed at great length by Burbules and Rice, few would want to argue against their value. Indeed, such ideals hold a powerful appeal, particularly for women who have been admonished since childhood to be "a good girl." That archetype of femininity, the "good girl," is intimate with these ideals, and has most likely worked toward them all her life out of a fear of losing not only her gender identity and her assigned social role, but also the approval of her family, her boyfriend, or her boss.[12] My point is that in our culture, now and in the past, these "personal" attributes are gender related.

Although the authors allude several times to "relations of dominance," "unequal partners in the social commonwealth," "the dimensions of power and privilege that divide and set interests in conflict," and the "power relations underlying traditional educational aims and practices," nowhere in their article do Burbules and Rice explicitly address the current relations that promote the practice and rewards of these virtues based on gendered identities. Thus a serious question remains: How can appeals to abstract virtues that currently have a differential impact on gendered individuals promote equitable nurturing conditions for all? The answer for the authors seems to be that "learning and developing as a person involves incorporating painful lessons, failures, and frustrations, without being paralyzed by them; it involves living with tensions, rather than striving to mask them with oversimplifications that might make the world seem more palatable."[13] The message for women and marginalized groups is clear. Despite all that has gone on before, despite our present inequitable conditions, each of us must still try to promote dialogue; the admonition is to have faith in the future. This is not a new message to most of us.

Beyond these problems, a grave concern persists regarding the kind of appeal that is exhibited in what I've just described. I worry that the whole approach, the fulcrum of analysis for the conditions necessary to establish and maintain dialogue, serves to shore up the long-disputed liberal humanist idea of the individual. This view is still embraced and still used to justify unequal educational practices. Although the argument has been carefully drawn to acknowledge and expose the limits, impediments, and difficulties we face in establishing the conditions for success, in its heavy investment in dispositions and virtues *possessed* by individuals, it tends to put into the foreground an episteme that has for too long given us the conforming illusion that the self, or subject of history, is in authorial command over the processes that constitute that history. One ruinous legacy of that liberal tradition has been to leave us with just this sort of subject-oriented epistemology, now quite naturalized in the name of personality, identity, continuity, stability, and free will.[14] In addition, this legacy has served to promote the idea of a reality — and thus our knowledge of it — that exists outside and separate from consciousness itself. The willing individual, then, gives meaning to this reality by representing or referring to it as accurately as possible. On this view, the task becomes one of "reasonably" talking about this reality in clear, concise speech and in an "accurate," transparent language that does not in itself produce any meaning, but that represents the meaning of the world as unobtrusively as possible.

The persistent idea of the transparency of representation, both visual and verbal, dates back at least to Aristotle and comes down to us via the Western tradition. Just as the "real" is generally assumed and promoted in the ubiquitous advertising images that surround us and in the snapshots we take, it evokes a world we already to seem to know.[15] The "right use" of language in the act of talking or reading and writing, for that matter, leaves understanding of what we say to each other up to the (virtuous) abilities possessed by individuals. The better developed our individual intellectual capacities and characters, the more richly endowed with the meritorious virtues of sensitivity, patience, restraint, honesty, and sincerity, the better able we will be to "communicate" with each other "reasonably" and "fairly." Burbules and Rice's claims that the communicative virtues are "developed in" us and "exercised" within a relational process recalls the well-known theory of socialization long favored in sociological and psychological literature. As the authors posit, socialization theory recognizes that the processes that form individual personality and character have both relational and social aspects; this acknowledgment, however, does not denote a relational ontology. To understand the virtues as properties "acquired," "possessed," and "practiced" by individuals, rather than as properties of the *relations themselves,* reinscribes the individualistic ontology characteristic of liberal humanist thought. This is not a matter of mere expression, but of posing a worldview centered around the individual, around his/her behavior and actions.

Any focus on the idea of selves continuously constituted by various discursive practices is effectively displaced by a focus on ourselves as sovereign selves, or groups of selves, and on our independent consciousness acting outside contingencies of history. We are also outside language and other interruptions. How well we have developed and enacted our dispositions, how "sensitive" we are to our own meanings and to those of others — meanings put there by separate but equally free self-cohering subjects in the privacy of their consciousness and their ability to translate their concerns — ends up as the major factor in determining the difficulties or ease we have in communicating.

The political consequences of this sort of liberal individualism have been long recognized by feminists and marginalized groups. And feminist teachers in the developing world are particularly aware of these consequences; their experiences in the classroom have made them wary of just the sort of "attitudinal" engagement described above.[16] These feminist teachers propose that, within inequitable relations, these very attitudinal, individualistic parameters encourage an empty pluralism and domesticate the historical agency of peoples in the developing world. Thus, they have been struggling against the formulation of knowledge and politics that these parameters set. They argue that managing conflict in the classroom by focusing on the creation of an ethos of the "personal" and "interpersonal" glosses over complex ethical and political issues, erasing the very politics of knowledge involved in teaching and learning about difference. For example, they have (as I have) observed that White students' efforts to be sensitive to different experiences often has led to the positioning of people of color as the central voices and the bearers of all knowledge in a class or course. As a consequence, White students often become observers, relieving themselves of responsibility for the discussion or seeing themselves as having nothing valuable to contribute. On the surface it appears that the students of color are being granted voice and agency, but it is necessary to consider what particular kind of voice it is that is being allowed. If it is a voice located in a different and separate space from the agency of White students, it can have the effect of codifying "difference" so that race (or gender) is conceptualized in terms of personal or individual experience. While it thus appears that in such a class the histories and cultures of marginalized peoples are now "legitimate" objects of study and discussion, the legitimation tends to take place at the attitudinal, interpersonal level rather than in terms of a fundamental challenge to dominant or hegemonic views of knowledge and history. Feminist teachers worry that the focus on personal attitudes and dispositions bypasses the complexly situated politics of knowledge and ends up reinstituting a "particular individual-oriented codification and commodification of gender and race."[17]

Re/doing

It is incredibly difficult, as we know, to open up new terrain that unsettles both the ideas of the "subject as content" and the "subject as structure," but that is what feminists using postmodern insights are attempting to do.[18] How to theorize, even how to talk "sensibly" and "reasonably" against both a "subject" that is "natural" and a "subject" that is merely "effects" is a present problem that we know has different ethical/political consequences for different groups. This situation has created an urgency in some of us because we believe that the familiar forms of presenting and representing our selves are no longer suited for presenting a perception that is in some sense new. How to talk about self and context as a problem that can be, in significant ways, unrelated to each other and entirely parts of each other at one and the same time is our difficulty. Teresa de Lauretis discusses this seeming "paradox" in terms of feminism as it is being constructed in feminist discourse today. She notes that "the subject I see emerging . . . is one that is at the same time inside and outside the ideology of gender, and conscious of being so, conscious of that twofold pull of that division, that doubled vision."[19]

The recognition of the difficulty of our talk has pushed many of us into effecting a doubled movement in our discourse, one often mis-taken by others. The effort here is to disrupt, and thus unmask, the domination of the claim to univocal meaning, the absence of ambiguity, the obsession with oneness, and the "natural" precedence of one term over others.[20] Because of present power relations, we want this double gesture not to lead directly to a new synthesis of opposites, but to an ongoing state of metamorphosis. The depolarization of false opposites can then begin to generate shifting arrangements of alignment and difference among forces that converge or conflict, depending on their relation to other forces with which they variably intersect. The point is to *disrupt* present gender and racial "differences," to create a new space for heterogeneity within personal identities, and to promote the "difference within" genders, for example, instead of the "difference between." It is crucial to realize that the double movement forms only a starting point, rather than a conclusion, on the part of feminist educators.

Making this talk understood will take practice because we are working toward positively unsettling traditional notions of discourse and any ideas of unitary positionality within it.[21] We are also now obliged to speak to others firmly from within our present positions, always realizing and remembering that our ideas are at best tentative, uncertain, unguaranteed. It will be even more difficult to bring others into our (new) talk, to facilitate an appreciation and a remembrance of our mutual goals even as we necessarily speak from our own presently constituted positions.

Because of these difficulties it is possible that some feminists will decide that the practice of dialogue at this particular historical juncture is not the most promising way to expend their energies and resources. This does not mean, of course, that they will necessarily refuse the "challenge" at another time.

So the question remains: Can we talk? My answer is, "You bet we can, but the discussion is just beginning." And, because some of us are bent on delaying the gratification of any conclusion until our subject matter is ready to come to voice, I think we're going to be talking for a long time.

NOTES

1. This problem is one of increasing interest within feminist discourse generally and has been addressed in a number of recent publications specific to education. For an introduction, see Denise Riley, *Am I That Name? Feminism and the Category of Women in*

History (Minneapolis: University of Minnesota Press, 1988). Patti Lather, in *Getting Smart: Feminist Research and Pedagogy With/in the Postmodern* (New York: Routledge, 1991), argues that a critical task is to take away the barriers in educational research and pedagogy that prevent people from speaking for themselves.

2. See particularly the work of Gayatri Spivak, Gloria Anzaldua, Hazel Carby, and bell hooks: Gayatri Spivak, "Can the Subaltern Speak?" in *Marxism and the Interpretation of Culture*, ed. Cary Nelson and Lawrence Grossberg (Urbana: University of Illinois Press, 1988); Gayatri Spivak, "Theory in the Margin" in *Consequences of Theory*, ed. Jonathan Arac and Barbara Johnson (Baltimore: Johns Hopkins University Press, 1991); Gloria Anzaldua, *Borderlands: La Frontera* (San Francisco: Spinsters/Aunt Lute, 1987); Hazel Carby, "White Women Listen! Black Feminism and the Boundaries of Sisterhood" in *The Empire Strikes Back: Race and Racism in 70's Britain*, ed. The Center for Contemporary Cultural Studies (London: Hutchinson, 1982); and bell hooks, *talking back: thinking feminist, thinking black* (Boston: South End Press, 1989).

3. The question has been raised particularly by Elizabeth Ellsworth and a number of others working in education. See Elizabeth Ellsworth, "Why Doesn't This Feel Empowering? Working through the Repressive Myths of Critical Pedagogy," *Harvard Educational Review, 59* (1989), 297–324, and subsequent responses in *Harvard Educational Review, 60* (1990), 388–405. See also Mary S. Leach and Bronwyn Davies, "Crossing the Boundaries: Educational Thought and Gender Equity," *Educational Theory, 40* (1990), 321–332; and Lather, *Getting Smart*, pp. 70–100.

4. This is expressed explicitly by Elizabeth Ellsworth, "The Question Remains: How Will You Hold Awareness of the Limits of Your Knowledge?" *Harvard Educational Review, 60* (1990), 396–405. See also Elizabeth Ellsworth, "Speaking Out of Place: Educational Politics from the Third Wave of Feminism," Paper presented at Bergamo Curriculum Theorizing Conference, Dayton, OH, October 17–21, 1990.

5. See "Correspondence," *Harvard Educational Review, 60* (1990), 388–395. Arguments surrounding these issues are set out by Peter McLaren in "Schooling the Postmodern Body: Critical Pedagogy and the Politics of Enfleshment," *Journal of Education, 170* (1988), 71–72, and Henry Giroux, "Border Pedagogy in the Age of Postmodernism," *Journal of Education, 170* (1988), 162–181.

6. Nicholas C. Burbules and Suzanne Rice, "Dialogue across Differences: Continuing the Conversation," *Harvard Educational Review, 61* (1991), 393–416.

7. Burbules and Rice, "Dialogue across Differences," p. 413.

8. Burbules and Rice, "Dialogue across Differences," p. 402.

9. Burbules and Rice, "Dialogue across Differences," p. 407.

10. Burbules and Rice, "Dialogue across Differences," p. 411.

11. Burbules and Rice, "Dialogue across Differences," p. 411.

12. See particularly Lucy Gilbert and Paula Webster, *Bound by Love: The Sweet Trap of Daughterhood* (Boston: Beacon Press, 1982), and Sandra Lee Bartky, *Femininity and Domination: Studies in the Phenomenology of Oppression* (New York: Routledge, 1990).

13. Burbules and Rice, "Dialogue across Differences," p. 413.

14. See, for example, Yehoshua Ariell, *Individualism and Nationalism in American Ideology* (Baltimore: Penguin Books, 1966); Robert Paul Wolff, *The Poverty of Liberalism* (Boston: MIT Press, 1968); Sandra Harding and Merrill B. Hintikka, eds., *Discovering Reality* (Boston: D. Reidel, 1983); and most recently, Elizabeth Fox-Genovese, *Feminism Without Illusions: A Critique of Individualism* (Chapel Hill: University of North Carolina Press, 1991).

15. For discussions focused on the politics of representation, see Linda Hutcheon, *The Politics of Postmodernism* (New York: Routledge, 1990).

16. For an examination of relations among ethnicity, ideology, and the academy, see Rosaura Sanchez, "Ethnicity, Ideology and Academia," *The American Review, 15* (1987) 80–88. See also Elsa Barkley Brown, "African-American Women's Quilting: A Framework for Conceptualizing and Teaching African-American Women's History," *Signs,*

14 (1989), 921–929. Especially see Chandra Talpade Mohanty on these issues; for example, Chandra Mohanty, "Under Western Eyes: Feminist Scholarship and Colonial Discourses," *Feminist Review, 30* (1988), 61–88, or "Feminist Encounters: Locating the Politics of Experience," *Copyright, 1* (1987), 30–44.

17. For interesting discussions, see E. San Juan, Jr., "The Cult of Ethnicity and the Fetish of Pluralism," *Cultural Critique, 18* (1991), 215–229; and Wahneema Lubiano, "Shuckin' Off the African-American Native Other," *Cultural Critique, 18* (1991), 149–186.

18. The connections between postmodernisms and feminisms have been made by many. See, for example, Jane Flax, *Thinking Fragments: Psychoanalysis, Feminism, and Postmodernism in the Contemporary West* (Berkeley: University of California Press, 1990), and Susan J. Hekman, *Gender and Knowledge: Elements of a Postmodern Feminism* (Boston: Northeastern University Press, 1990).

19. Teresa de Lauretis, *Technologies of Gender: Essays on Theory, Film and Fiction* (Bloomington: Indiana University Press, 1987), p. 10.

20. See particularly Gayatri Spivak, "Displacement and the Discourse of Women," in *Displacement: Derrida and After,* ed. Mark Krupnick (Bloomington: University of Indiana Press, 1983), pp. 169–195.

21. See Paul Rabinow, *The Foucault Reader* (New York: Pantheon, 1984), p. 47.

Can We Be Heard?
Burbules and Rice Reply to Leach

When we submitted our article "Dialogue across Differences: Continuing the Conversation" for publication, we were prepared for many responses that would take issue with what we said. We were even prepared for responses that misunderstood us and attributed to us positions we did not advocate. What we were not prepared for were responses that attributed to us positions that we explicitly denied in our article. Mary Leach's response, to our great dismay, does just this. Could we have made our points so badly?

In this response we will try, first, to reply to these issues by juxtaposing some of Leach's criticisms with what we actually said in our article. Second, we will explain more fully what we mean by "communicative virtues," and why we think they are educationally significant. Third, we will describe what we see as points of underlying concern that we think we share with Leach, even if we may not agree about their precise origins or what to do about them.

What We Said and Didn't Say

First of all, through a selective and surprisingly ungenerous use and interpretation of a few quotes from our article, Leach tries to read into our positions an affinity with liberal humanism, individualism, metaphysical realism, and a belief in the possibility of a "transparent" and "right use" of language. While we are not as convinced as she apparently is that these are completely discredited and untenable positions, the fact is that we do not hold to any of them. Even a cursory reading of our summary of postmodernism in the first part of the article should have shown that we fully understand, and generally support, the postmodern criticisms of these modernist views.

Of greater concern to us is that what we did say in the article is frequently given a characterization by Leach that might make a nice foil for her own assertions, but that ignores explicit statements that we actually made. Our purpose in this response is not to defend these views — of course they might be mistaken — but to see that they receive attention for what they are.

For example, Leach says that we believe dialogue across differences "will promote understanding, cooperation, and accommodation." What we said — more than once — is that dialogue across differences will frequently fail, even given good will and effort, particularly when the communicative situation is distorted by relations of power and domination (pp. 403–404, 405, 407–408, 413). The value of a notion such as "dialogue across differences" is not only that it provides an educational aim to work towards, but also that it provides a critical reference point for seeing how far we actually are from being able to achieve it.

Leach says that we believe that an "attitudinal" change on the part of individuals within dialogue will allow them to gain "a better sense of the context and personal histories" of other participants. What we said is that, while such sensitivity is certainly a desirable educational goal, an attitudinal change is *not* sufficient to make it possible, and that even when dialogue proceeds successfully, the resulting conversation may *heighten* a sense of difference and conflict among participants, not eliminate it (pp. 402, 404, 405, 409).

Leach says that we believe that the communicative virtues are the "most important" conditions for dialogue across differences, and that we define the virtues as "essential personal characteristics." What we said is that the communicative virtues alone *cannot* provide solutions to many situations of communicative inequality (p. 411). And we used the phrase "essential personal characteristics" in only one place in the article, not to define the virtues or to espouse "essentialism," but to refer specifically to what we see as *one* necessary (but not sufficient) condition for dialogue across differences: "There is no doubt that one of the essential personal characteristics that pre-exists and predetermines educational possibilities within a given setting is the attitude of the participants, not only to the particular differences that may divide them, but to the fact of difference itself" (p. 412).

Leach says that we write as if the communicative virtues are routinely acquired in "the present and past, not . . . some future time when equitable relations are effected." The implication seems to be that we think the communicative virtues are unrelated to the formation of nondominating human relations and more supportive institutional arrangements. What we said is that many oppressive contextual and institutional factors do inhibit the acquisition and exercise of the communicative virtues, and that we are far from creating the conditions in which these virtues can be expected of everyone:

> Clearly these subcommunities are not all equal partners in the social commonwealth: there are dimensions of power and privilege that divide them and set their interests in conflict. . . . It is unrealistic and unfair to ask groups already put upon

35

also to take on the burden of trying to understand, and make themselves understood by, those who harm them or benefit from their deprivation. . . . There are contexts of hostility, resentment, or domination in which only further harm can be done by attempts to communicate across conflicts and gulfs of misunderstanding. We do not wish for a moment to deny that more harm can and often does occur, or to posit the naive hope that if we just keep speaking with one another all conflicts can be resolved. . . . [For example,] tolerance and patience may be virtues when practiced by a teacher trying to understand and appreciate a student's perspective, but not when invoked to protect racist or sexist speech that intimidates, harms, or silences others. (pp. 403–404, 408, 411–412)

And we said that it is a positive educational *aim* to create the kind of communicative relations in which the virtues can flourish (pp. 412–413) — an aim that our society is quite obviously far from satisfying (p. 412).

We hope that this clarifies some of our original arguments. It is disturbing to us that a thoughtful and engaged reader, as Leach is, could have misunderstood us so seriously. Our only explanation is that, because we chose to direct our article to a broad audience and to try to find a way to make the central claims of postmodernism clear and plausible for readers who are not centrally immersed in that literature, we failed to use the authorized postmodern terminology for expressing our positions.

Apparently, if one does not accept the complete erasure of the individual within a "relational ontology," then one *must* be an individualist; if one does not accept the totally constructed and local character of knowledge, then one *must* be mired in an Enlightenment "episteme"; if one does not abandon entirely the aim of "reasonable" and "fair" communication, then one *must* believe in an unproblematically "accurate, transparent use of language"; and so on. We trust that readers will recognize the flaws underlying this style of argument, and we want to point out that what we consider the best work in postmodern theory — for example, the work of Seyla Benhabib, Richard Bernstein, Nancy Fraser, Hans-Georg Gadamer, Jurgen Habermas, Linda Nicholson, and Richard Rorty — avoids such dualistic, either/or characterizations of these complex problems.

However, there are also some interesting and important issues raised by Leach's criticisms, and we appreciate the opportunity to engage them and, we hope, advance the discussion further. We would like to remind readers that our primary arguments in the original article concerned the postmodern/antimodern distinction, the nature of difference, and the possibilities of dialogue. Leach devotes most of her attention, however, to our discussion of communicative virtues, even though it constituted a very small part of the article and — as we suggested in a footnote — was only being presented there in a preliminary and incomplete way. Nevertheless, Leach's response has helped us both by pointing out significant gaps in the account provided there, and by showing us some of the ways in which that account may be read and understood by some audiences. Of course, it is our responsibility to try to anticipate and correct such impressions, if we can, and we obviously failed to do so effectively in "Dialogue across Differences." We appreciate the chance to elaborate our view of the communicative virtues in light of Leach's criticisms.[1]

What Are the Communicative Virtues?

Leach offers three critical arguments against our conception of the communicative virtues: that it is grounded in a faulty theory of socialization; that it reinscribes an individualistic ontology; and that it "prescribes" virtues that are related problematically to gender.

We completely agree with Leach about the shortcomings of traditional socialization theory. Particularly problematic, in our view, are those versions of this theory that do not account for the ways in which persons actively construct identity and make sense of the world. Hence, we are puzzled by Leach's claim that we "posit" socialization theory, because the phrase, or citations to that literature, appear nowhere in our article — moreover, the developmental model provided by virtue ethics, which we *do* draw on, differs significantly from that provided by socialization theory. Indeed, one of the attractions of a virtues approach to communicative relations is that it helps to illuminate active dimensions of self-formation. In our view, the development of virtues occurs only through participation in practices, including communicative practices — which, of course, does imply a supporting social and material context. But instead of considering character or identity as something stamped upon a person by his or her social group, the emphasis is placed upon how a person actively takes up certain traits of character as a part of responding to and interacting with others.

Both the acquisition and practice of virtues are relational processes. To say that character is developed through participation in practices implies, at the outset, that one develops in relations with others. Virtues are concerned with choice and action, and because we are called on to choose and act under many diverse circumstances, there is no way to state in advance of participation in specific situations how, precisely, one ought to choose and act. Thus, the virtues are not abstract, decontextualized ideals: what it means to be patient, for example, can only be determined in the context of specific relations, and so it may be nuanced differently in relations between adults and children than it is in relations between adults. Part of the process of acquiring the communicative virtues, then, entails learning *when* their expression is warranted, and when it may not be, and what is involved in expressing the virtues appropriately in different contexts. We often need to rely on our partners in these situations to help us understand whether we are enacting them well. This is a much more complex model of acquisition, development, and expression of character than the sort of "socialization" account Leach attributes to us.[2]

Although we offered no arguments in the original article concerning either individualistic or relational ontologies, we do not consider our approach to the communicative virtues to be individualistic in the way Leach claims. We focus on *communicative* virtues not in order to argue that "selves" are "independent consciousnesses" that exist outside language and history, but, on the contrary, to highlight the centrality of various communicative practices in all aspects of human well-being. Our very identity and our ability to resolve conflicts peacefully, to coordinate action, and even to think all depend on our communicative relations. This approach is fully consistent with the ontological claim that we are relational and historical beings: "One becomes a person in and through relationships with other people; being a person requires that one have a history of relationships with [others]."[3]

Leach wants to say that virtues are properties of relations themselves, not of individual persons, but this sets up another unhelpful dichotomy. It is true that communicative relations can (for better or worse) catch us up in the spirit of a give-and-take; for example, we have all had the experience of an intensive conversation taking on a life of its own, drawing the participants into patterns of communicative interaction that they do not fully control or direct as separate individuals. There is a sense in which it does make sense to call the *conversation* itself "honest," or whatever. But it is also true that there are things that the participants do in interaction that create and maintain the conditions of such a communicative relation; if they do not actively engage in these practices, the fabric of the relation can suffer.[4]

We are also sympathetic with Leach's concern that particular communicative virtues are "gendered." But the sense in which they are so, and the implications of this genderedness, need to be assessed carefully in light of certain conceptual points regarding virtues in general. First, virtues are not *synonymous* with cultural or gender-related styles of self-presentation, and whether one is animated by the virtues cannot be determined simply from outward appearances and actions. Such a determination requires assessing whether self-presentation is related to a genuine concern for others, or whether it is a merely perfunctory convention of social interaction.[5] So, for example, when Leach criticizes students who *appear* "sensitive" to others, but who seem to lack any genuine concern, she approaches a virtues account of the situation. She is critical of such students not because they fail to manifest the behavior of "listening," but because they seem to be play-acting instead of expressing true sensitivity to the experiences and perspectives of diverse others. Second, as noted above, virtues need to be conceived as context-sensitive. Keeping this aspect of the virtues in mind helps to prevent us from confusing manifestations of the virtues that are beneficial with those that are not. Patience is a virtue, slavishness is not, and the manifestation of utter indignation in the face of sexist or racist epithets does not necessarily reveal an agent's lack of patience or tolerance, any more than do bland and token efforts at "sensitivity" reveal its presence. Third, we believe that it is important to think of the virtues as a *constellation* of dispositions, not discrete modes of behavior. The point of virtue ethics is not to prescribe particular virtues for specific individuals, but rather to inquire into the *conditions that make certain human practices possible.* The communicative virtues, for example, summarize some of the conditions that make dialogue across differences possible. When such dialogue is open and equitable, *all* participants will need to be respectful, tolerant, sincere, etc. — in the original article, that is all we claimed on this subject.

It is because we value communicative openness and equitability that the desirability of this whole constellation of virtues becomes clearer. Certain of these virtues (such as tolerance, patience, and careful listening) relate more to receptiveness, while others (such as honesty and sincerity) are tied more closely to speaking. Communicative relations in which one partner possesses only the first sort of virtues and the other the second would hardly be open and equitable. As we have stressed, possession of these virtues is not sufficient to the task of overcoming the numerous obstacles that block and distort communication; yet lacking them, one will definitely be excluded from, and may exclude others from, numerous communicative contexts.

In light of these conceptual clarifications, the status of Leach's claim regarding the "genderedness" of communicative virtues can be evaluated more clearly. There are certainly reasons to question why women are motivated by some of these virtues more often than are many men. We agree with Leach that women are more inclined to acquire such virtues as patience and careful listening; we believe this is because from an early age they are drawn into various practices and relations that involve responsiveness to others. Nowhere is this clearer, of course, than in mothering relations. We would not argue that all mothers are especially patient or careful listeners, but rather that the practice of mothering does tend to foster and develop these qualities in many women, some of whom come to approve them in their own right as valuable and praiseworthy — that is, as virtues.[6] Of course it is inequitable that women continue to carry such a heavy burden for mothering and other forms of caring work. But the object of criticism here ought to be the current sexual division of labor, *not* the skills, dispositions, and virtues that are required for sustaining and nurturing human life. No one is well-served — least of all women — by the denigration of these virtues as the characteristics of the archetypical "good girl."

Conversely, there is at least some evidence that women tend, generally, to speak less honestly and sincerely than men do.[7] Perhaps this is to be expected if speaking forthrightly in public forums is interpreted, for women, as shrillness, or if honest and sincere complaints directed at a spouse can result in physical or psychological abuse. Yet we cannot imagine that anyone would seriously argue that honesty and sincerity are generally undesirable qualities for women — or men — to possess. The argument, again, should be against those features of contemporary life that make it potentially dangerous for women to express themselves in these ways, rather than against these qualities.

Admittedly, there has been a dangerous tendency to romanticize all "women's work" undertaken in the service of others. When examined through the lens of virtue ethics, such romanticization becomes problematic because it fails to discriminate between the virtues that can be, and often are, expressed in such work and tendencies toward women's self-abnegation. As should be clear from our comments in the original article, and here, we do not endorse the wholesale exercise of certain "dispositions" regardless of personal history or context. Yet Leach seems to believe that we are advocating just this position, that we are encouraging women and other marginalized groups and individuals to be passive and quiescent in their communicative interactions with more privileged partners. This position runs directly against the conception of virtue we advocate.

Our approach also does not prescribe certain communicative virtues for women and others for men. Indeed, we believe that any honest assessment of efforts to create and sustain "coalitions across recognized and respected deep divides of socially constructed and historically embedded differences among individuals and groups," as Leach calls for, will conclude that such efforts — whether they involve men and women; White women and women of color; heterosexual, bisexual, and lesbian women; or any such differences — must be animated by the communicative virtues. Leach herself calls for "respect for differences."

While we believe that a virtues perspective carries important implications for understanding how we create and sustain communicative relations in our daily interactions, we also want to stress the *critical* dimensions of this perspective. Once we recognize that the quality of human life depends heavily on our communicative relations, then we are prompted to identify, and struggle against, the ideological and institutional arrangements that diminish these relations. As our analysis indicates above, this approach provides strong critical leverage for challenging, among other things, how our social (including educational) institutions have been created in ways that make it difficult for both women and men to acquire and enact the full range of communicative virtues.

Yet these communicative virtues are not abstract ideals. Despite all the social constraints that interfere with open communicative relations, the communicative virtues *are* manifested in actual experience; often, they are most apparent in informal relations between, for example, parents and children or among friends. Indeed, one of the things that gives us confidence in a virtues approach is the persistence of these characteristics in practice across different types of communicative relations, across different cultures, and across history. One identifies these virtues, and assesses what their appropriate expression entails, through actual experiences of trying to make one's self understood and to understand others. Such experiences tell us that open and inclusive discussion, even across significant difference and conflict, is possible; coalitions of "unassimilated differences" can be and *are* formed and sustained. But it also tells us that such discussion is only possible when the parties involved are animated by patience, tolerance, sincerity, honesty, etc. — whether one chooses to characterize these as "virtues," as we do, or as something else.

Certainly, we know as well as anyone that these sorts of communicative relations can be extremely difficult to achieve, especially in formal contexts such as public schools and universities. But it is because we have a standard of communicative conduct, including the exercise of certain virtues, that we can identify how and why these contexts fail to support such relations, and how they might be made more congenial.

Doesn't Leach Agree?

The unavoidability of a discussion of the communicative virtues — or something very much like them — can be seen from the very values that motivate Leach's response and are stated in her own conclusion: Can we talk? Can we make this talk understood? Can we bring others into our (new) talk? These questions raise important issues.

The concern with promoting contexts in which marginalized group members can have a "voice" — *and be listened to* — is one that clearly animated our article.[8] Leach says that our position is not sufficiently "relational," but a *relational* view of communication must look at the conditions in which understanding can occur, and this will not be simply a matter of what can be said, but also of what can be heard. The success of such communication depends on contributions from *both* parts of this relation — from the speaker's awareness of audience, context, and appropriateness, and from the hearer's attentiveness, concern, and willingness to set aside presuppositions (to the extent possible) in order to appreciate what is being said on its own terms. Yes — if it needs to be repeated — much, much more also must be the case for successful communication to occur: power imbalances, prejudices, and prior experiences of harm can make either of these roles risky, threatening, or impractical for some people.

Who was the audience, then, for our appeals to the educational benefit of dialogue across differences? Leach writes as if our primary audience were members of marginalized groups. She accuses us of saying, in effect, "Just be more patient and tolerant, be a 'good girl' (or good whatever), speak your mind nicely and reasonably, and maybe someone will listen to you." But by emphasizing, as we repeatedly did, the virtue of listening; by recommending, as we repeatedly did, the need to valorize and respect the voices of silenced individuals and groups; by pointing out, as we repeatedly did, that the reason for valuing dialogue across differences is to *encourage* a climate in which multiple discourses can receive free play — in all of these we were clearly speaking to the *primary* responsibility of persons situated in privileged or dominant positions to acknowledge the limits of their capacity to speak to, speak about, or speak for marginalized others. This is, we assume, at least close to what Leach would want to say, too, and it is precisely opposite to the way she chooses to read us.

What benefit is it to gain your voice if no one is listening? What value is the multiplication of discourses if they cannot engage one another? Why work to find a language in which to express your thoughts, feelings, and experiences, if the only people you can expect to understand you are those who already share the same thoughts, feelings, and experiences?[9] The very value of the capacity for being able to talk is fundamentally linked to being able to be heard; and *this* relation depends on people being able and willing to say what needs to be said in a way that can be heard, and on people being able and willing to listen in a way that encourages what needs to be said. We consider these communicative virtues, and we are trying to present a case that their development should be central to our educational aspirations.

NOTES

1. The promised fuller account of communicative virtues is now under way. One part of this development will be available in Suzanne Rice and Nicholas C. Burbules, "Communicative Virtues and Educational Relations," in *Philosophy of Education 1992: Proceedings of the Forty-Eighth Annual Meeting of the Philosophy of Education Society,* ed. Henry Alexander (Normal, IL: Philosophy of Education Society, 1993), and in subsequent work.

2. It is ironic, by the way, that part of Leach's criticism of the communicative virtues itself relies heavily on a traditional model of socialization. In this model, a woman unproblematically internalizes patience, tolerance, etc., "out of a fear of losing not only her gender identity and her assigned social role, but also the approval of her family, her boyfriend, or her boss." We are concerned not only with the theoretical problems apparent in this account, which we will discuss later in this section, but also with its tacit denigration of the moral status of women who actively *choose* to embrace the virtues we have discussed. Leach's implication seems to be that women who acquire and practice these virtues do so not because they have considered them

thoughtfully and carefully, and found them praiseworthy, but because they just happen to have been socialized into a particular society.

3. Caroline Whitbeck, "A Different View of Reality: Feminist Ontology," in *Women, Knowledge, and Reality,* ed. Ann Garry and Marilyn Pearsall (Boston: Unwin Hyman, 1989), p. 68.

4. There is a substantial literature on this topic, much of it coming from feminist points of view. See, for example, Mary Field Belenky, Blythe McVicker Clinchy, Nancy Rule Goldberger, and Jill Mattuck Tarule, *Women's Ways of Knowing: The Development of Self, Voice, and Mind* (New York: Basic Books, 1986); Deborah Tannen, *Talking Voices: Repetition, Dialogue, and Imagery in Conversational Discourse* (New York: Cambridge University Press, 1989); and Deborah Tannen, *You Just Don't Understand: Women and Men in Conversation* (New York: William Morrow, 1990).

5. Betty A. Sichel, *Moral Education: Character, Community, and Ideals* (Philadelphia: Temple University Press, 1988), pp. 32–33.

6. See Sara Ruddick, *Maternal Thinking: Toward a Politics of Peace* (New York: Ballantine, 1989).

7. Mary Louise Pratt, "Linguistic Utopias," in *The Linguistics of Writing: Arguments Between Language and Literature,* ed. N. Fabb, D. Attridge, A. Durant, and C. MacCabe (New York: Methuen, 1987), pp. 48–66.

8. We have found a lucid discussion of the myriad uses and misuses of the concept of "voice" to analyze cross-cultural settings in Margaret D. LeCompte, "Collaborative Research and Evaluation: Some Notes on Power, Agenda, and Voice," University of Colorado at Boulder, unpublished manuscript.

9. This was, we thought, the point of our recounting of the Feminist Alliance Project (p. 406).

Why Doesn't This Feel Empowering?
Working through the Repressive Myths
of Critical Pedagogy

ELIZABETH ELLSWORTH

In this chapter, Elizabeth Ellsworth paints a complex portrait of the practice of teaching for liberation. She reflects on her own role as a White, middle-class woman and professor engaged with a diverse group of students developing an antiracist course. Grounded in a clearly articulated political agenda and her experience as a feminist teacher, Ellsworth provides a critique of "empowerment," "student voice," "dialogue," and "critical reflection," and raises provocative issues about the nature of action for social change and knowledge.

In the spring of 1988, the University of Wisconsin-Madison was the focal point of a community-wide crisis provoked by the increased visibility of racist acts and structures on campus and within the Madison community. During the preceding year, a fraternity had been suspended for portraying racially demeaning stereotypes at a "Fiji Island party," including a 15-foot-high cutout of a "Fiji native," a dark-skinned caricature with a bone through its nose. On December 1, 1987, the Minority Affairs Steering Committee released a report, initiated and researched by students, documenting the university's failure to address institutional racism and the experiences of marginalization of students of color on campus. The report called for the appointment of a person of color to the position of vice chancellor of ethnic minority affairs/affirmative action; effective strategies to recruit and retain students of color, faculty, and staff; establishment of a multicultural center; implementation of a mandatory six-credit ethnic studies requirement; revamping racial and sexual harassment grievance procedures; and initiation of a cultural and racial orientation program for all students. The release of the report and the university's responses to it, and to additional incidents such as the fraternity party, became the focus of ongoing campus and community-wide debates, demonstrations, and organizing efforts.

In January 1988, partly in response to this situation, I facilitated a special topics course at UW-Madison called "Media and Anti-Racist Pedagogies," Curriculum and Instruction 607, known as C&I 607. In this chapter, I will offer an interpretation of C&I 607's interventions against campus racism and traditional educational forms at the university. I will then use that interpretation to support a critique of current discourses on critical pedagogy.[1] The literature on critical

Harvard Educational Review   Vol. 59   No. 3   August 1989, 297–324

pedagogy represents attempts by educational researchers to theorize and opera-
tionalize pedagogical challenges to oppressive social formations. While the attempts I am concerned with here share fundamental assumptions and goals,
their different emphases are reflected in the variety of labels given to them, such
as "critical pedagogy," "pedagogy of critique and possibility," "pedagogy of student voice," "pedagogy of empowerment," "radical pedagogy," "pedagogy for
radical democracy," and "pedagogy of possibility."[2]

I want to argue, on the basis of my interpretation of C&I 607, that key assumptions, goals, and pedagogical practices fundamental to the literature on critical
pedagogy — namely, "empowerment," "student voice," "dialogue," and even the
term "critical" — are repressive myths that perpetuate relations of domination.
By this I mean that when participants in our class attempted to put into practice
prescriptions offered in the literature concerning empowerment, student voice,
and dialogue, we produced results that were not only unhelpful, but actually
exacerbated the very conditions we were trying to work against, including Eurocentrism, racism, sexism, classism, and "banking education." To the extent that
our efforts to put discourses of critical pedagogy into practice led us to reproduce relations of domination in our classroom, these discourses were "working
through" us in repressive ways, and had themselves become vehicles of repres-
sion. To the extent that we disengaged ourselves from those aspects and moved
in another direction, we "worked through" and out of the literature's highly
abstract language ("myths") of who we "should" be and what "should" be happening in our classroom, and into classroom practices that were context specific
and seemed to be much more responsive to our own understandings of our
social identities and situations.

This chapter concludes by addressing the implications of the classroom practices we constructed in response to racism in the university's curriculum, pedagogy, and everyday life. Specifically, it challenges educational scholars who situate themselves within the field of critical pedagogy to come to grips with the
fundamental issues this work has raised — especially the question, What diversity
do we silence in the name of "liberatory" pedagogy?

PEDAGOGY AND POLITICAL INTERVENTIONS ON CAMPUS

The nationwide eruption in 1987–1988 of racist violence in communities and on
campuses, including the University of Wisconsin-Madison, pervaded the context
in which Curriculum and Instruction 607, "Media and Anti-Racist Pedagogies,"
was planned and facilitated. The increased visibility of racism in Madison was
also partly due to the UW Minority Student Coalition's successful documentation
of the UW system's resistance to and failure to address monoculturalism in the
curriculum, to recruit and retain students and professors of color, and to alleviate the campus culture's insensitivity or hostility to cultural and racial diversity.

At the time that I began to construct a description of C&I 607, students of
color had documented the extent of their racial harassment and alienation on
campus. Donna Shalala, the newly appointed, feminist chancellor of UW-Madison, had invited faculty and campus groups to take their own initiatives against
racism on campus. I had just served on a university committee investigating an

incident of racial harassment against one of my students. I wanted to design a course in media and pedagogy that not only would work to clarify the structures of institutional racism underlying university practices and its culture in spring 1988, but that also would use that understanding to plan and carry out a political intervention within that formation. This class would not debate whether or not racist structures and practices were operating at the university; rather, it would investigate *how* they operated, with what effects and contradictions — and where they were vulnerable to political opposition. The course concluded with public interventions on campus, which I will describe later. For my purposes here, the most important interruption of existing power relations within the university consisted of transforming business-as-usual — that is, prevailing social relations — in a university classroom.

Before the spring of 1988, I had used the language of critical pedagogy in course descriptions and with students. For example, syllabi in the video production for education courses stated that goals of the courses included the production of "socially responsible" videotapes, the fostering of "critical production" practices and "critical reception and analysis" of educational videotapes. Syllabi in the media criticism courses stated that we would focus on "critical media use and analysis in the classroom" and the potential of media in "critical education." Students often asked what was meant by critical — critical of what, from what position, to what end? — and I referred them to answers provided in the literature. For example, critical pedagogy supported classroom analysis and rejection of oppression, injustice, inequality, silencing of marginalized voices, and authoritarian social structures.[3] Its critique was launched from the position of the "radical" educator who recognizes and helps students to recognize and name injustice, who empowers students to act against their own and others' oppression (including oppressive school structures), who criticizes and transforms her or his own understanding in response to the understandings of students.[4] The goal of critical pedagogy was a critical democracy, individual freedom, social justice, and social change — a revitalized public sphere characterized by citizens capable of confronting public issues critically through ongoing forms of public debate and social action.[5] Students would be empowered by social identities that affirmed their race, class, and gender positions, and provided the basis for moral deliberation and social action.[6]

The classroom practices of critical educators may in fact engage with actual, historically specific struggles, such as those between students of color and university administrators. But the overwhelming majority of academic articles appearing in major educational journals, although apparently based on actual practices, rarely locate theoretical constructs within them. In my review of the literature I found, instead, that educational researchers who invoke concepts of critical pedagogy consistently strip discussions of classroom practices of historical context and political position. What remains are the definitions cited above, which operate at a high level of abstraction. I found this language more appropriate (yet hardly more helpful) for philosophical debates about the highly problematic concepts of freedom, justice, democracy, and "universal" values than for thinking through and planning classroom practices to support the political agenda of C&I 607.

Given the explicit antiracist agenda of the course, I realized that even naming C&I 607 raised complex issues. To describe the course as "Media and Critical Pedagogy," or "Media, Racism, and Critical Pedagogy," for example, would be to hide the politics of the course, making them invisible to the very students I was trying to attract and work with — namely, students committed or open to working against racism. I wanted to avoid colluding with many academic writers in the widespread use of code words such as "critical," which hide the actual political agendas I assume such writers share with me — namely, antiracism, antisexism, anti-elitism, anti-heterosexism, anti-ableism, anticlassism, and anti-neoconservatism.

I say "assume" because, while the literature on critical pedagogy charges the teacher with helping students to "identify and choose between sufficiently articulated and reasonably distinct moral positions,"[7] it offers only the most abstract, decontextualized criteria for choosing one position over others, criteria such as "reconstructive action"[8] or "radical democracy and social justice."[9] To reject the term "critical pedagogy" and name the course "Media and Anti-Racist Pedagogies" was to assert that students and faculty at UW-Madison in the spring of 1988 were faced with ethical dilemmas that called for political action. While a variety of "moral assessments" and political positions existed about the situation on campus, this course would attempt to construct a classroom practice that would act *on the side* of antiracism. I wanted to be accountable for naming the political agenda behind this particular course's critical pedagogy.

Thinking through the ways in which our class's activities could be understood as political was important, because while the literature states implicitly or explicitly that critical pedagogy is political, there have been no sustained research attempts to explore whether or how the practices it prescribes actually alter specific power relations outside or inside schools. Further, when educational researchers advocating critical pedagogy fail to provide a clear statement of their political agendas, the effect is to hide the fact that as critical pedagogues, they are in fact seeking to appropriate public resources (classrooms, school supplies, teacher/professor salaries, academic requirements and degrees) to further various "progressive" political agendas that they believe to be for the public good — and therefore deserving of public resources. But however good the reasons for choosing the strategy of subverting repressive school structures from within, it has necessitated the use of code words such as "critical," "social change," "revitalized public sphere," and a posture of invisibility. As a result, the critical education "movement" has failed to develop a clear articulation of the need for its existence, its goals, priorities, risks, or potentials. As Liston and Zeichner argue, debate within the critical education movement itself over what constitutes a radical or critical pedagogy is sorely needed.[10]

By prescribing moral deliberation, engagements in the full range of views present, and critical reflection, the literature on critical pedagogy implies that students and teachers can and should engage each other in the classroom as fully rational subjects. According to Valerie Walkerdine, schools have participated in producing "self-regulating" individuals by developing in students capacities for engaging in rational argument. Rational argument has operated in ways that set up as its opposite an irrational Other, which has been understood historically as the province of women and other exotic Others. In schools, rational deliberation, reflection, and consideration of all viewpoints has become a vehicle for regulating conflict and the power to speak, for transforming "conflict into rational argument by means of universalized capacities for language and reason."[11] But students and professor entered C&I 607 with investments of privilege and struggle already made in favor of some ethical and political positions concerning racism and against other positions. The context in which this course was developed highlighted that fact. The demands that the Minority Student Coalition delivered to the administration were not written in the spirit of engaging in rationalist, analytical debates with those holding other positions. In a racist society and its institutions, such debate has not and cannot be "public" or "democratic" in the sense of including the voices of all affected parties and affording them equal weight and legitimacy. Nor can such debate be free of conscious and unconscious concealment of interests, or assertion of interests that some participants hold as non-negotiable no matter what arguments are presented.

As Barbara Christian has written, "what I write and how I write is done in order to save my own life. And I mean that literally. For me literature is a way of knowing that I am not hallucinating, that whatever I feel/know *is*."[12] Christian is an African-American woman writing about the literature of African-American women, but her words are relevant to the issues raised by the context of C&I 607. I understood the words written by the Minority Student Coalition and spoken by other students/professors of difference on campus to have a similar function as a reality check for survival.[13] It is inappropriate to respond to such words by subjecting them to rationalist debates about their validity. Words spoken for survival come already validated in a radically different arena of proof and carry no option or luxury of choice. (This is not to say, however, that the positions of students of color, or of any other group, were to be taken up unproblematically — an issue I will address below.)

I drafted a syllabus and circulated it for suggestions and revisions to students I knew to be involved in the Minority Student Coalition, and to colleagues who shared my concerns. The goal of "Media and Anti-Racist Pedagogies," as stated in the revised syllabus, was to define, organize, carry out, and analyze an educational initiative on campus that would win semiotic space for the marginalized discourses of students against racism. Campus activists were defining these discourses and making them available to other groups, including the class, through documents, demonstrations, discussions, and press conferences.

The syllabus also listed the following assumptions underlying the course:

1. Students who want to acquire knowledge of existing educational media theory and criticism for the purpose of guiding their own educational practice can best do so in a learning situation that interrelates theory with concrete attempts at using media for education.

2. Current situations of racial and sexual harassment and elitism on campus and in the curriculum demand meaningful responses from both students and faculty, and responses can be designated in a way that accomplishes both academic and political goals.

3. Often, the term "critical education" has been used to imply, but also to hide positions and goals of antiracism, anticlassism, antisexism, and so forth. Defining this course as one that explores the possibility of using media to construct antiracist pedagogies asserts that these are legitimate and imperative goals for educators.

4. What counts as an appropriate use of media for an antiracist pedagogy cannot be specified outside of the contexts of actual educational situations; therefore student work on this issue should be connected to concrete initiatives in actual situations.

5. Any antiracist pedagogy must be defined through an awareness of the ways in which oppressive structures are the result of *intersections* between racist, classist, sexist, ableist, and other oppressive dynamics.

6. Everyone who has grown up in a racist culture has to work at unlearning racism — we will make mistakes in this class, but they will be made in the context of our struggle to come to grips with racism.

Naming the political agenda of the course, to the extent that I did, seemed relatively easy. I was in the fourth year of a tenure-track position in my department, and felt that I had "permission" from colleagues to pursue the line of research and practice out of which this course had clearly grown. The administration's response to the crisis on campus gave further "permission" for attempts to alleviate racism in the institution. However, the directions in which I should proceed became less clear once the class was underway. As I began to live out and interpret the consequences of how discourses of "critical reflection," "empowerment," "student voice," and "dialogue" had influenced my conceptualization of the goals of the course and my ability to make sense of my experiences in the class, I found myself struggling against (struggling to unlearn) key assumptions and assertions of current literature on critical pedagogy, and straining to recognize, name, and come to grips with crucial issues of classroom practice that critical pedagogy cannot or will not address.

FROM CRITICAL RATIONALISM
TO THE POLITICS OF PARTIAL NARRATIVES

The students enrolled in "Media and Anti-Racist Pedagogies" included Asian-American, Chicano/a, Jewish, Puerto Rican, and Anglo-European men and women from the United States, and Asian, African, Icelandic, and Canadian international students. It was evident after the first class meeting that all of us agreed, but with different understandings and agendas, that racism was a problem on campus that required political action. The effects of the diverse social positions and political ideologies of the students enrolled, my own position and experiences as a woman and a feminist, and the effects of the course's context on the form and content of our early class discussions quickly threw the rationalist assumptions underlying critical pedagogy into question.

These rationalist assumptions have led to the following goals: the teaching of analytic and critical skills for judging the truth and merit of propositions, and the interrogation and selective appropriation of potentially transformative moments in the dominant culture.[14] As long as educators define pedagogy against oppressive formations in these ways, the role of the critical pedagogue will be to guarantee that the foundation for classroom interaction is reason. In other words, the critical pedagogue is one who enforces the rules of reason in the classroom — "a series of rules of thought that any ideal rational person might adopt if his/her purpose was to achieve propositions of universal validity."[15] Under these conditions, and given the coded nature of the political agenda of critical pedagogy, only one "political" gesture appears to be available to the critical pedagogue. She/he can ensure that students are given the chance to arrive logically at the "universally valid proposition" underlying the discourse of critical pedagogy — namely, that all people have a right to freedom from oppression guaranteed by the democratic social contract, and that in the classroom, this proposition be given equal time vis-à-vis other "sufficiently articulated and reasonably distinct moral positions."[16]

Yet educators who have constructed classroom practices dependent upon analytic critical judgment can no longer regard the enforcement of rationalism as a self-evident political act against relations of domination. Literary criticism, cultural studies, post-structuralism, feminist studies, comparative studies, and media studies have by now amassed overwhelming evidence of the extent to which the myths of the ideal rational person and the "universality" of propositions have been oppressive to those who are not European, White, male, middle-class, Christian, able-bodied, thin, and heterosexual.[17] Writings by many literary and cultural critics, both women of color and White women who are concerned with explaining the intersections and interactions among relations of racism, colonialism, sexism, and so forth, are not employing, either implicitly or explicitly, concepts and analytical methods that could be called feminist post-structuralism.[18] While post-structuralism, like rationalism, is a tool that can be used to dominate, it has also facilitated a devastating critique of the violence of rationalism against its Others. It has demonstrated that as a discursive practice, rationalism's regulated and systematic use of elements of language constitutes rational competence "as a series of exclusions — of women, people of color, of nature as historical agent, of the true value of art."[19] In contrast, post-structuralist thought is not bound to reason, but "to discourse, literally narratives about the world that are admittedly *partial*. Indeed, one of the crucial features of discourse is the intimate tie between knowledge and interest, the latter being understood as a 'standpoint' from which to grasp 'reality.'"[20]

The literature on critical pedagogy implies that the claims made by documents, demonstrations, press conferences, and classroom discussions of students of color and White students against racism could rightfully be taken up in the classroom and subjected to rational deliberation over their truth in light of competing claims. But this would force students to subject themselves to the logics of rationalism and scientism which have been predicated on and made possible through the exclusion of socially constructed irrational Others — women, people of color, nature, aesthetics. As Audre Lorde writes, "The master's tools will never dismantle the master's house,"[21] and to call on students of color to justify and explicate their claims in terms of the master's tools — tools such as rationalism, fashioned precisely to perpetuate their exclusion — colludes with the oppressor in keeping "the oppressed occupied with the master's concerns."[22] As Barbara Christian describes:

> The literature of people who are not in power has always been in danger of extinction or cooptation, not because we do not theorize, but because what we can even imagine, far less who we can reach, is constantly limited by societal structures. For me, literary criticism is promotion as well as understanding, a response to the writer to whom there is often no response, to folk who need the writing as much as they need anything. I know, from literary history, that writing disappears unless there is a response to it. Because I write about writers who are now writing, I hope to help ensure that their tradition has continuity and survives.[23]

In contrast to the enforcement of rational deliberation, but like Christian's promotion and response, my role in C&I 607 would be to interrupt institutional limits on how much time and energy students of color, White students, and professors against racism could spend on elaborating their positions and playing them out to the point where internal contradictions and effects on the positions of other social groups could become evident and subject to self-analysis.

With Barbara Christian, I saw the necessity to take the voices of students and professors of difference at their word — as "valid" — but not without response.[24] Students' and my own narratives about experiences of racism, ableism, elitism, fat oppression, sexism, anti-Semitism, heterosexism, and so on are partial — partial in the sense that they are unfinished, imperfect, limited; and partial in the sense that they project the interests of "one side" over others. Because those voices are partial and partisan, they must be made problematic, but not because they have broken the rules of thought of the ideal rational person by grounding their knowledge in immediate emotional, social, and psychic experiences of oppression,[25] or are somehow lacking or too narrowly circumscribed.[26] Rather, they must be critiqued because they hold implications for other social movements and their struggles for self-definition. This assertion carries important implications for the "goal" of classroom practices against oppressive formations, which I will address later.

HAVE WE GOT A THEORY FOR YOU![27]

As educators who claim to be dedicated to ending oppression, critical pedagogues have acknowledged the socially constructed and legitimated authority that teachers/professors hold over students.[28] Yet theorists of critical pedagogy have failed to launch any meaningful analysis of or program for reformulating the institutionalized power imbalances between themselves and their students, or of the essentially paternalistic project of education itself. In the absence of such an analysis and program, their efforts are limited to trying to transform negative effects of power imbalances within the classroom into positive ones. Strategies such as student empowerment and dialogue give the illusion of equality while in fact leaving the authoritarian nature of the teacher/student relationship intact.

"Empowerment" is a key concept of this approach, which treats the symptoms but leaves the disease unnamed and untouched. Critical pedagogies employing this strategy prescribe various theoretical and practical means for sharing, giving, or redistributing power to students. For example, some authors challenge teachers to reject the vision of education as inculcation of students by the more powerful teacher. In its place, they urge teachers to accept the possibility of education through "reflective examination" of the plurality of moral positions before the presumably rational teacher and students.[29] Here, the goal is to give students the analytical skills they need to make them as free, rational, and objective as teachers supposedly are to choose positions on their objective merits. I have already argued that in a classroom in which "empowerment" is made dependent on rationalism, those perspectives that would question the political interests (sexism, racism, colonialism, for example) expressed and guaranteed by rationalism would be rejected as "irrational" (biased, partial).

A second strategy is to make the teacher more like the student by redefining the teacher as learner of the student's reality and knowledge. For example, in their discussion of the politics of dialogic teaching and epistemology, Shor and Freire suggest that "the teacher selecting the objects of study knows them *better* than the students as the course begins, but the teacher *re-learns* the objects through studying them with their students."[30] The literature explores only one reason for expecting the teacher to "re-learn" an object of study through the student's less adequate understanding, and that is to enable the teacher to devise more effective strategies for bringing the student "up" to the teacher's level of understanding. Giroux, for example, argues for a pedagogy that "is attentive to the histories, dreams, and experiences that . . . students bring to school. It is only by beginning with these subjective forms that critical educators can develop a language and set of practices"[31] that can successfully mediate differences between student understandings and teacher understandings in "pedagogically progressive" ways.[32] In this example, Giroux leaves the implied superiority of the teacher's understanding and the undefined "progressiveness" of this type of pedagogy unproblematized and untheorized.

A third strategy is to acknowledge the "directiveness"[33] or "authoritarianism"[34] of education as inevitable, and judge particular power imbalances between teacher and student to be tolerable or intolerable depending on "towards what and with whom [they are] directive."[35] "Acceptable" imbalances are those in which authority serves "common human interests by sharing information, promoting open and informed discussion, and maintaining itself only through the respect and trust of those who grant the authority."[36] In such cases, authority becomes "emancipatory authority," a kind of teaching in which teachers would make explicit and available for rational debate "the political and moral referents for authority they assume in teaching particular forms of knowledge, in taking stands against forms of oppression, and in treating students as if they ought also to be concerned about social justice and political action."[37] Here, the question of "empowerment for what" becomes the final arbiter of a teacher's use or misuse of authority.

But critical pedagogues consistently answer the question of "empowerment for what?" in ahistorical and depoliticized abstractions. These include empowerment for "human betterment,"[38] for expanding "the range of possible social identities people may become,"[39] and "making one's self present as part of a moral and political project that links production of meaning to the possibility for human agency, democratic community, and transformative social action."[40] As a result, student empowerment has been defined in the broadest possible humanist terms, and becomes a "capacity to act effectively" in a way that fails to challenge any identifiable social or political position, institution, or group.

The contortions of logic and rhetoric that characterize these attempts to define "empowerment" testify to the failure of critical educators to come to terms with the essentially paternalistic project of traditional education. "Emancipatory authority" is one such contortion, for it implies the presence of or potential for an emancipated teacher.[41] Indeed, it asserts that teachers "can link knowledge to power by bringing to light and teaching the subjugated histories, experiences, stories, and accounts of those who suffer and struggle."[42] Yet I cannot unproblematically bring subjugated knowledges to light when I am not free of my own learned racism, fat oppression, classism, ableism, or sexism. No teacher is free of these learned and internalized oppressions. Nor are accounts of one group's suffering and struggle immune from reproducing narratives oppressive to another's — the racism of the Women's Movement in the United States is one example.

As I argued above, "emancipatory authority" also implies, according to Shor and Freire, a teacher who knows the object of study "better" than do the students. Yet I did not understand racism better than my students did, especially those students of color coming into class after six months (or more) of campus activism and whole lives of experience and struggle against racism — nor could I ever hope to. My experiences with and access to multiple and sophisticated strategies for interpreting and interrupting sexism (in White middle-class contexts) do not provide me with a ready-made analysis of or language for understanding my own implications in racist structures. My understanding and experience of racism will always be constrained by my white skin and middle-class privilege. Indeed, it is impossible for anyone to be free from these oppressive formations at this historical moment. Furthermore, while I had the institutional power and authority in the classroom to enforce "reflective examination" of the plurality of moral and political positions before us in a way that supposedly gave my own assessments equal weight with those of students, in fact my institutional role as professor would always weight my statements differently from those of students.

Given my own history of white-skin, middle-class, able-bodied, thin privilege and my institutionally granted power, it made more sense to see my task as one of redefining "critical pedagogy" so that it did not need utopian moments of "democracy," "equality," "justice," or "emancipated" teachers — moments that are unattainable (and ultimately undesirable, because they are always predicated on the interests of those who are in the position to define utopian projects). A preferable goal seemed to be to become capable of a sustained encounter with currently oppressive formations and power relations that refuse to be theorized away or fully transcended in a utopian resolution — and to enter into the encounter in a way that owned up to my own implications in those formations and was capable of changing my own relation to and investments in those formations.

THE REPRESSIVE MYTH OF THE SILENT OTHER

At first glance, the concept of "student voice" seemed to offer a pedagogical strategy in this direction. This concept has become highly visible and influential in current discussions of curriculum and teaching, as evidenced by its appearance in the titles of numerous presentations at the 1989 American Educational Research Association Convention. Within current discourses on teaching, it functions to efface the contradiction between the emancipatory project of critical pedagogy and the hierarchical relation between teachers and students. In other words, it is a strategy for negotiating between the directiveness of dominant educational relationships and the political commitment to make students autonomous of those relationships (how does a teacher "make" students autonomous without directing them?). The discourse on student voice sees the student as "empowered" when the teacher "helps" students to express their subjugated knowledges.[43] The targets of this strategy are students from disadvantaged and subordinated social-class, racial, ethnic, and gender groups — or alienated middle-class students without access to skills of critical analysis, whose voices have been silenced or distorted by oppressive cultural and educational formations. By speaking, in their "authentic voices," students are seen to make themselves visible and define themselves as authors of their own world. Such self-definition presumably gives students an identity and political position from which to act as agents of social change.[44] Thus, while it is true that the teacher is directive, the student's own daily life experiences of oppression chart her/his path toward self-definition and agency. The task of the critical educator thus becomes "finding ways of working with students that enable the full expression of multiple 'voices' engaged in dialogic encounter," encouraging students of different race, class, and gender positions to speak in self-affirming ways about their experiences and how they have been mediated by their own social positions and those of others.[45]

Within feminist discourses seeking to provide both a place and power for women to speak, "voice" and "speech" have become commonplace as metaphors for women's feminist self-definitions — but with meanings and effects quite different from those implied by discourses of critical pedagogy. Within feminist movements, women's voices and speech are conceptualized in terms of self-definitions that are oppositional to those definitions of women constructed by others, usually to serve interests and contexts that subordinate women to men. But while critical educators acknowledge the existence of unequal power relations in classrooms, they have made no systematic examination of the barriers that this imbalance throws up to the kind of student expression and dialogue they prescribe.

The concept of critical pedagogy assumes a commitment on the part of the professor/teacher toward ending the student's oppression. Yet the literature offers no sustained attempt to problematize this stance and confront the likelihood that the professor brings to social movements (including critical pedagogy) interests of her or his own race, class, ethnicity, gender, and other positions. She/he does not play the role of disinterested mediator on the side of the oppressed group.[46] As an Anglo, middle-class professor in C&I 607, I could not unproblematically "help" a student of color to find her/his authentic voice as a student of color. I could not unproblematically "affiliate" with the social groups my students represent and interpret their experience to them. In fact, I brought to the classroom privileges and interests that were put at risk in fundamental ways by the demands and defiances of student voices. I brought a social subjectivity that has been constructed in such a way that I have not and can never participate unproblematically in the collective process of self-definition, naming of oppression, and struggles for visibility in the face of marginalization engaged in by students whose class, race, gender, and other positions I do not share. Critical pedagogues are always implicated in the very structures they are trying to change.

Although the literature recognizes that teachers have much to learn from their students' experiences, it does not address the ways in which there are things that I as professor could *never know* about the experiences, oppression, and understandings of other participants in the class. This situation makes it impossible for any single voice in the classroom — including that of professor — to assume the position of center or origin of knowledge or authority, of having privileged access to authentic experience or appropriate language. A recognition, contrary to all Western ways of knowing and speaking, that all knowings are partial, that there are fundamental things each of us cannot know — a situation alleviated only in part by the pooling of partial, socially constructed knowledges in classrooms — demands a fundamental retheorizing of "education" and "pedagogy," an issue I will begin to address below.

When educational researchers writing about critical pedagogy fail to examine the implications of the gendered, raced, and classed teacher and student for the theory of critical pedagogy, they reproduce, by default, the category of generic "critical teacher" — a specific form of the generic human that underlies classical liberal thought. Like the generic human, the generic critical teacher is not, of course, generic at all. Rather, the term defines a discursive category predicated on the current mythical norm, namely: young, White, Christian, middle-class, heterosexual, able-bodied, thin, rational man. Gender, race, class, and other differences became only variations on or additions to the generic human — "underneath, we are all the same."[47] But voices of students and professors of difference solicited by critical pedagogy are not additions to that norm, but oppositional challenges that require a dismantling of the mythical norm and its uses as well as alternatives to it. There has been no consideration of how voices of, for example, White women, students of color, disabled students, White men against masculinist culture, and fat students will necessarily be constructed in opposition to the teacher/institution when they try to change the power imbalances they inhabit in their daily lives, including their lives in schools.

Critical pedagogues speak of student voices as "sharing" their experiences and understandings of oppression with other students and with the teacher in the interest of "expanding the possibilities of what it is to be human."[48] Yet White women, women of color, men of color, White men against masculinist culture, fat people, gay men and lesbians, people with disabilities, and Jews do not speak of the oppressive formations that condition their lives in the spirit of "sharing."

Rather, the speech of oppositional groups is a "talking back," a "defiant speech"[49] that is constructed within communities of resistance and is a condition of survival.

In C&I 607, the defiant speech of students and professor of difference constituted fundamental challenges to and rejections of the voices of some classmates and often of the professor. For example, it became clear very quickly that in order to name her experience of racism, a Chicana student had to define her voice in part through oppression to — and rejection of — definitions of "Chicana" assumed or taken for granted by other student/professor voices in the classroom. And in the context of protests by students of color against racism on campus, her voice had to be constructed in oppression to the institutional racism of the university's curriculum and policies — which were represented in part by my discourses and actions as Anglo-American, middle-class woman professor. Unless we found a way to respond to such challenges, our academic and political work against racism would be blocked. This alone is a reason for finding ways to express and engage with student voices, one that distances itself from the abstract, philosophical reasons implied by the literature on critical pedagogy when it fails to contextualize its projects. Furthermore, grounding the expression of and engagement with student voices in the need to construct contextualized political strategies rejects both the voyeuristic relation that the literature reproduces when the voice of the professor is not problematized, and the instrumental role critical pedagogy plays when student voice is used to inform more effective teaching strategies.

The lessons learned from feminist struggles to make a difference through defiant speech offer both useful critiques of the assumptions of critical pedagogy and starting points for moving beyond its repressive myths.[50] Within feminist movements, self-defining feminist voices have been understood as constructed collectively in the context of a larger feminist movement or women's marginalized subcultures. Feminist voices are made possible by the interactions among women within and across race, class, and other differences that divide them. These voices have never been solely or even primarily the result of a pedagogical interaction between an individual student and a teacher. Yet discourses of the pedagogy of empowerment consistently position students as individuals with only the most abstract of relations to concrete contexts of struggle. In their writing about critical pedagogy, educational researchers consistently place teachers/professors at the center of the consciousness-raising activity. For example, Peter McLaren describes alienated middle-class youth this way:

> These students do not recognize their own self-representation and suppression by the dominant society, and in our vitiated learning environments they are not provided with the requisite theoretical constructs to help them understand why they feel as badly as they do. Because teachers lack a critical pedagogy, these students are not provided with the ability to think critically, a skill that would enable them to better understand why their lives have been reduced to feelings of meaningless, randomness, and alienation.[51]

In contrast, many students came into "Media and Anti-Racist Pedagogies" with oppositional voices already formulated within various antiracism and other movements. These movements had not necessarily relied on intellectuals/teachers to interpret their goals and programs to themselves or to others.

Current writings by many feminists working from antiracism and feminist post-structuralist perspectives recognize that any individual woman's politicized voice will be partial, multiple, and contradictory.[52] The literature on critical pedagogy also recognizes the possibility that each student will be capable of identifying a multiplicity of authentic voices in her/himself. But it does not confront the ways in which any individual student's voice is already a "teeth gritting" and often contradictory intersection of voices constituted by gender, race, class, ability, ethnicity, sexual orientation, or ideology. Nor does it engage with the fact that the particularities of historical context, personal biography, and subjectivities split between the conscious and unconscious will necessarily render each expression of student voice partial and predicated on the absence and marginalization of alternative voices. It is impossible to speak from all voices at once, or from any one, without the traces of the others being present and interruptive. Thus the very term "student voice" is highly problematic. Pluralizing the concept as "voices" implies correction through addition. This loses sight of the contradictory and partial nature of all voices.

In C&I 607, for example, participants expressed much pain, confusion, and difficulty in speaking, because of the ways in which discussions called up their multiple and contradictory social positionings. Women found it difficult to prioritize expressions of racial privilege and oppression when such prioritizing threatened to perpetuate their gender oppression. Among international students, both those who were of color and those who were White found it difficult to join their voices with those of U.S. students of color when it meant a subordination of their oppression as people living under U.S. imperialist policies and as students for whom English was a second language. Asian-American women found it difficult to join their voices with other students of color when it meant subordinating their specific oppression as Asian Americans. I found it difficult to speak as a White woman about gender oppression when I occupied positions of institutional power relative to all students in the class, men and women, but positions of gender oppression relative to students who were White men, and in different terms, relative to students who were men of color.

Finally, the argument that women's speech and voice have not been and should not be constructed primarily for the purpose of communicating women's experiences to men is commonplace within feminist movements. This position takes the purposes of such speech to be survival, expansion of women's own understandings of their oppression and strength, sharing common experiences among women, building solidarity among women, and political strategizing. Many feminists have pointed to the necessity for men to "do their own work" at unlearning sexism and male privilege, rather than looking to women for the answers. I am similarly suspicious of the desire by the mostly White, middle-class men who write the literature on critical pedagogy to elicit "full expression" of student voices. Such a relation between teacher/student becomes voyeuristic when the voice of the pedagogue himself goes unexamined.

Furthermore, the assumption present in the literature that silence in front of a teacher or professor indicates "lost voice," "voicelessness," or lack of social identity from which to act as a social agent betrays deep and unacceptable gender, race, and class biases. It is worth quoting bell hooks at length about the fiction of the silence of subordinated groups:

> Within feminist circles silence is often seen as the sexist defined "right speech of womanhood" — the sign of woman's submission to patriarchal authority. This emphasis on woman's silence may be an accurate remembering of what has taken place in the households of women from WASP backgrounds in the United States but in Black communities (and in other diverse ethnic communities) women have not been silent. Their voices can be heard. Certainly for Black women our struggle has not been to emerge from silence to speech but to change the nature and direction of our speech. To make a speech that compels listeners, one that is heard. . . . Dialogue, the sharing of speech and recognition, took place not between mother and child or mother and male authority figure, but with other Black women. I can remember watching, fascinated, as our mother talked with her mother, sisters, and women friends. The intimacy and intensity of their speech — the satisfaction they received from talking to one another, the pleasure, the joy. It was in this world of woman speech, loud talk, angry words, women with tongues sharp, tender sweet tongues, touching our world with their words, that I made speech my birthright — and the right to voice, to authorship, a privilege I would not be denied. It was in that world and because of it that I came to dream of writing, to write.[53]

White women, men and women of color, impoverished people, people with disabilities, gays and lesbians, are not silenced in the sense implied by the literature on critical pedagogy. They just are not talking in their authentic voices, or they are declining/refusing to talk at all, to critical educators who have been unable to acknowledge the presence of knowledges that are challenging and most likely inaccessible to their own social positions. What they/we say, to whom, in what context, depending on the energy they/we have for the struggle on a particular day, is the result of conscious and unconscious assessments of the power relations and safety of the situation.

As I understand it at the moment, what got said — and how — in our class was the product of highly complex strategizing for the visibility that speech gives without giving up the safety of silence. More than that, it was a highly complex negotiation of the politics of knowing and being known. Things were left unsaid, or they were encoded, on the basis of speakers' conscious and unconscious assessments of the risks and costs of disclosing their understandings of themselves and of others. To what extent had students occupying socially constructed positions of privilege at a particular moment risked being known by students occupying socially constructed positions of subordination at the same moment? To what extent had students in those positions of privilege relinquished the security and privilege of being the knower?[54]

As long as the literature on critical pedagogy fails to come to grips with issues of trust, risk, and the operations of fear and desire around such issues of identity and politics in the classroom, their rationalistic tools will continue to fail to loosen deep-seated, self-interested investments in unjust relations of, for example, gender, ethnicity, and sexual orientation.[55] These investments are shared by both teachers and students, yet the literature on critical pedagogy has ignored its own implications for the young, White, Christian, middle-class, heterosexual, able-bodied man/pedagogue that it assumes. Against such ignoring, Mohanty argues that to desire to ignore is not cognitive, but performative. It is the incapacity or refusal "to acknowledge one's own implication in the information."[56] "[Learning] involves a necessary implication in the radical alterity of the unknown, in the desire(s) not to know, in the process of this unresolvable dialectic."[57]

FROM DIALOGUE TO WORKING TOGETHER ACROSS DIFFERENCES

Because student voice has been defined as "the measures by which students and teacher participate in dialogue,"[58] the foregoing critique has serious consequences for the concept of "dialogue" as it has been articulated in the literature on critical pedagogy. Dialogue has been defined as a fundamental imperative of critical pedagogy and the basis of the democratic education that ensures a democratic state. Through dialogue, a classroom can be made into a public sphere, a locus of citizenship in which

> students and teachers can engage in a process of deliberation and discussion aimed at advancing the public welfare in accordance with fundamental moral judgments and principles. . . . School and classroom practices should, in some manner, be organized around forms of learning which serve to prepare students for responsible roles as transformative intellectuals, as community members, and as critically active citizens outside of schools.[59]

Dialogue is offered as a pedagogical strategy for constructing these learning conditions, and consists of ground rules for classroom interaction using language. These rules include the assumptions that all members have equal opportunity to speak, all members respect other members' rights to speak and feel safe to speak, and all ideas are tolerated and subjected to rational critical assessment against fundamental judgments and moral principles. According to Henry Giroux, in order for dialogue to be possible, classroom participants must exhibit "trust, sharing, and commitment to improving the quality of human life."[60] While the specific form and means of social change and organization are open to debate, there must be agreement around the goals of dialogue: "all voices and their differences become unified both in their efforts to identify and recall moments of human suffering and in their attempts to overcome conditions that perpetuate such suffering."[61]

However, for the reasons outlined above — the students' and professor's asymmetrical positions of difference and privilege — dialogue in this sense was both impossible and undesirable in C&I 607. In fact, the unity of efforts and values unproblematically assumed by Giroux was not only impossible but potentially repressive as well. Giroux's formula for dialogue requires and assumes a classroom of participants unified on the side of the subordinated against the subordinators, sharing and trusting in an "us-ness" against "them-ness." This formula fails to confront dynamics of subordination present among classroom participants and within classroom participants in the form of multiple and contradictory subject positions. Such a conception of dialogue invokes the "all too easy polemic that opposes victims to perpetrators," in which a condition for collective purpose among "victims" is the desire for home, for synchrony, for sameness.[62] Biddy Martin and Chandra Mohanty call for creating new forms of collective struggle that do not depend upon the repressions and violence needed by "dialogue" based on and enforcing a harmony of interests. They envision collective struggle that starts from an acknowledgement that "unity" — interpersonal, personal, and political — is necessarily fragmentary, unstable, not given, but chosen and struggled for — but not on the basis of "sameness."[63]

But despite early rejections of fundamental tenets of dialogue, including the usually unquestioned emancipatory potentials of rational deliberation and "unity," we remained in the grip of other repressive fictions of classroom dialogue for most of the semester. I expected that we would be able to ensure all members a safe place to speak, equal opportunity to speak, and equal power in influencing decisionmaking — and as a result, it would become clear what had to be done and why. It was only at the end of the semester that I and the students recognized that we had given this myth the power to divert our attention and classroom practices away from what we needed to be doing. Acting as if our classroom were a safe space in which democratic dialogue was possible and happening did not make it so. If we were to respond to our context and the social identities of the people in our classroom in ways that did not reproduce the oppressive formations we were trying to work against, we needed classroom practices that confronted the power dynamics inside and outside of our classroom that made democratic dialogue impossible. During the last two weeks of the semester, we reflected in class on our group's process — how we spoke to and/or silenced each other across our differences, how we divided labor, made decisions, and treated each other as visible and/or invisible. As students had been doing with each other all along, I began to have informal conversations with one or two students at a time who were extremely committed on personal, political, and academic levels to breaking through the barriers we had encountered and to understanding what had happened during the semester. These reflections and discussions led me to the following conclusions.

Our classroom was not in fact a safe space for students to speak out or talk back about their experiences of oppression both inside and outside of the classroom. In our class, these included experiences of being gay, lesbian, fat, women of color working with men of color, White women working with men of color, men of color working with White women and men.[64] Things were not being said for a number of reasons. These included fear of being misunderstood and/or disclosing too much and becoming too vulnerable; memories of bad experiences in other contexts of speaking out; resentment that other oppressions (sexism, heterosexism, fat oppression, classism, anti-Semitism) were being marginalized in the name of addressing racism — and guilt for feeling such resentment; confusion abut levels of trust and commitment surrounding those who were allies to another group's struggles; resentment by some students of color for feeling that they were expected to disclose "more" and once again take the burden of doing the pedagogic work of educating White students/professor about the consequences of White middle-class privilege; and resentment by White students for feeling that they had to prove they were not the enemy.

Dialogue in its conventional sense is impossible in the culture at large because at this historical moment, power relations between raced, classed, and gendered students and teachers are unjust. The injustice of these relations and the way in which those injustices distort communication cannot be overcome in a classroom, no matter how committed the teacher and students are to "overcoming conditions that perpetuate suffering." Conventional notions of dialogue and democracy assume rationalized, individualized subjects capable of agreeing on universalizable "fundamental moral principles" and "quality of human life" that become self-evident when subjects cease to be self-interested and particularistic about group rights. Yet social agents are not capable of being fully rational and disinterested; and they are subjects split between the conscious and unconscious and among multiple social positionings. Fundamental moral and political principles are not absolute and universalizable, waiting to be discovered by the disinterested researcher/teacher; they are "established intersubjectively by subjects capable of interpretation and reflection."[65] Educational researchers attempting to construct meaningful discourses about the politics of classroom practices must begin to theorize the consequences for education of the way in which knowledge, power, and desire are mutually implicated in each other's formations and deployments.

By the end of the semester, participants in the class agreed that commitment to rational discussion about racism in a classroom setting was not enough to make that setting a safe space for speaking out and talking back. We agreed that a safer space required high levels of trust and personal commitment to individuals in the class, gained in part through social interactions outside of class — potlucks, field trips, participation in rallies and other gatherings. Opportunities to know the motivations, histories, and stakes of individuals in the class should have been planned early in the semester.[66] Furthermore, White students/professor should have shared the burden of educating themselves about the consequences of their White-skin privilege, and to facilitate this, the curriculum should have included significant amounts of literature, film, and videos by people of color and White people against racism — so that the students of color involved in the class would not always be looked to as "experts" in racism or the situation on the campus.

Because all voices within the classroom are not and cannot carry equal legitimacy, safety, and power in dialogue at this historical moment, there are times when the inequalities must be named and addressed by constructing alternative ground rules for communication. By the end of the semester, participants in C&I 607 began to recognize that some social groups represented in the class had had consistently more speaking time than others. Women, international students for whom English was a second language, and mixed groups sharing ideological and political languages and perspectives began to have very significant interactions outside of class. Informal, overlapping affinity groups formed and met unofficially for the purpose of articulating and refining positions based on shared oppression, ideological analyses, or interests. They shared grievances about the dynamics of the larger group and performed reality checks for each other. Because they were "unofficial" groups constituted on the spot in response to specific needs or simply as a result of casual encounters outside of the classroom, alliances could be shaped and reshaped as strategies in context.

The fact that affinity groups did form within the larger group should not be seen as a failure to construct a unity of voices and goals — a possibility unproblematically assumed and worked for in critical pedagogy. Rather, affinity groups were necessary for working against the way current historical configurations of oppression were reproduced in the class. They provided some participants with safer home bases from which they gained support, important understandings, and a language for entering the larger classroom interactions each week. Once we acknowledged the existence, necessity, and value of these affinity groups, we began to see our task not as one of building democratic dialogue between free and equal individuals, but of building a coalition among the multiple, shifting, intersecting, and sometimes contradictory groups carrying unequal weights of legitimacy within the culture and the classroom. Halfway through the semester, students renamed the class Coalition 607.

At the end of the semester, we began to suspect that it would have been appropriate for the large group to experiment with forms of communication other than dialogue. These could have brought the existence and results of affinity group interactions to bear more directly on the larger group's understandings and practices. For example, it seemed that we needed times when one affinity group (women of color, women and men of color, feminists, White men against masculinist culture, White women, gays, lesbians) could "speak out" and "talk back" about their experience of Coalition 607's group process or their experience of racial, gender, or other injustice on the campus, while the rest of the class listened without interruption. This would have acknowledged that we were not interacting in class dialogue solely as individuals, but as members of larger social groups, with whom we shared common and also differing experiences of oppression, a language for naming, fighting, and surviving that oppression, and a shared sensibility and style. The differences among the affinity groups that composed the class made communication within the class a form of cross-cultural or cross-subcultural exchange rather than the free, rational, democratic exchange between equal individuals implied in critical pedagogy literature.

But I want to emphasize that this does not mean that discourses of students of difference were taken up and supported unconditionally by themselves and their allies. There had been intense consciousness-raising on the UW-Madison campus between African-American students, Asian-American students, Latino/a, Chicano/a students, Native-American students, and men and women of color, about the different forms racism had taken across the campus, depending on ethnicity and gender — and how no single group's analysis could be adopted to cover all other students of color.

Early in the semester, it became clear to some in Coalition 607 that some of the antiracism discourses heard on campus were structured by highly problematic gender politics, and White women and women of color could not adopt those discourses as their own without undercutting their own struggles against sexism on campus and in their communities. We began to define coalition-building not only in terms of what we shared — a commitment to work against racism — but in terms of what we did not share — gender, sexual orientation, ethnicity, and other differences. These positions gave us different stakes in, experiences of, and perspectives on racism. These differences meant that each strategy we considered for fighting racism on campus had to be interrogated for the implications it held for struggles against sexism, ableism, elitism, fat oppression, and so forth.

We agreed to a final arbiter of the acceptability of demands/narratives by students of color and our class's actions on campus. Proposals would be judged in light of our answers to this question: to what extent do our political strategies and alternative narratives about social difference succeed in alleviating campus racism while at the same time managing *not to undercut* the efforts of other social groups to win self-definition?

A PEDAGOGY OF THE UNKNOWABLE

Like the individual students themselves, each affinity group possessed only partial narratives of its oppression — partial in that they were self-interested and predicated on the exclusion of the voices of others, and partial in the sense that the meaning of an individual's or group's experience is never self-evident or complete. No one affinity group could ever "know" the experiences and knowledges of other affinity groups or the social positions that were not their own. Nor can social subjects, who are split between the conscious and unconscious, and cut across by multiple, intersecting, and contradictory subject positions, ever fully "know" their own experiences. As a whole, Coalition 607 could never know with certainty whether the actions it planned to take on campus would undercut the struggle of other social groups, or even that of its own affinity groups. But this situation was not a failure; it was not something to overcome. Realizing that there are partial narratives that some social groups or cultures have and others can never know, but that are necessary to human survival, is a condition to embrace and use as an opportunity to build a kind of social and educational interdependency that recognizes differences as "different strengths" and as "forces for change."[67] In the words of Audre Lorde, "Difference must be not merely tolerated, but seen as a fund of necessary polarities between which our creativity can spark like a dialectic. Only then does the necessity for interdependency become unthreatening."[68]

In the end, Coalition 607 participants made an initial gesture toward acting out the implications of the unknowable and the social, educational, and political interdependency that it necessitates. The educational interventions against racism that we carried out on campus were put forth as Coalition 607's statement about its members' provisional, partial understanding of racial oppression on the UW-Madison campus at the moment of its actions. These statements were not offered with the invitation for audiences to participate in dialogue, but as a speaking out from semiotic spaces temporarily and problematically controlled by Coalition 607's students. First, we took actions on campus by interrupting business-as-usual (that is, social relations of racism, sexism, classism, Eurocentrism as usual) in the public spaces of the library mall and administrative offices. (The mall is a frequent site for campus protests, rallies, and graffiti, and was chosen for this reason.) These interruptions consisted of three events.

At noon on April 28, 1988, a street theater performance on the library mall, "Meet on the Street," presented an ironic history of university attempts to coopt and defuse the demands of students of color from the 1950s through the 1980s. The affinity group that produced this event invited members of the university and Madison communities who were not in the class to participate. That night, after dark, "Scrawl on the Mall" used overhead and movie projectors to project towering images, text, and spontaneously written "graffiti" on the white walls of the main campus library. Class members and passersby drew and wrote on transparencies for the purpose of deconstructing, defacing, and transforming racist discourses and giving voice to perspectives and demands of students of color and White students against racism. For example, students projected onto the library a page from the administration's official response to the Minority Student Coalition demands, and "edited" it to reveal how it failed to meet those demands. Throughout the semester, a third group of students interrupted business-as-usual in the offices of the student newspaper and university administrators by writing articles and holding interviews that challenged the university's and the newspaper's response to the demands by students of color.

These three events disrupted power relations, however temporarily, within the contexts in which they occurred. Students of color and White students against racism opened up semiotic space for discourses normally marginalized and silenced within the everyday uses of the library mall and administrators' offices. They appropriated means of discourse production — overhead projectors, microphones, language, images, newspaper articles — and controlled, however problematically, the terms in which students of color and racism on campus would be defined and represented within the specific times and spaces of the events. They made available to other members of the university community, with unpredictable and uncontrollable effects, discourses of antiracism that might otherwise have remained unavailable, distorted, more easily dismissed, or seemingly irrelevant. Thus students engaged in the political work of changing material conditions within a public space, allowing them to make visible and assert the legitimacy of their own definitions, in their own terms, of racism and antiracism on the UW campus.

Each of the three actions was defined by different affinity groups according to differing priorities, languages of understanding and analysis, and levels of comfort with various kinds of public action. They were "unified" through their activity of mutual critique, support, and participation, as each group worked through, as much as possible, ways in which the others supported or undercut its own understandings and objectives. Each affinity group brought its proposal for action to the whole class to check out in what ways that action might affect the other groups' self-definitions, priorities, and plans for action. Each group asked the others for various types of labor and support to implement its proposed action. During these planning discussions, we concluded that the results of our interventions would be unpredictable and uncontrollable, and dependent upon the subject positions and changing historical contexts of our audiences on the mall and in administrative offices. Ultimately, our interventions and the process by which we arrived at them had to make sense — both rationally and emotionally — to *us*, however problematically we understand "making sense" to be a political action. Our actions had to make sense as interested interpretations and constant rewritings of ourselves in relation to shifting interpersonal and political contexts. Our interpretations had to be based on attention to history, to concrete experiences of oppression, and to subjugated knowledges.[69]

CONCLUSION

For me, what has become more frightening than the unknown or unknowable, are social, political, and educational projects that predicate and legitimate their actions on the kind of knowing that underlies current definitions of critical pedagogy. In this sense, current understandings and uses of "critical," "empowerment," "student voice," and "dialogue" are only surface manifestations of deeper contradictions involving pedagogies, both traditional and critical. The kind of knowing I am referring to is that in which objects, nature, and "Others" are seen to be known or ultimately knowable, in the sense of being "defined, delineated, captured, understood, explained, and diagnosed" at a level of determination never accorded to the "knower" herself or himself.[70]

The experience of Coalition 607 has left me wanting to think through the implications of confronting unknowability. What would it mean to recognize not only that a multiplicity of knowledges are present in the classroom as a result of the way difference has been used to structure social relations inside and outside the classroom, but that these knowledges are contradictory, partial, and irreducible? They cannot be made to "make sense" — they cannot be known, in terms of the single master discourse of an educational project's curriculum or theoretical framework, even that of critical pedagogy. What kinds of classroom practice are made possible and impossible when one affinity group within the class has lived out and arrived at a currently useful "knowledge" about a particular oppressive formation on campus, but the professor and some of the other students can never know or understand that knowledge in the same way? What practice is called for when even the combination of all partial knowledges in a classroom results in yet another partial knowing, defined by structuring absences that mark the "terror and loathing of any difference?"[71] What kinds of interdependencies between groups and individuals inside and outside of the classroom would recognize that every social, political, or educational project the class takes up locally will already, at the moment of its definition, lack knowledges necessary to answer broader questions of human survival and social justice? What kind of educational project could redefine "knowing" so that it no longer describes the activities of those in power "who started to speak, to speak alone and for everyone else, on behalf of everyone else?"[72] What kind of educational project would redefine the silence of the unknowable, freeing it from "the male-defined context, of Absence, Lack, and Fear," and make of that silence "a language of its own" that changes the nature and direction of speech itself?[73]

Whatever form it takes in the various, changing, locally specific instances of classroom practices, I understand a classroom practice of the unknowable right now to be one that would support students/professors in the never-ending "moving about" Trinh Minh-ha describes:

> After all, she is this Inappropriate/d Other who moves about with always at least two/four gestures: that of affirming "I am like you" while pointing insistently to the

difference; and that of reminding "I am different" while unsettling every definition of otherness arrived at.[74]

In relation to education, I see this moving about as a strategy that affirms "you know me/I know you" while pointing insistently to the interested partialness of those knowings; and constantly reminding us that "you can't know me/I can't know you" while unsettling every definition of knowing arrived at. Classroom practices that facilitate such moving about would support the kind of contextually politically and historically situated identity politics called for by Alcoff, hooks, and others.[75] That is, one in which "identity" is seen as "nonessentialized and emergent from a historical experience" as a necessary stage in a process, a starting point — not an ending point.[76] Identity in this sense becomes a vehicle for multiplying and making more complex the subject positions possible, visible, and legitimate at any given historical moment, requiring disruptive changes in the way social technologies of gender, race, ability, and so on define "Otherness" and use it as a vehicle for subordination.

Gayatri Spivak calls the search for a coherent narrative "counterproductive" and asserts that what is needed is "persistent critique" of received narratives and a priori lines of attack.[77] Similarly, unlike post-liberal or post-Marxist movements predicated on repressive unities, Minh-ha's moving about refuses to reduce profoundly heterogeneous networks of power/desire/interest to any one a priori, coherent narrative. It refuses to know and resist oppression from any a priori line of attack, such as race, class, or gender solidarity.

But participants in Coalition 607 did not simply unsettle every definition of knowing, assert the absence of a priori solidarities, or replace political action (in the sense defined at the beginning of this chapter) with textual critique. Rather, we struggled, as S. P. Mohanty would have us do, to "develop a sense of the profound *contextuality* of meanings [and oppressive knowledges] in their play and their ideological effects."[78]

Our classroom was the site of dispersed, shifting, and contradictory contexts of knowing that coalesced differently in different moments of student/professor speech, action, and emotion. This situation meant that individuals and affinity groups constantly had to change strategies and priorities of resistance against oppressive ways of knowing and being known. The antagonist became power itself as it was deployed within our classroom — oppressive ways of knowing and oppressive knowledges.

This position, informed by post-structuralism and feminism, leaves no one off the hook, including critical pedagogues. We cannot act as if our membership in or alliance with an oppressed group exempts us from the need to confront the "grey areas which we all have in us."[79] As Minh-ha reminds us, "There are no social positions exempt from becoming oppressive to others . . . any group — any position — can move into the oppressor role," depending upon specific historical contexts and situations.[80] Or as Mary Gentile puts it, "everyone is someone else's 'Other.'"[81]

Various groups struggling for self-definition in the United States have identified the mythical norm deployed for the purpose of setting the standard of humanness against which Others are defined and assigned privilege and limitations. At this moment in history, that norm is young, White, heterosexual, Christian, able-bodied, thin, middle-class, English-speaking, and male. Yet, as Gentile argues, no individual embodies, in the essentialist sense, this mythical norm.[82] Even individuals who most closely approximate it experience a dissonance. As someone who embodies some but not all of the current mythical norm's socially constructed characteristics, my colleague Albert Selvin wrote in response to the first draft of this chapter: "I too have to fight to differentiate myself from a position defined for me — whose terms are imposed on me — which limits and can destroy me — which does destroy many White men or turns them into helpless agents. . . . I as a White man/boy was not allowed — by my family, by society — to be anything *but* cut off from the earth and the body. That condition is not/was not an essential component or implication of my maleness."[83]

To assert multiple perspectives in this way is not to draw attention away from the distinctive realities and effects of the oppression of any particular group. It is not to excuse or relativize oppression by simply claiming, "we are all oppressed." Rather, it is to clarify oppression by preventing "oppressive simplifications," and insisting that it be understood and struggled against contextually.[84] For example, the politics of appearance in relation to the mythical norm played a major role in our classroom. Upon first sight, group members tended to draw alliances and assume shared commitments because of the social positions we presumed others to occupy (radical, heterosexual, antiracist person of color, and so on). But not only were these assumptions often wrong, at times they denied ideological and personal commitments to various struggles by people who appeared outwardly to fit the mythical norm.

The terms in which I can and will assert and unsettle "difference" and unlearn my positions of privilege in future classroom practices are wholly dependent on the Others/others whose presence — with their concrete experiences of privileges and oppression, and subjugated or oppressive knowledges — I am responding to and acting with in any given classroom. My moving about between the positions of privileged speaking subject and Inappropriate/d Other cannot be predicted, prescribed, or understood beforehand by any theoretical framework or methodological practice. It is in this sense that a practice grounded in the unknowable is profoundly contextual (historical) and interdependent (social). This reformulation of pedagogy and knowledge removes the critical pedagogue from two key discursive positions she/he has constructed for her/himself in the literature — namely, origin of what can be known and origin of what should be done. What remains for me is the challenge of constructing classroom practices that engage with the discursive and material spaces that such a removal opens up. I am trying to unsettle received definitions of pedagogy by multiplying the ways in which I am able to act on and in the university both as the Inappropriate/d Other and as the privileged speaking/making subject trying to unlearn that privilege.

In a follow-up to Coalition 607, Curriculum and Instruction 800 planned, produced, and "made sense" of a day-long film and video event against oppressive knowledges and ways of knowing in the curriculum, pedagogy, and everyday life at UW-Madison. We did not focus on any one formation (race *or* class *or* gender *or* ableism). Rather, we engaged with each other and worked against oppressive social formations on campus in ways that tried to "find a commonality in the experience of difference without compromising its distinctive realities and effects."[85]

The classroom practice that seems most capable of accomplishing this is one that facilitates a kind of communication across differences that is best represented by this statement: "If you can talk to me in ways that show you understand that your knowledge of me, the world, and 'the Right thing to do' will always be partial, interested, and potentially oppressive to others, and if I can do the same, then we can work together on shaping and reshaping alliances for constructing circumstances in which students of difference can thrive."

NOTES

1. By "critique" I do not mean a systematic analysis of the specific articles or individual authors' positions that make up this literature, for the purpose of articulating a "theory" of critical pedagogy capable of being evaluated for its internal consistency, elegance, powers of prediction, and so on. Rather, I have chosen to ground the following critique in my interpretation of my experiences in C&I 607. That is, I have attempted to place key discourses in the literature on critical pedagogy *in relation to* my interpretation of my experience in C&I 607 — by asking which interpretations and "sense making" do those discourses facilitate, which do they silence and marginalize, and what interests do they appear to serve?

2. By "the literature on critical pedagogy," I mean those articles in major educational journals and special editions devoted to critical pedagogy. For the purpose of this article, I systematically reviewed more than thirty articles appearing in journals such as *Harvard Educational Review, Curriculum Inquiry, Educational Theory, Teachers College Record, Journal of Curriculum Theorizing,* and *Journal of Curriculum Studies* between 1984 and 1988. The purpose of this review was to identify key and repeated claims, assumptions, goals, and pedagogical practices that currently set the terms of debate within this literature. "Critical pedagogy" should not be confused with "feminist pedagogy," which constitutes a separate body of literature with its own goals and assumptions.

3. Some of the more representative writing on this point can be found in Michelle Fine, "Silencing in the Public Schools," *Language Arts, 64* (1987), 157–174; Henry A. Giroux, "Radical Pedagogy and the Politics of Student Voice," *Interchange, 17* (1986), 48–69; and Roger Simon, "Empowerment as a Pedagogy of Possibility," *Language Arts, 64* (1987), 370–382.

4. See Henry A. Giroux and Peter McLaren, "Teacher Education and the Politics of Engagement: The Case for Democratic Schooling," *Harvard Educational Review, 56* (1986), 213–238; and Ira Shor and Paulo Freire, "What is the 'Dialogical Method' of Teaching?" *Journal of Education, 169* (1987), 11–31.

5. Shor and Freire, "What is the 'Dialogical Method'?" and Henry A. Giroux, "Literacy and the Pedagogy of Voice and Political Empowerment," *Educational Theory, 38* (1988), 61–75.

6. Daniel P. Liston and Kenneth M. Zeichner, "Critical Pedagogy and Teacher Education," *Journal of Education, 169* (1987), 117–137.

7. Liston and Zeichner, "Critical Pedagogy," p. 120.

8. Liston and Zeichner, "Critical Pedagogy," p. 127.

9. Giroux, "Literacy and the Pedagogy of Voice," p. 75.

10. Liston and Zeichner, "Critical Pedagogy," p. 128.

11. Valerie Walkerdine, "On the Regulation of Speaking and Silence: Subjectivity, Class, and Gender in Contemporary Schooling," in *Language, Gender, and Childhood,* ed. Carolyn Steedman, Cathy Urwin, and Valerie Walkerdine (London: Routledge & Kegan Paul, 1985), p. 205.

12. Barbara Christian, "The Race for Theory," *Cultural Critique, 6* (Spring 1987), 51–63.
13. By the end of the semester, many of us began to understand ourselves as inhabiting intersections of multiple, contradictory, overlapping social positions not reducible either to race, or class, or gender, and so on. Depending upon the moment and the context, the degree to which any one of us "differs" from the mythical norm (see conclusion) varies along multiple axes, and so do the consequences. I began using the terms "students of difference" "professor of difference," to refer to social positionings in relation to the mythical norm (based on ability, size, color, sexual preference, gender, ethnicity, and so on). This reminded us of the necessity to reconstruct how, within specific situations, particular socially constructed differences from the mythical norm (such as color) get taken up as vehicles for institutions such as the university to act out and legitimate oppressive formations of power. This enabled us to open up our analysis of racism on campus for the purpose of tracing its relations to institutional sexism, ableism, elitism, anti-Semitism, and other oppressive formations.
14. Giroux and McLaren, "Teacher Education and the Politics of Engagement," p. 229.
15. Stanley Aronowitz, "Postmodernism and Politics," *Social Text, 18* (1987/1988), 99–115.
16. Liston and Zeichner, "Critical Pedagogy," p. 120.
17. For an excellent theoretical discussion and demonstration of the explanatory power of this approach, see Julian Henriques, Wendy Hollway, Cathy Urwin, Couze Venn, and Valerie Walkerdine, *Changing the Subject: Psychology, Social Regulation, and Subjectivity* (New York: Methuen, 1984); Gloria Anzaldua, *Borderlands/La Frontera: The New Mestiza* (San Francisco: Spinsters/Aunt Lute, 1987); Teresa de Lauretis, ed., *Feminist Studies/Critical Studies* (Bloomington: Indiana University Press, 1986); Hal Foster, ed., *Discussions in Contemporary Culture* (Seattle: Bay Press, 1987); Chris Weedon, *Feminist Practice and Poststructuralist Theory* (New York: Basil Blackwell, 1987).
18. Weedon, *Feminist Practice and Poststructuralist Theory.*
19. Aronowitz, "Postmodernism and Politics," p. 103.
20. Aronowitz, "Postmodernism and Politics," p. 103.
21. Audre Lorde, *Sister Outsider* (New York: Crossing Press, 1984), p. 112.
22. Lorde, *Sister Outsider,* p. 112.
23. Christian, "The Race for Theory," p. 63.
24. For a discussion of the thesis of the "epistemic privilege of the oppressed," see Uma Narayan, "Working Together Across Difference: Some Considerations on Emotions and Political Practice," *Hypatia, 3* (1988), 31–47.
25. For an excellent discussion of the relation of the concept of "experience" to feminism, essentialism, and political action, see Linda Alcoff, "Cultural Feminism versus Post-Structuralism: The Identity Crisis in Feminist Theory," *Signs, 13* (1988), 405–437.
26. Narayan, "Working Together Across Difference," pp. 31–47.
27. This subtitle is borrowed from Maria C. Lugones and Elizabeth V. Spelman's critique of imperialistic, ethnocentric, and disrespectful tendencies in White feminists' theorizing about women's oppression, "Have We Got a Theory for You! Feminist Theory, Cultural Imperialism, and the Demand for 'The Woman's Voice,'" *Women's Studies International Forum* (1983), 573–581.
28. Nicholas C. Burbules, "A Theory of Power in Education," *Educational Theory, 36* (1986), 95–114; Giroux and McLaren, "Teacher Education and the Politics of Engagement," pp. 224–227.
29. Liston and Zeichner, "Critical Pedagogy and Teacher Education," p. 120.
30. Shor and Freire, "What is the 'Dialogical Method' of Teaching?" p. 14.
31. Giroux, "Radical Pedagogy," p. 64.
32. Giroux, "Radical Pedagogy," p. 66
33. Shor and Freire, "What is the 'Dialogical Method' of Teaching?" p. 22.
34. Burbules, "A Theory of Power in Education"; and Giroux and McLaren, "Teacher Education and the Politics of Engagement," pp. 224–227.
35. Shor and Freire, "What is the 'Dialogical Method' of Teaching?" p. 23.

36. Burbules, "A Theory of Power in Education," p. 108.
37. Giroux and McLaren, "Teacher Education and the Politics of Engagement," p. 226.
38. Walter C. Parker, "Justice, Social Studies, and the Subjectivity/Structure Problem," *Theory and Research in Social Education, 14* (1986), p. 227.
39. Simon, "Empowerment as a Pedagogy of Possibility," p. 372.
40. Giroux, "Literacy and the Pedagogy of Voice," pp. 68–69.
41. Giroux and McLaren, "Teacher Education and the Politics of Engagement," p. 225.
42. Giroux and McLaren, "Teacher Education and the Politics of Engagement," p. 227.
43. Shor and Freire, "What is the 'Dialogical Method' of Teaching?" p. 30; Liston and Zeichner, "Critical Pedagogy," p. 122.
44. Simon, "Empowerment as a Pedagogy of Possibility," p. 80.
45. Simon, "Empowerment as a Pedagogy of Possibility," p. 375.
46. Aronowitz, "Postmodernism and Politics," p. 111.
47. Alcoff, "Cultural Feminism versus Post-Structuralism," p. 420.
48. Simon, "Empowerment as a Pedagogy of Possibility."
49. bell hooks, "Talking Back," *Discourse, 8* (1986/1987), 123–128.
50. bell hooks, *talking back: thinking feminist, thinking black* (Boston: South End Press, 1989).
51. Peter McLaren, *Life in Schools* (New York: Longman, 1989).
52. Alcoff, "Cultural Feminism versus Post-Structuralism"; Anzaldua, *Borderlands/La Frontera;* de Lauretis, *Feminist Studies/Critical Studies;* hooks, *talking back;* Trihn T. Minh-ha, *Woman, Native, Other* (Bloomington: Indiana University Press, 1989); Weedon, *Feminist Practice and Poststructuralist Theory.*
53. hooks, "Talking Back," p. 124.
54. Susan Hardy Aiken, Karen Anderson, Myra Dinerstein, Judy Lensink, and Patricia MacCorquodale, "Trying Transformations: Curriculum Integration and the Problem of Resistance," *Signs, 12* (1987), 225–275.
55. Aiken et al., "Trying Transformations," p. 263.
56. Shoshana Felman, "Psychoanalysis and Education: Teaching Terminable and Interminable," *Yale French Studies, 63* (1982), 21–44.
57. S. P. Mohanty, "Radical Teaching, Radical Theory: The Ambiguous Politics of Meaning," in *Theory in the Classroom,* ed. Cary Nelson (Urbana: University of Illinois Press, 1986), p. 155.
58. Giroux and McLaren, "Teacher Education and the Politics of Engagement," p. 235.
59. Giroux and McLaren, "Teacher Education and the Politics of Engagement," p. 237.
60. Giroux, "Literacy and the Pedagogy of Voice," p. 72.
61. Giroux, "Literacy and the Pedagogy of Voice," p. 72.
62. Biddy Martin and Chandra Talpade Mohanty, "Feminist Politics: What's Home Got to Do with It?" in *Feminist Studies/Critical Studies,* ed. Theresa de Lauretis (Bloomington: Indiana University Press, 1986), pp. 208–209.
63. Martin and Mohanty, "Feminist Politics," p. 208.
64. Discussions with students after the semester ended and comments from students and colleagues on the draft of this article have led me to realize the extent to which some international students and Jews in the class felt unable or not safe to speak about experiences of oppression inside and outside of the class related to those identities. Anti-Semitism, economic and cultural imperialism, and the rituals of exclusion of international students on campus were rarely named and never fully elaborated in the class. The classroom practices that reproduced these particular oppressive silences in C&I 607 must be made the focus of sustained critique in the follow-up course, C&I 800, "Race, Class, Gender, and the Construction of Knowledge in Educational Media."
65. John W. Murphy, "Computerization, Postmodern Epistemology, and Reading in the Postmodern Era," *Educational Theory, 38* (1988), 175–182.
66. Lugones and Spelman assert that the only acceptable motivation for following Others into their worlds is friendship. Self-interest is not enough, because "the task at hand

for you is one of extraordinary difficulty. It requires that you be willing to devote a great part of your life to it and that you be willing to suffer alienation and self-disruption . . . whatever the benefits you may accrue from such a journey, they cannot be concrete enough for you at this time and they are not worth your while" ("Have We Got a Theory for You," p. 576). Theoretical or political "obligation" is inappropriate, because it puts Whites/Anglos "in a morally self-righteous position" and makes people of color vehicles of redemption for those in power (p. 581). Friendship, as an appropriate and acceptable "condition" under which people become allies in struggles that are not their own, names my own experience and has been met with enthusiasm by students.

67. Lorde, *Sister Outsider,* p. 112.
68. Lorde, *Sister Outsider,* p. 112.
69. Martin and Mohanty, "Feminist Politics," p. 210.
70. Alcoff, "Cultural Feminism versus Post-Structuralism," p. 406.
71. Lorde, *Sister Outsider,* p. 113.
72. Trinh T. Minh-ha, "Introduction," *Discourse, 8* (1986/1987), p. 7.
73. Minh-ha, "Introduction," p. 8.
74. Minh-ha, "Introduction," p. 9.
75. Alcoff, "Cultural Feminism versus Post-Structuralism"; bell hooks, "The Politics of Radical Black Subjectivity," *Zeta Magazine,* April 1989, pp. 52–55.
76. hooks, "The Politics of Radical Black Subjectivity," p. 54.
77. Gayatri Chakravorty Spivak, "Can the Subaltern Speak?" in *Marxism and the Interpretation of Culture,* ed. Cary Nelson and Lawrence Grossberg (Urbana: University of Illinois Press, 1988), p. 272.
78. S. P. Mohanty, "Radical Teaching, Radical Theory," p. 169.
79. Minh-ha, "Introduction," p. 6.
80. A. Selvin, personal correspondence (October 24, 1988).
81. Mary Gentile, *Film Feminisms: Theory and Practice* (Westport, CT: Greenwood Press, 1985), p. 7.
82. Gentile, *Film Feminisms,* p. 7.
83. A. Selvin, personal correspondence.
84. Gentile, *Film Feminisms,* p. 7.
85. Gentile, *Film Feminisms,* p. 7.

This chapter is a revised version of a paper presented at the Tenth Conference on Curriculum Theory and Classroom Practice, Bergamo Conference Center, Dayton, Ohio, October 25–29, 1988. It was part of a symposium entitled "Reframing the Empirical 'I/Eye': Feminist, Neo-Marxist, and Post-structuralist Challenges to Research in Education." I want to thank Mimi Orner, Ph.D. candidate and teaching assistant in the Department of Curriculum and Instruction, UW-Madison, for her insights and hours of conversations about the meanings of C&I 607. They have formed the backbone of this chapter.

Freire and a Feminist Pedagogy
of Difference

KATHLEEN WEILER

*In this chapter, Kathleen Weiler presents a feminist critique that challenges tradi-
tional Western knowledge systems. As an educator, Weiler sees this critique impacting
both the theory and practice of education. She begins with a discussion of the liberatory pedagogy of Paulo Freire, and the profound importance of his work. She then
offers a critical reflection of Freire's work and, in particular, questions his assumption of a uniform experience of oppression, as well as his abstract goals for liberation.
A feminist pedagogy, she claims, offers a more complex vision of liberatory pedagogy.*

*Weiler traces the growth of feminist epistemology from the early consciousness-rais-
ing groups to current women's studies programs. She identifies three ways that a
feminist pedagogy that incorporates a critical analysis of Freire's work builds on and
enriches his pedagogy: in its questioning of the role and authority of the teacher; in
its recognition of the importance of personal experience as a source of knowledge; and
in its exploration of the perspectives of people of different races, classes, and cultures.*

We are living in a period of profound challenges to traditional Western epistemology and political theory. These challenges, couched in the language of postmodernist theory and in postcolonialist critiques, reflect the rapid transformation of the economic and political structure of the world order: the impact of
transnational capital; the ever more comprehensive integration of resources,
labor, and markets; the pervasiveness of media and consumer images. This interdependent world system is based on the exploitation of oppressed groups,
but the system at the same time calls forth oppositional cultural forms that give
voice to the conditions of these groups. White male bourgeois dominance is
being challenged by people of color, women, and other oppressed groups, who
assert the validity of their own knowledge and demand social justice and equality
in numerous political and cultural struggles. In the intellectual sphere, this shifting world system has led to a shattering of Western metanarratives and to the
variety of stances of postmodernist and cultural-identity theory. A major theoretical challenge to traditional Western knowledge systems is emerging from
feminist theory, which has been increasingly influenced by postmodernist and
cultural-identity theory. Feminist theory, like other contemporary approaches,
validates difference, challenges universal claims to truth, and seeks to create
social transformation in a world of shifting and uncertain meanings.

In education, these profound shifts are evident on two levels: first, at the level
of practice, as excluded and formerly silenced groups challenge dominant ap-

Harvard Educational Review   Vol. 61 No. 4 November 1991, 449–474.

proaches to learning and to definitions of knowledge; and second, at the level of theory, as modernist claims to universal truth are called into question.[1] These challenges to accepted truths have been raised not only to the institutions and theories that defend the status quo, but also to the critical or liberatory pedagogies that emerged in the 1960s and 1970s. Feminist educational critics, like other theorists influenced by postmodernism and theories of difference, want to retain the vision of social justice and transformation that underlies liberatory pedagogies, but they find that their claims to universal truths and their assumptions of a collective experience of oppression do not adequately address the realities of their own confusing and often tension-filled classrooms. This consciousness of the inadequacy of classical liberatory pedagogies has been particularly true for feminist educators, who are acutely aware of the continuing force of sexism and patriarchal structures and of the power of race, sexual preference, physical ability, and age to divide teachers from students and students from one another.

Paulo Freire is without question the most influential theorist of critical or liberatory education. His theories have profoundly influenced literacy programs throughout the world and what has come to be called critical pedagogy in the United States. His theoretical works, particularly *Pedagogy of the Oppressed*, provide classic statements of liberatory or critical pedagogy based on universal claims of truth.[2] Feminist pedagogy as it has developed in the United States provides a historically situated example of a critical pedagogy in practice. Feminist conceptions of education are similar to Freire's pedagogy in a variety of ways, and feminist educators often cite Freire as the educational theorist who comes closest to the approach and goals of feminist pedagogy.[3] Both feminist pedagogy as it is usually defined and Freirean pedagogy rest upon visions of social transformation; underlying both are certain common assumptions concerning oppression, consciousness, and historical change. Both pedagogies assert the existence of oppression in people's material conditions of existence and as a part of consciousness; both rest on a view of consciousness as more than a sum of dominating discourses, but as containing within it a critical capacity — what Antonio Gramsci called "good sense"; and both thus see human beings as subjects and actors in history and hold a strong commitment to justice and a vision of a better world and of the potential for liberation.[4] These ideals have powerfully influenced teachers and students in a wide range of educational settings, both formal and informal.

But in action, the goals of liberation or opposition to oppression have not always been easy to understand or achieve. As universal goals, these ideals do not address the specificity of people's lives; they do not directly analyze the contradictions between conflicting oppressed groups or the ways in which a single individual can experience oppression in one sphere while being privileged or oppressive in another. Feminist and Freirean teachers are in many ways engaged in what Teresa de Lauretis has called "shifting the ground of signs," challenging accepted meanings and relationships that occur at what she calls "political or more often micropolitical" levels, groupings that "produce no texts as such, but by shifting the 'ground' of a given sign . . . effectively intervene upon codes of perception as well as ideological codes."[5] But in attempting to challenge dominant values and to "shift the ground of signs," feminist and Freirean teachers raise conflicts for themselves and for their students, who also are historically situated and whose own subjectivities are often contradictory and in process. These conflicts have become increasingly clear as both Freirean and feminist pedagogies are put into practice. Attempting to implement these pedagogies without acknowledging the conflict not only of divided consciousness — what Audre Lorde calls "the oppressor within us" — but also the conflicts among groups trying to work together to name and struggle against oppression — among teachers and students in classrooms, or among political groups working for change in very specific areas — can lead to anger, frustration, and a retreat to safer or more traditional approaches.[6] The numerous accounts of the tensions of trying to put liberatory pedagogies into practice demonstrate the need to reexamine the assumptions of the classic texts of liberatory pedagogy and to consider the various issues that have arisen in attempts at critical and liberatory classroom practice.[7]

As a White feminist writing and teaching from the traditions of both critical pedagogy and feminist theory, these issues are of particular concern to me. In this article, I examine and critique the classic liberatory pedagogy of Paulo Freire, particularly as it is presented in *Pedagogy of the Oppressed*, his most famous and influential text. I then examine the development and practice of feminist pedagogy, which emerged in a particular historical and political moment in the United States, and which, as a situated pedagogy, provides an example of some of the difficulties of putting these ideals into practice and suggests at the same time some possible theoretical and practical directions for liberatory pedagogies in general. I argue that an exploration of the conflicts and concerns that have arisen for feminist teachers attempting to put into practice their versions of a feminist pedagogy can help enrich and re-envision Freirean goals of liberation and social progress. This emerging pedagogy does not reject the goals of justice — the end of oppression, and liberation — but frames them more specifically in the context of historically defined struggles and calls for the articulation of interests and identity on the part of teacher and theorist as well as student. This approach questions whether the oppressed cannot act also as oppressors and challenges the idea of a commonality of oppression. It raises questions about common experience as a source of knowledge, the pedagogical authority of the teacher, and the nature of political and pedagogical struggle.

THE PEDAGOGY OF PAULO FREIRE

Freire's pedagogy developed in particular historical and political circumstances of neocolonialism and imperialism. As is well known, Freire's methods developed originally from his work with peasants in Brazil and later in Chile and Guinea-Bissau.[8] Freire's thought thus needs to be understood in the context of the political and economic situation of the developing world. In Freire's initial formulation, oppression was conceived in class terms and education was viewed in the context of peasants' and working people's revolutionary struggles. Equally influential in Freire's thought and pedagogy were the influence of radical Christian thought and the revolutionary role of liberation theology in Latin America. As is true for other radical Christians in Latin America, Freire's personal knowledge of extreme poverty and suffering challenged his deeply felt Christian faith grounded in the ethical teachings of Jesus in the Gospels. Freire's pedagogy is thus founded on a moral imperative to side with the oppressed that emerges from both his Christian faith and his knowledge and experience of suffering in the society in which he grew up and lived. Freire has repeatedly stated that his pedagogical method cannot simply be transferred to other settings, but that each historical site requires the development of a pedagogy appropriate to that setting. In his most recent work, he has also addressed sexism and racism as systems of oppression that must be considered as seriously as class oppression.[9] Nonetheless, Freire is frequently read without consideration for the context of the specific settings in which his work developed and without these qualifications in mind. His most commonly read text still is his first book to be published in English, *Pedagogy of the Oppressed.* In this classic text, Freire presents the epistemological basis for his pedagogy and discusses the concepts of oppression, conscientization, and dialogue that are at the heart of his pedagogical project, but as he enacted it in settings in the developing world and as it has been appropriated by radical teachers in other settings.

Freire organizes his approach to liberatory pedagogy in terms of a dualism between the oppressed and the oppressors and between humanization and dehumanization. This organization of thoughts in terms of opposing forces reflects Freire's own experiences of literacy work with the poor in Brazil, a situation in which the lines between oppressor and oppressed were clear. For Freire, humanization is the goal of liberation; it has not yet been achieved, nor can it be achieved so long as the oppressors oppress the oppressed. That is, liberation and humanization will not occur if the roles of oppressor and oppressed are simply reversed. If humanization is to be realized, new relationships among human beings must be created:

> Because it is a distortion of being more fully human, sooner or later being less human leads the oppressed to struggle against those who made them so. In order for this struggle to have meaning, the oppressed must not, in seeking to regain their humanity (which is a way to create it), become in turn oppressors of the oppressors, but rather restorers of the humanity of both.[10]

The struggle against oppression leading to humanization is thus utopian and visionary. As Freire says elsewhere, "To be utopian is not to be merely idealistic or impractical but rather to engage in denunciation and annunciation."[11] By denunciation, Freire refers to the naming and analysis of existing structures of oppression; by annunciation, he means the creation of new forms of relationships and being in the world as a result of mutual struggle against oppression. Thus Freire presents a theoretical justification for a pedagogy that aims to critique existing forms of oppression and to transform the world, thereby creating new ways of being, or humanization.

Radical educators throughout the world have used *Pedagogy of the Oppressed* as the theoretical justification for their work. As an eloquent and impassioned statement of the need for and possibility of change through reading the world and the word, there is no comparable contemporary text.[12] But when we look at *Pedagogy of the Oppressed* from the perspective of recent feminist theory and pedagogy, certain problems arise that may reflect the difficulties that have some-times arisen when Freire's ideas are enacted in specific settings. The challenges of recent feminist theory do not imply the rejection of Freire's goals for what he calls a pedagogy for liberation; feminists certainly share Freire's emphasis on seeing human beings as the subjects and not the objects of history. A critical feminist rereading of Freire, however, points to ways in which the project of Freirean pedagogy, like that of feminist pedagogy, may be enriched and re-en-visioned.

From a feminist perspective, *Pedagogy of the Oppressed* is striking in its use of the male referent, a usage that was universal when the book was written in the 1960s.[13] Much more troublesome, however, is the abstract quality of terms such as humanization, which do not address the particular meanings imbued by men and women, Black and White, or other groups. The assumption of *Pedagogy of the Oppressed* is that in struggling against oppression, the oppressed will move toward true humanity. But this leaves unaddressed the forms of oppression ex-perienced by different actors, the possibility of struggles among people op-pressed differently by different groups — what Cameron McCarthy calls "non-synchrony of oppression."[14] This assumption also presents humanization as a universal, without considering the various definitions this term may bring forth from people of different groups. When Freire speaks of the oppressed needing to fight the tendency to become "sub-oppressors," he means that the oppressed have only the pattern of oppression before them as a way of being in a position other than the one they are in. As Freire writes, "Their ideal is to be men; but for them, to be men is to be oppressors. This is their model of humanity."[15] What is troubling here is not that "men" is used for human beings, but that the model of oppressor implied here is based on the immediate oppressor of men — in this case, bosses over peasants or workers. What is not addressed is the possibility of simultaneous contradictory positions of oppression and dominance: the man oppressed by his boss could at the same time oppress his wife, for example, or the White woman oppressed by sexism could exploit the Black woman. By fram-ing this discussion in such abstract terms, Freire slides over the contradictions and tensions within social settings in which overlapping forms of oppression exist.

This usage of "the oppressed" in the abstract also raises difficulties in Freire's use of experience as the means of acquiring a radical literacy, "reading the world and the word." At the heart of Freire's pedagogy is the insistence that all people are subjects and knowers of the world. Their political literacy will emerge from their reading of the world — that is, their own experience. This reading will lead to collective knowledge and action. But what if that experience is divided? What if different truths are discovered in reading the world from different positions? For Freire, education as the practice of freedom "denies that men are abstract, isolated, independent, and unattached to the world. . . . Authentic reflection considers neither abstract man nor the world without men, but men in their relations with the world."[16] But implicit in this vision is the assumption that, when the oppressed perceive themselves in relation to the world, they will act together collectively to transform the world and to move toward their own hu-manization. The nature of their perception of the world and their oppression is implicitly assumed to be uniform for all the oppressed. The possibility of a contradictory experience of oppression among the oppressed is absent. As Freire says:

> Accordingly, the point of departure must always be with men in the "here and now," which constitutes the situation within which they are submerged, from which they emerge, and in which they intervene. Only by starting from this situation — which determines their perception of it — can they begin to move.[17]

The assumption again is that the oppressed, these men, are submerged in a common situation of oppression, and that their shared knowledge of that oppression will lead them to collective action.

Central to Freire's pedagogy is the practice of conscientization; that is, coming to a consciousness of oppression and a commitment to end that oppression. Conscientization is based on this common experience of oppression. Through this reading of the world, the oppressed will come to knowledge. The role of the teacher in this process is to instigate a dialogue between teacher and student, based on their common ability to know the world and to act as subjects in the world. But the question of the authority and power of the teacher, particularly those forms of power based on the teacher's subject position as raced, classed, gendered, and so on, is not addressed by Freire. There is, again, the assumption that the teacher is "on the same side" as the oppressed, and that as teachers and students engage together in a dialogue about the world, they will uncover together the same reality, the same oppression, and the same liberation. In *Pedagogy of the Oppressed*, the teacher is presented as a generic man whose interests will be with the oppressed as they mutually discover the mechanisms of oppression. The subjectivity of the Freirean teacher is, in this sense, what Gayatri Chakravorty Spivak refers to as "transparent."[18] In fact, of course, teachers are not abstract; they are women or men of particular races, classes, ages, abilities, and so on. The teacher will be seen and heard by students not as an abstraction, but as a particular person with a certain defined history and relationship to the world. In a later book, Freire argues that the teacher has to assume authority, but must do so without becoming authoritarian. In this recognition of the teacher's authority, Freire acknowledges the difference between teacher and students:

> The educator continues to be different from the students, but, and now for me this is the central question, the difference between them, if the teacher is democratic, if his or her political dream is a *liberating* one, is that he or she cannot permit the necessary difference between the teacher and the students to become "antagonistic."[19]

In this passage, Freire acknowledges the power of the teacher by virtue of the structural role of "teacher" within a hierarchical institution and, under the best of circumstances, by virtue of the teacher's greater experience and knowledge. But Freire does not go on to investigate what the other sources of "antagonism" in the classroom might be. However much he provides a valuable guide to the use of authority by the liberatory teacher, he never addresses the question of other forms of power held by the teacher by virtue of race, gender, or class that may lead to antagonisms. Without naming these sources of tension, it is difficult to address or build upon them to challenge existing structures of power and subjectivities. Without recognizing more clearly the implicit power and limitations of the position of teacher, calls for a collective liberation or for opposition to oppression slide over the surface of the tensions that may emerge among teachers and students as subjects with conflicting interests and histories and with different kinds of knowledge and power. A number of questions are thus left unaddressed in *Pedagogy of the Oppressed:* How are we to situate ourselves in relation to the struggle of others? How are we to address our own contradictory positions as oppressors and oppressed? Where are we to look for liberation when our collective "reading of the world" reveals contradictory and conflicting experiences and struggles? The Freirean vision of the oppressed as undifferentiated and as the source of unitary political action, the transparency of the subjectivity of the Freirean teacher, and the claims of universal goals of liberation and social transformation fail to provide the answers to these questions.

Calling into question the universal and abstract claims of *Pedagogy of the Oppressed* is certainly not to argue that Freire's pedagogy should be rejected or discarded. The ethical stance of Freire in terms of praxis and his articulation of people's worth and ability to know and change the world are an essential basis for radical pedagogies in opposition to oppression. Freire's thought illuminates the central question of political action in a world increasingly without universals. Freire, like liberation theologians such as Sharon Welch, positions himself on the side of the oppressed; he claims the moral imperative to act in the world. As Peter McLaren has commented in reference to Freire's political stand, "The task of liberating others from their suffering may not emerge from some transcendental fiat, yet it nevertheless compels us to affirm our humanity in solidarity with victims."[20] But in order better to seek the affirmation of our own humanity and to seek to end suffering and oppression, I am arguing for a more situated theory of oppression and subjectivity, and for the need to consider the contradictions of such universal claims of truth or process.

In the next section of this chapter, I explore feminist pedagogy as an example of a situated pedagogy of liberation. Like Freirean pedagogy, feminist pedagogy is based on assumptions of the power of consciousness raising, the existence of oppression and the possibility of ending it, and the desire for social transformation. But in its historical development, feminist pedagogy has revealed the shortcomings that emerge in the attempt to enact a pedagogy that assumes a universal experience and abstract goals. In the attempt of feminist pedagogy to address these issues, a more complex vision of a liberatory pedagogy is being developed and explored.

FEMINIST PEDAGOGY, CONSCIOUSNESS RAISING, AND WOMEN'S LIBERATION

Feminist pedagogy in colleges and universities has developed in conjunction with the growth of women's studies and what is inclusively called "the new scholarship on women." These developments within universities — the institutionalization of women's studies as programs and departments and the challenge to existing canons and disciplines by the new scholarship on women and by feminist theory — are reflected in the classroom teaching methods that have come to be loosely termed feminist pedagogy. Defining exactly what feminist pedagogy means in practice, however, is difficult. It is easier to describe the various methods used in specific women's studies courses and included by feminist teachers claiming the term feminist pedagogy than it is to provide a coherent definition.[21] But common to the claims of feminist teachers is the goal of providing students with the skills to continue political work as feminists after they have left the university. Nancy Schniedewind makes a similar claim for what she calls "feminist process," which she characterizes as "both a feminist vision of equalitarian personal relations and societal forms and the confidence and skills to make their knowledge and vision functional in the world."[22]

The pedagogy of feminist teachers is based on certain assumptions about knowledge, power, and political action that can be traced beyond the academy to the political activism of the women's movement in the 1960s. This same commitment to social change through the transformative potential of education underlay Freire's pedagogy in Brazil during the same period. Women's studies at the university level have since come to encompass a wide variety of political stances and theoretical approaches. Socialist feminism, liberal feminism, radical feminism, and postmodern feminism all view issues from their different perspectives. Nonetheless, feminist pedagogy continues to echo the struggles of its origins and to retain a vision of social activism. Virtually all women's studies courses and programs at least partially reflect this critical, oppositional, and activist stance, even within programs now established and integrated into the bureaucratic structures of university life. As Linda Gordon points out:

> Women's studies did not arise accidentally, as the product of someone's good idea, but was created by a social movement for women's liberation with a sharp critique of the whole structure of society. By its very existence, women's studies constitutes a critique of the university and the body of knowledge it imparts.[23]

Despite tensions and splits within feminism at a theoretical level and in the context of women's studies programs in universities, the political commitment of women's liberation that Gordon refers to continues to shape feminist pedagogy. Thus, like Freirean pedagogy, feminist pedagogy is grounded in a vision of social change. And, like Freirean pedagogy, feminist pedagogy rests on truth claims of the primacy of experience and consciousness that are grounded in historically situated social change movements. Key to understanding the methods and epistemological claims of feminist pedagogy is an understanding of its origins in more grassroots political activity, particularly in the consciousness-raising groups of the women's liberation movement of the late 1960s and early 1970s.

Women's consciousness-raising groups began to form more or less spontaneously in northeastern and western U.S. cities in late 1967 among White women who had been active in the civil rights and new left movements.[24] In a fascinating parallel to the rise of the women's suffrage movement out of the abolitionist movement in the mid-nineteenth century, these activist and politically committed women came to apply the universal demands for equality and justice of the civil rights movement to their own situation as women.[25] While public actions such as the Miss America protest of 1968, mass meetings, and conferences were organized in this early period, the unique organizational basis for the women's liberation movement was grounded in the small groups of women who came together for what came to be known as consciousness raising. Early conscious-ness-raising groups, based on friendship and common political commitment, focused on the discussion of shared experiences of sexuality, work, family, and participation in the male-dominated left political movement. Consciousness rais-ing focused on collective political change rather than on individual therapy. The groups were unstructured and local — they could be formed anywhere and did not follow formal guidelines — but they used the same sorts of methods because these methods addressed common problems. One woman remembers the first meeting of what became her consciousness-raising group:

> The flood broke loose gradually and then more swiftly. We talked about our families, our mothers, our fathers, our siblings; we talked about our men; we talked about school; we talked about "the movement" (which meant new left men). For hours we talked and unburdened our souls and left feeling high and planning to meet again the following week.[26]

Perhaps the clearest summary of consciousness raising from this period can be found in Kathie Sarachild's essay, "Consciousness Raising: A Radical Weapon."[27] In this article, Sarachild, a veteran of the civil rights movement in the South and a member of Redstockings, one of the earliest and most influen-tial women's groups, presents an account that is both descriptive and proscrip-tive.[28] She makes it clear that consciousness raising arose spontaneously among small groups of women and that she is describing and summarizing a collective process that can be used by other groups of women. Fundamental to Sarachild's description of consciousness raising is its grounding in the need for political action. She describes the emergence of the method of consciousness raising among a group of women who considered themselves radicals in the sense of demanding fundamental changes in society. As Sarachild comments:

> We were interested in getting to the roots of problems in society. You might say we wanted to pull up weeds in the garden by their roots, not just pick off the leaves at the top to make things look good momentarily. Women's liberation was started by women who considered themselves radicals in this sense.[29]

A second fundamental aspect of consciousness raising is the reliance on experi-ence and feeling. According to Sarachild, the focus on examining women's own experience came from a profound distrust of accepted authority and truth. These claims about what was valuable and true tended to be accepting of existing assumptions about women's "inherent nature" and "proper place." In order to call those truths into question (truths we might now call hegemonic and that Foucault, for example, would tie to structures of power), women had nowhere to turn except to their own experience. Sarachild describes the process in her group:

> In the end the group decided to raise its consciousness by studying women's lives by topics like childhood, jobs, motherhood, etc. We'd do any outside reading we wanted to and thought was important. But our starting point for discussion, as well

as our test of the accuracy of what any of the books said, would be the actual experience we had in these areas.[30]

The last aspect of consciousness raising was a common sharing of experience in a collective, leaderless group. As Michele Russell points out, this sharing is similar to the practice of "testifying" in the Black church, and depends upon openness and trust in the group.[31] The assumption underlying this sharing of stories was the existence of commonality among women; as Sarachild puts it, "we made the assumption, an assumption basic to consciousness raising, that most women were like ourselves — not different."[32]

The model for consciousness raising among the Redstockings, as with other early groups, came from the experiences of many of the women as organizers in the civil rights movement in the South. Sarachild, for instance, cites the example of the Student Nonviolent Coordinating Committee, and quotes Stokely Carmichael when she argues for the need for people to organize in order to understand their own conditions of existence and to fight their own struggles. Other sources cited by Sarachild include the nineteenth-century suffragist Ernestine Rose, Mao Zedong, Malcolm X, and the practice of "speaking bitterness" in the Chinese revolution described by William Hinton in *Fanshen*.[33] Both the example of the civil rights movement and the revolutionary tradition of the male writers that provided the model for early consciousness raising supported women's commitment to political action and social change.[34] As Sarachild comments:

> We would be the first to dare to say and do the undareable, what women really felt and wanted. The first job now was to raise awareness and understanding, our own and others — awareness that would prompt people to organize and to act on a mass scale.[35]

Thus consciousness raising shared the assumptions of earlier revolutionary traditions: that understanding and theoretical analysis were the first steps to revolutionary change, and that neither was adequate alone; theory and practice were intertwined as praxis. As Sarachild puts it, "Consciousness raising was seen as both a method for arriving at the truth and a means for action and organizing."[36] What was original in consciousness raising, however, was its emphasis on experience and feeling as the guide to theoretical understanding, an approach that reflected the realities of women's socially defined subjectivities and the conditions of their lives. Irene Peslikis, another member of Redstockings, wrote, "When we think of what it is that politicizes people it is not so much books or ideas but experience."[37]

While Sarachild and other early feminists influenced by a left political tradition explored the creation of theory grounded in women's feelings and experiences, they never lost the commitment to social transformation.[38] In their subsequent history, however, consciousness raising and feminist pedagogy did not always retain this political commitment to action. As the women's movement expanded to reach wider groups of women, consciousness raising tended to lose its commitment to revolutionary change. This trend seems to have been particularly true as the women's movement affected women with a less radical perspective and with little previous political involvement. Without a vision of collective action and social transformation, consciousness raising held the possibility of what Berenice Fisher calls "a diversion of energies into an exploration of feelings and 'private' concerns to the detriment of political activism."[39] The lack of structure and the local natures of consciousness-raising groups only reinforced these tendencies toward a focus on individual rather than collective change. The one site in which the tradition of consciousness raising did find institutional expression was in academia, in the growth of women's studies courses and programs stimulated by the new scholarship on women. The founders of these early courses and programs tended to be politically committed feminists who themselves had experienced consciousness raising and who, like Freire, assumed that education could and should be a means of social change.

The first women's studies courses, reflecting the growth of the women's movement in what has come to be called the second wave of feminism, were taught in the late 1960s.[40] In 1970, Paul Lauter and Florence Howe founded The Feminist Press, an important outlet for publishing early feminist scholarship and recovering lost texts by women writers.[41] In 1977, the founding of the National Women's Studies Association provided a national organization, a journal, and yearly conferences that gave feminists inside and outside of academia a forum to exchange ideas and experiences. By the late 1980s, respected journals such as *Signs* and *Feminist Studies* were well established, and women's studies programs and courses were widespread (if not always enthusiastically supported by administrations) in colleges and universities.[42] At the same time, feminist research and theory — what has come to be called "the new scholarship on women" — put forth a profound challenge to traditional disciplines.[43] The growth of women's studies programs and feminist scholarship thus provided an institutional framework and theoretical underpinning for feminist pedagogy, the attempt to express feminist values and goals in the classroom. But while feminist scholarship has presented fundamental challenges to traditional androcentric knowledge, the attempt to create a new pedagogy modeled on consciousness raising has not been as successful or coherent a project. Serious challenges to the goal of political transformation through the experience of feminist learning have been raised in the attempt to create a feminist pedagogy in the academy. The difficulties and contradictions that have emerged in the attempt to create a feminist pedagogy in traditional institutions like universities raise serious questions for all liberatory pedagogies and echo some of the problems raised by the unitary and universal approach of *Pedagogy of the Oppressed*. But in engaging these questions, feminist pedagogy suggests new directions that can enrich Freirean pedagogies of liberation.

Feminist pedagogy has raised three areas of concern that are particularly useful in considering the ways in which Freirean and other liberatory pedagogies can be enriched and expanded. The first of these concerns the role and authority of the teacher; the second addresses the epistemological question of the source of the claims for knowledge and truth in personal experience and feeling; the last, emerging from challenges by women of color and postmodernist feminist theorists, raises the question of difference. Their challenges have led to a shattering of the unproblematic and unitary category "woman," as well as of an assumption of the inevitable unity of "women." Instead, feminist theorists have increasingly emphasized the importance of recognizing difference as a central category of feminist pedagogy. The unstated assumption of a universal experience of "being a woman" was exploded by the critiques of postmodern feminists and by the growing assertion of lesbians and women of color that the universal category "woman" in fact meant "White, heterosexual, middle-class woman," even when used by White, heterosexual, socialist feminists, or women veterans of the civil rights movement who were committed to class or race struggles.[44] These theoretical challenges to the unity of both "woman" and "women" have in turn called into question the authority of women as teachers and students in the classroom, the epistemological value of both feeling and experience, and the nature of political strategies for enacting feminist goals of social change. I turn next to an exploration of these key issues of authority, experience, feeling, and difference within feminist pedagogy and theory.

The Role and Authority of the Teacher

In many respects, the feminist vision of the teacher's authority echoes that Freirean image of the teacher who is a joint learner with students and who holds authority by virtue of greater knowledge and experience. But as we have seen, Freire fails to address the various forms of power held by teachers depending on their race, gender, and the historical and institutional settings in which they work. In the Freirean account, they are in this sense "transparent." In the actual practice of feminist pedagogy, the central issues of difference, positionality, and the need to recognize the implications of subjectivity or identity for teachers and students have become central. Moreover, the question of authority in institutional settings makes problematic the possibility of achieving the collective and nonhierarchical vision of early consciousness-raising groups within university classrooms. The basic elements of early consciousness-raising groups — an emphasis on feeling, experience, and sharing, and a suspicion of hierarchy and authority — continue to influence feminist pedagogy in academic settings. But the institutionalized nature of women's studies in the hierarchical and bureaucratic structure of academia creates tensions that run counter to the original commitment to praxis in consciousness-raising groups. Early consciousness-raising groups were homogeneous, antagonistic to authority, and had a commitment to political change that had directly emerged from the civil rights and new left movements. Feminist pedagogy within academic classrooms addresses heterogeneous groups of students within a competitive and individualistic culture in which the teacher holds institutional power and responsibility (even if she may want to reject that power).[45] As bell hooks comments, "The academic setting, the academic discourse [we] work in, is not a known site for truthtelling."[46] The very success of feminist scholarship has meant the development of a rich theoretical tradition with deep divisions and opposing goals and methods.[47] Thus the source of the teacher's authority as a "woman" who can call upon a "common woman's knowledge" is called into question; at the same time the feminist teacher is "given" authority by virtue of her role within the hierarchical structure of the university.

The question of authority in feminist pedagogy seems to be centered around two different conceptions. The first refers to the institutionally imposed authority of the teacher within a hierarchical university structure. The teacher in this role must give grades, is evaluated by administrators and colleagues in terms of expertise in a body of knowledge, and is expected to take responsibility for meeting the goals of an academic course as it is understood within the wider university. This hierarchical structure is clearly in opposition to the collective goals of a common women's movement and is miles from the early structureless consciousness-raising groups in which each woman was an expert on her own life. Not only does the university structure impose this model of institutional authority, but students themselves expect it. As Barbara Hillyer Davis comments: "The institutional pressure to [impart knowledge] is reinforced by the students' well-socialized behavior. If I will tell them 'what I want,' they will deliver it. They are exasperated with my efforts to depart from the role of dispenser of wisdom."[48] Feminist educators have attempted to address this tension between their ideals of collective education and the demands of the university by a variety of expedients: group assignments and grades, contracts for grades, pass/fail courses, and such techniques as self-revelation and the articulation of the dynamics of the classroom.[49]

Another aspect of institutionalized authority, however, is the need for women to *claim* authority in a society that denies it to them. As Culley and Portuges have pointed out, the authority and power of the woman feminist teacher is already in question from many of her students precisely because she is a woman:

> As women, our own position is precarious, and the power we are supposed to exercise is given grudgingly, if at all. For our own students, for ourselves, and for our superiors, we are not clearly "us" or "them." The facts of class, of race, of ethnicity, of sexual preference — as well as gender — may cut across the neat divisions of teacher/student.[50]

Thus the issue of institutional authority raises the contradictions of trying to achieve a democratic and collective ideal in a hierarchical institution, but it also raises the question of the meaning of authority for feminist teachers, whose right to speak or to hold power is itself under attack in a patriarchal (and racist, homophobic, classist, and so on) society. The question of asserting authority and power is a central concern to feminists precisely because as women they have been taught that taking power is inappropriate. From this perspective, the feminist teacher's acceptance of authority becomes in itself liberating to her and to her students. It becomes a claim to authority in terms of her own value as a scholar and a teacher in a patriarchal society that structurally denies or questions that authority as it is manifest in the organization and bureaucracy of the university. Women students, after all, are socialized to be deferential, and both men and women students are taught to accept male authority. It is instructive for students to see women assert authority. But this use of authority will lead to positive social change only if those teachers are working also to empower students in a Freirean sense.[51] As Susan Stanford Friedman argues:

> What I and other women have needed is a theory of feminist pedagogy consistent with our needs as women operating at the fringes of patriarchal space. As we attempt to move on to academic turf culturally defined as male, we need a theory that first recognizes the androcentric denial of *all* authority to women and, second, points out a way for us to speak with an authentic voice not based on tyranny.[52]

These concerns lead to a conception of authority and power in a positive sense, both in terms of women asserting authority as women, and in terms of valuing intellectual work and the creation of theory as a means of understanding and, thus, of changing the world.

The authority of the intellectual raises issues for feminists in the academy that are similar to those faced by other democratic and collective political movements, such as those described by Freire. There is a contradiction between the idea of a women's movement including all women and a group of what Berenice Fisher calls "advanced women."[53] Feminists who question the whole tradition of androcentric thought are deeply suspicious of women who take a position of "experts" who can translate and interpret other women's experiences. Fisher articulates these tensions well:

> Who are intellectuals in relation to the women's movement? . . . Are intellectuals sorts of leaders, sage guides, women who give voice to or clarify a broader urge toward social change? Is intellectual work essentially elitist, a matter of mere privilege to think, to write, to create? Is it simply a patriarchal mode of gaining and maintaining power, a way of negating women's everyday experience, a means of separating some women from the rest of the "community?"[54]

Fisher argues that feminist intellectuals are struggling with these questions in their scholarship, teaching, and roles within the universities and the wider women's movement. She does not reject the authority of the feminist intellectual, but she also does not deny the need to address and clarify these contradictions. She, like Charlotte Bunch, is an embodiment of this attempt to accept both the authority and responsibility of the feminist intellectual who is creating theory.

In terms of feminist pedagogy, the authority of the feminist teacher as intellectual and theorist finds expression in the goal of making students themselves theorists of their own lives by interrogating and analyzing their own experience. In an approach very similar to Freire's concept of conscientization, this strategy moves beyond the naming or sharing of experience to the creation of a critical understanding of the forces that have shaped that experience. This theorizing is antithetical to traditional views of women. As Bunch points out, traditionally

> women are supposed to worry about mundane survival problems, to brood about fate, and to fantasize in a personal manner. We are not meant to think analytically about society, to question the ways things are, to consider how things could be different. Such thinking involves an active, not a passive, relationship to the world.[55]

Thus feminist educators like Fisher and Bunch accept their authority as intellectuals and theorists, but they consciously attempt to construct their pedagogy to recognize and encourage the capacity of their students to theorize and to recognize their own power.[56] This is a conception of authority not in the institutional terms of a bureaucratized university system, but rather an attempt to claim the authority of theorist and guide for students who are themselves potential theorists.

Feminist concerns about the authority of the feminist teacher address questions of classroom practice and theory ignored by Freire — in his formulation of the teacher and student as two "knowers" of the world, and in his assertion that the liberatory teacher should acknowledge and claim authority but not authoritarianism. The feminist exploration of authority is much richer and addresses more directly the contradictions between goals of collectivity and hierarchies of knowledge. Feminist teachers are much more conscious of the power of various subject positions than is represented in Freire's "transparent" liberatory teacher. An acknowledgment of the realities of conflict and tensions based on contradictory political goals, as well as of the meaning of historically experienced oppression for both teachers and students, leads to a pedagogy that respects difference not just as significant for students, but for teachers as well.

Personal Experience as a Source of Knowledge and Truth

As feminists explore the relationship of authority, theory, and political action, they raise questions about the categories and claims for truth underlying both consciousness raising and feminist pedagogy. These claims rest on categories of experience and feeling as guides to theoretical understanding and political change. Basic to the Freirean method of conscientization is the belief in the ability of all people to be knowers and to read both the word and the world. In Freirean pedagogy, it is through the interrogation of their own experiences that the oppressed will come to an understanding of their own power as knowers and creators of the world; this knowledge will contribute to the transformation of their world. In consciousness-raising groups and in feminist pedagogy in the university, a similar reliance on experience and feeling has been fundamental to the development of a feminist knowledge of the world that can be the basis for social change. Underlying both Freirean and early feminist pedagogy is an assumption of a common experience as the basis for political analysis and action. Both experience and feeling were central to consciousness raising and remain central to feminist pedagogy in academia; they are claimed as a kind of "inner knowing," shaped by society but at the same time containing an oppositional quality. Feeling is looked to as a guide to a deeper truth than that of abstract rationality. Experience, which is interpreted through ideologically constructed categories, also can be the basis for an opposition to dominant schemes of truth if what is experienced runs counter to what is set forth and accepted as "true." Feminist educators, beginning with women in the early consciousness-raising groups, have explored both experience and feeling as sources of knowledge, and both deserve closer examination.

In many ways, feeling or emotion has been seen traditionally as a source of women's knowledge about the world. As we have seen, in the early consciousness-raising groups, feelings were looked to as the source of a "true" knowledge of the world for women living in a society that denied the value of their perceptions. Feelings or emotions were seen as a way of testing accepted claims of what is universally true about human nature or, specifically, about women. Claims such as Freud's theory of penis envy, for example, were challenged by women first because these theoretical descriptions of women's psychology did not match women's own feelings about their lives. As feminist pedagogy has developed, with a continued emphasis on the function of feelings as a guide to knowledge about the world, emotions have been seen as links between a kind of inner truth or inner self and the outer world — including ideology, culture, and other discourses of power.[57] However, as feminist educators have explored the uses of feeling or emotion as a source of knowledge, several difficulties have become clear. First of all, there is a danger that the expression of strong emotion can be simply cathartic and can deflect the need for action to address the underlying causes of that emotion. Moreover, it is not clear how to distinguish among a wide range of emotions as the source of political action. At a more theoretical level, there are contradictions involved in claiming that the emotions are a source for knowledge and at the same time arguing that they are manipulated and shaped by dominant discourses. Both consciousness-raising groups and feminist theorists have asserted the social construction of feelings and their manipulation by the dominant culture; at the same time, they look to feelings as a source of truth. Berenice Fisher points to the contradiction implicit in these claims:

> In theoretical terms, we cannot simultaneously claim that all feelings are socially conditioned and that some feelings are "true." We would be more consistent to acknowledge that society only partly shapes our emotions, leaving an opening where we can challenge and change the responses to which we have been socialized. That opening enables the consciousness-raising process to take place and gives us the space in which to reflect on the new emotional responses that our process evokes.[58]

In this formulation, Fisher seems to be arguing for a kind of Gramscian "good sense," a locus of knowing in the self that is grounded in feeling as a guide to theoretical understanding. Feelings thus are viewed as a kind of cognition — a source of knowledge.

Perhaps the most eloquent argument for feelings as a source of oppositional knowledge is found in the work of Audre Lorde. Lorde, a Black lesbian feminist theorist and poet, writes from the specificity of her own socially defined and shaped life. For her, feeling is the source of poetry, a means of knowing that challenges White, Western, androcentric epistemologies. She specifically ties her own feelings as a Black woman to a non-Western way of knowing. She writes:

> As we come more into touch with our own ancient, non-European consciousness of living as a situation to be experienced and interacted with, we learn more and more to cherish our feelings, to respect those hidden sources of power from where true knowledge and, therefore, lasting action comes.[59]

Lorde is acutely aware of the ways in which the dominant society shapes our sense of who we are and what we feel. As she points out, "Within living structures defined by profit, by linear power, by institutional dehumanization, our feelings were not meant to survive."[60] Moreover, Lorde is conscious of the oppressor within us: "For we have, built into all of us, old blueprints of expectation and response, old structures of oppression, and these must be altered at the same time as we alter the living conditions which are the result of those structures."[61] But although Lorde does not deny what she calls "the oppressor within," she retains a belief in the power of deeper feeling to challenge the dominant definitions of truth and to point the way to an analysis that can lead to an alternative vision:

> As we begin to recognize our deepest feelings, we begin to give up, of necessity, being satisfied with suffering and self-negation, and with the numbness which so

often seems like their only alternative in society. Our acts against oppression become integral with self, motivated and empowered from within.[62]

For Lorde, then, feelings are a guide to analysis and to action. While they are shaped by society and are socially constructed in that sense, Lorde insists on a deeper reality of feeling closer in touch with what it means to be human. This formulation echoes the Freirean vision of humanization as a new way of being in the world other than as oppressor and oppressed. Both Freire and Lorde retain a Utopian faith in the possibility that human beings can create new ways of being in the world out of collective struggle and a human capacity to feel. Lorde terms this the power of the erotic; she speaks of the erotic as "a measure between the beginnings of our sense of self and the chaos of our strongest feelings," a resource "firmly rooted in the power of our unexpressed or unrecognized feeling."[63] Because the erotic can challenge the dominant, it has been denied as a source of power and knowledge. But for Lorde, the power of the erotic provides the basis for visionary social change.

In her exploration of feelings and of the erotic as a source of knowledge about the world, Lorde does not reject analysis and rationality. But she questions the depth of critical understanding of those forces that shape our lives that can be achieved using only the rational and abstract methods of analysis given to us by dominant ideology. In Foucault's terms, she is seeking a perspective from which to interrogate dominant regimes of truth; central to her argument is the claim that an analysis framed solely in the terms of accepted discourse cannot get to the root of structures of power. That is what her well-known phrase, "The Master's Tools Will Never Dismantle the Master's House," implies. As she argues:

> Rationality is not unnecessary. It serves the chaos of knowledge. It serves feeling. It serves to get from this place to that place. But if you don't honor those places, then the road is meaningless. Too often, that's what happens with the worship of rationality and that circular, academic analytic thinking. But ultimately, I don't see feel/think as a dichotomy. I see them as a choice of ways and combinations.[64]

Lorde's discussion of feeling and the erotic as a source of power and knowledge is based on the assumption that human beings have the capacity to feel and know, and can engage in self-critique; people are not completely shaped by dominant discourse. The oppressor may be within us, but Lorde insists that we also have the capacity to challenge our own ways of feeling and knowing. When tied to a recognition of positionality, this validation of feeling can be used to develop powerful sources of politically focused feminist education.

For Lorde and Fisher, this kind of knowing through an exploration of feeling and emotion requires collective inquiry and constant reevaluation. It is a contingent and positioned claim to truth. Similar complexities arise in the use of experience as the basis for feminist political action. Looking to experience as the source of knowledge and the focus of feminist learning is perhaps the most fundamental tenet of feminist pedagogy. This is similar to the Freirean call to "read the world" to seek the generative themes that codify power relationships and social structures. The sharing of women's experiences was the touchstone of early consciousness-raising groups and continues to be a fundamental method of feminist pedagogy. That women need to examine what they have experienced and lived in concrete ways, in their own bodies, is a materialistic conception of experience. In an early essay, Adrienne Rich pointed to this materiality of experience: "To think like a woman in a man's world means . . . remembering that every mind resides in a body; remaining accountable to the female bodies in which we live; constantly retesting given hypotheses against lived experience."[65] As became clear quite early in the women's movement, claims about experience as a source of women's knowledge rested on certain assumptions about commonalities in women's lives. Women were conceived of as a unitary and relatively undifferentiated group. Sarachild, for example, spoke of devising "new theories which . . . reflect the actual experience and feelings and necessities of women."[66] Underlying this approach was the assumption of a common woman's experience, one reflecting the world of the White, middle-class, heterosexual women of the early feminist movement. But as the critiques of lesbians, women of color, and postmodernist feminist theorists have made clear, there is no single woman's experience to be revealed. Both experience and feeling thus have been called into question as the source of an unproblematic knowledge of the world that will lead to praxis. As Diana Fuss comments: "'female experience' is never as unified, as knowable, as universal, and as stable as we presume it to be."[67]

Challenges to the concept of a unitary women's experience by both women of color and by postmodern critics has not meant the abandonment of experience as a source of knowledge for feminist teachers. Of course experience, like feeling, is socially constructed in the sense that we can only understand it and speak about it in ideas and terms that are part of an existing ideology and language. But in a stance similar to that of Lorde in her use of the erotic, feminist teachers have explored the ways in which women have experienced the material world through their bodies. This self-examination of lived experience is then used as a source of knowledge that can illuminate the social processes and ideology that shape us. As Fuss suggests, "Such a position permits the introduction of narratives of lived experience into the classroom while at the same time challenging us to examine collectively the central role social and historical practices play in shaping and producing these narratives."[68] One example of this approach is found in the work of Frigga Haug and the group of German feminists of which she is a part.[69] Haug and this group use what they call collective memory work to explore their feelings about their own bodies in order to uncover the social construction of their selves:

> Our collective empirical work set itself the high-flown task of identifying the ways in which individuals construct themselves into existing structures, and are thereby themselves formed; the way in which they reconstruct social structures; the points at which change is possible, the points where our chains chafe most, the point where accommodations have been made.[70]

This collective exploration of "the point where . . . chains chafe most" recalls the Freirean culture circles, in which peasants would take such examples as their personal experiences with the landlord as the starting point for their education or conscientization. Basic to their approach is a belief in reflection and a rejection of a view of people as "fixed, given, unchangeable." By working collectively on "memory work," a sharing and comparison of their own lives, Haug and her group hope to uncover the workings of hegemonic ideology in their own subjectivities. Another example of such collective work can be found in the Jamaican women's theater group, Sistren. Founded in 1977, Sistren is a collaborative theater group made up of working-class Jamaican women who create and write plays based on a collaborative exploration of their own experiences. The life histories of the women of Sistren have been collected in *Lionheart Girl: Life Stories of Jamaican Women*. In the compilation of this book, the Sistren collective used the same process of the collective sharing and analysis of experience that is the basis for their theater work. As the company's director Honor Ford-Smith writes:

> We began meeting collectively at first. Starting with our childhood, we made drawings of images based on such themes as where we had grown up, symbols of oppression in our lives, our relationships with men, our experience with race and the kind of work we had done.[71]

For Haug and her group, the Sistren collective, the early consciousness-raising groups, and the Freirean culture circles, collective sharing of experience is the source of knowledge of the forces that have shaped and continue to shape them. But their recognition of the shifting meaning of experience as it is explored through memory insists on the profoundly social and political nature of who we are.

The Question of Difference

Both women of color writing from a perspective of cultural feminism and postmodernist feminist theorists converge in their critique of the concept of a universal "women's experience." While the idea of a unitary and universal category "woman" has been challenged by women of color for its racist assumptions, it has also been challenged by recent analyses of feminist theorists influenced by postmodernism, who point to the social construction of subjectivity and who emphasize the "unstable" nature of the self. Postmodernist feminist critics such as Chris Weedon have argued that socially given identities such as "woman" are "precarious, contradictory, and in process, constantly being reconstituted in discourse each time we speak."[72] This kind of analysis considers the ways in which "the subject" is not an object; that is, not fixed in a static social structure, but constantly being created, actively creating the self, and struggling for new ways of being in the world through new forms of discourse or new forms of social relationships. Such analysis calls for a recognition of the positionality of each person in any discussion of what can be known from experience. This calling into question the permanence of subjectivities is what Jane Flax refers to as the "unstable self."[73] If we view individual selves as being constructed and negotiated, then we can begin to consider what exactly those forces are in which individuals shape themselves and by which they are shaped. The category of "woman" is itself challenged as it is seen more and more as a part of a symbolic system of ideology. Donna Haraway calls all such claims of identity into question:

> With the hard-won recognition of their social and historical constitution, gender, race, and class cannot provide the basis for belief in "essential" unity: There is nothing about being "female" that naturally binds women. There is not even such a state as "being" female, itself a highly complex category constructed in contested sexual discourses and other social practices. Gender, race, or class consciousness is

an achievement forced on us by the terrible historical experience of the contradictory social realities of patriarchy, colonialism, and capitalism.[74]

These analyses support the challenges to assumptions of an essential and universal nature of women and women's experience that have come from lesbian critics and women of color.[75]

Both women of color and lesbian critics have pointed to the complexity of socially given identities. Black women and other women of color raise challenges to the assumption that the sharing of experience will create solidarity and a theoretical understanding based upon a common women's standpoint. Lesbian feminists, both White and of color, point to the destructive nature of homophobia and what Adrienne Rich has called compulsory heterosexuality. As is true of White, heterosexual, feminist educators, these theorists base their analysis upon their own experiences, but those experiences reveal not only the workings of sexism, but of racism, homophobia, and class oppression as well. This complex perspective underlies the Combahee River Collective Statement, a position paper written by a group of African-American feminists in Boston in the 1970s. This statement makes clear what a grounded theory of experience means for women whose value is denied by the dominant society in numerous ways. The women in the Combahee River Collective argue that "the most profound and potentially most radical politics come directly out of our own identity, as opposed to working to end somebody else's oppression."[76] For African-American women, an investigation of the shaping of their own identities reveals the ways in which sexism and racism are interlocking forms of oppression:

> As children we realized that we were different from boys and that we were treated differently. For example, we were told in the same breath to be quiet both for the sake of being "ladylike" and to make us less objectionable in the eyes of white people. As we grew older we became aware of the threat of physical and sexual abuse from men. However, we had no way of conceptualizing what was so apparent to us, what we *knew* was really happening.[77]

When African-American teachers like Michele Russell or Barbara Omolade describe their feminist pedagogy, they ground that pedagogy in an investigation of experience in material terms. As Russell describes her teaching of an introductory Black Studies class for women at Wayne County Community College in Detroit: "We have an hour together. . . . The first topic of conversation — among themselves and with me — is what they went through just to make it in the door, on time. That, in itself becomes a lesson."[78] And Omolade points out in her discussion of her teaching at Medgar Evers College in New York, a college whose students are largely African-American women:

> No one can teach students to "see," but an instructor is responsible for providing the coherent ordering of information and content. The classroom process is one of information-sharing in which students learn to generalize their particular life experiences within a community of fellow intellectuals.[79]

Thus the pedagogy of Russell and Omolade is grounded in experience as a source of knowledge in a particularly materialistic way; the knowledge generated reveals the overlapping forms of oppression lived by women of color in this society.

The investigation of the experiences of women of color, lesbian women, women whose very being challenges existing racial, sexual, heterosexual, and class dominance, leads to a knowledge of the world that both acknowledges differences and points to the need for an "integrated analysis and practice based upon the fact that the major systems of oppression are interlocking."[80] The turning to experience thus reveals not a universal and common women's essence, but, rather, deep divisions in what different women have experienced, and in the kinds of knowledge they discover when they examine their own experience. The recognition of the differences among women raises serious challenges to feminist pedagogy by calling into question the authority of the teacher/theorist, raising feelings of guilt and shame, and revealing tensions among students as well as between teacher and students. In classes of African-American women taught by African-American teachers, the sharing of experience can lead to the same sense of commonality and sharing that was true of early consciousness-raising groups. But in settings in which students come from different positions of privilege or oppression, the sharing of experience raises conflicts rather than building solidarity. In these circumstances, the collective exploration of experience leads not to a common knowledge and solidarity based on sameness, but to the tensions of an articulation of difference. Such exploration raises again the problems left unaddressed by Freirean pedagogy: the overlapping and multiple forms of oppression revealed in "reading the world" of experience.

CONCLUSION

Both Freirean and feminist pedagogies are based on political commitment and identification with subordinate and oppressed groups; both seek justice and empowerment. Freire sets out these goals of liberation and social and political transformation as universal claims, without exploring his own privileged position or existing conflicts among oppressed groups themselves. Writing from within a tradition of Western modernism, his theory rests on a belief of transcendent and universal truth. But feminist theory influenced by postmodernist thought and by the writings of women of color challenges the underlying assumptions of these universal claims. Feminist theorists in particular argue that it is essential to recognize, as Julie Mitchell comments, that we cannot "live as human subjects without in some sense taking on a history."[81] The recognition of our own histories means the necessity of articulating our own subjectivities and our own interests as we try to interpret and critique the social world. This stance rejects the universalizing tendency of much "malestream" thought, and insists on recognizing the power and privilege of who we are. As Biddy Martin and Chandra Mohanty comment:

> The claim to a lack of identity or positionality is itself based on privilege, on the refusal to accept responsibility for one's implication in actual historical or social relations, or a denial that positionalities exist or that they matter, the denial of one's own personal history and the claim to a total separation from it.[82]

Fundamental to recent feminist theory is a questioning of the concept of a coherent subject moving through history with a single essential identity. Instead, feminist theorists are developing a concept of the constant creation and negotiation of selves within structures of ideology and material constraints.[83] This line of theoretical analysis calls into question assumptions of the common interests of the oppressed, whether conceived of as women or peasants; it challenges the use of such universal terms as oppression and liberation without locating these claims in a concrete historical or social context. The challenges of recent feminist theory and, in particular, the writings of feminists of color point to the need to articulate and claim a particular historical and social identity, to locate ourselves, and to build coalitions from a recognition of the partial knowledges of our own constructed identities. Recognizing the standpoint of subjects as shaped by their experience of class, race, gender, or other socially defined identities has powerful implications for pedagogy, in that it emphasizes the need to make conscious the subject positions not only of students but of teachers as well. These lines of theoretical analysis have implications for the ways in which we can understand pedagogy as contested, as a site of discourse among subjects, teachers, and students whose identities are, as Weedon puts it, contradictory and in process. The theoretical formulation of the "unstable self," the complexity of subjectivities, what Giroux calls "multi-layered subjects," and the need to position ourselves in relation to our own histories raise important issues for liberatory pedagogies. If all people's identities are recognized in their full historical and social complexity as subject positions that are in process, based on knowledges that are partial and that reflect deep and conflicting differences, how can we theorize what a liberatory pedagogy actively struggling against different forms of oppression may look like? How can we build upon the rich and complex analysis of feminist theory and pedagogy to work toward a Freirean vision of social justice and liberation?

In the complexity of issues raised by feminist pedagogy, we can begin to acknowledge the reality of tensions that result from different histories, from privilege, oppression, and power as they are lived by teachers and students in classrooms. To recognize these tensions and differences does not mean abandonment of the goals of social justice and empowerment, but it does make clear the need to recognize contingent and situated claims and to acknowledge our own histories and selves in process. One significant area of feminist work has been grounded in the collective analysis of experience and emotion, as exemplified by the work of Haug and her group in Germany or by the Jamaican women's theater group, Sistren. In many respects, these projects look back to consciousness raising, but with a more developed theory of ideology and an acute consciousness of difference. As Berenice Fisher argues, a collective inquiry "requires the slow unfolding of layers of experience, both the contradictory experiences of a given woman and the conflicting experiences of different women."[84] Another approach builds on what Bernice Reagon calls the need for coalition building, a recognition and validation of difference. This is similar to what has come to be known as identity politics, exemplified in what Minnie Bruce Pratt is seeking in her discussion of trying to come to terms with her own identity as a privileged Southern White woman.[85] Martin and Mohanty speak of this as a sense of "home," a recognition of the difficulties of coming to terms with privilege or oppression, of the benefits of being an oppressor, or of the rage of being oppressed.[86] This is a validation of both difference and conflict, but also an attempt to build coalitions around common goals rather than a denial of differences.[87] It is clear that this kind of pedagogy and exploration of experiences in a society in which privilege and oppression are lived is risky and filled with pain. Such a pedagogy suggests a more complex realization of the Freirean vision of the collective conscientization and struggle against oppression, one which acknowledges difference and conflict, but which, like Freire's vision, rests on a belief in the human capacity to feel, to know, and to change.

NOTES

1. See as representative Henry Giroux, ed., *Postmodernism, Feminism and Cultural Politics* (Albany: State University of New York Press, 1991); Cleo Cherryholmes, *Power and Criticism: Poststructural Investigations in Education* (New York: Teachers College Press, 1988); Henry Giroux and Roger Simon, eds., *Popular Culture, Schooling and Everyday Life* (Westport, CT: Bergin & Garvey, 1989); Deborah Britzman, *Practice Makes Practice* (Albany: State University of New York Press, 1991); Patti Lather, *Getting Smart: Feminist Research and Pedagogy With/in the Postmodern* (New York: Routledge, 1991).
2. Paulo Freire, *Pedagogy of the Oppressed* (New York: Herder & Herder, 1971), p. 28.
3. Margo Culley and Catherine Portuges, "Introduction," in *Gendered Subjects* (Boston: Routledge & Kegan Paul, 1985). For comparisons of Freirean and feminist pedagogy, see also Frances Maher, "Classroom Pedagogy and the New Scholarship on Women," in *Gendered Subjects*, pp. 29–48, and "Toward a Richer Theory of Feminist Pedagogy: A Comparison of 'Liberation' and 'Gender' Models for Teaching and Learning," *Journal of Education, 169*, No. 3 (1987), 91–100.
4. Antonio Gramsci, *Selections from the Prison Notebooks* (New York: International Publishers, 1971).
5. Teresa de Lauretis, *Alice Doesn't: Feminism, Semiotics, Cinema* (Bloomington: Indiana University Press, 1984), p. 178.
6. Audre Lorde, *Sister Outsider* (Trumansburg, NY: The Crossing Press, 1984).
7. See, for example, Elizabeth Ellsworth, "Why Doesn't This Feel Empowering? Working through the Repressive Myths of Critical Pedagogy," *Harvard Educational Review, 59* (1989), 297–324; Ann Berlak, "Teaching for Outrage and Empathy in the Liberal Arts," *Educational Foundations, 3*, No. 2 (1989), 69–94; Deborah Britzman, "Decentering Discourses in Teacher Education: Or, the Unleashing of Unpopular Things," in *What Schools Can Do: Critical Pedagogy and Practice*, ed. Candace Mitchell and Kathleen Weiler (Albany: State University of New York Press, 1992).
8. Freire's method of codifications and generative themes have been discussed frequently. Perhaps the best introduction to these concrete methods can be found in Paulo Freire, *Education for Critical Consciousness* (New York: Seabury,1973).
9. See, for example, Paulo Freire, *The Politics of Education* (Westport, CT: Bergin & Garvey, 1985); Paulo Freire and Donaldo Macedo, *Literacy: Reading the Word and the World* (Westport, CT: Bergin & Garvey, 1987); Paulo Freire and Ira Shor, *A Pedagogy For Liberation* (London: Macmillan, 1987); Myles Horton and Paulo Freire, *We Make the Road by Walking: Conversations on Education and Social Change*, ed. Brenda Bell, John Gaventa, and John Peters (Philadelphia: Temple University Press, 1990).
10. Freire, *Pedagogy of the Oppressed*, p. 28.
11. Paulo Freire, "The Adult Literacy Process as Cultural Action for Freedom," in *The Politics of Education*, p. 57.
12. Freire and Macedo, *Literacy: Reading the Word and the World*.
13. See Simone de Beauvoir, *The Second Sex* (New York: Knopf, 1953), for a more striking use of the male referent.

14. Cameron McCarthy, "Rethinking Liberal and Radical Perspectives on Racial Inequality in Schooling: Making the Case for Nonsynchrony," *Harvard Educational Review, 58* (1988), 265–280.

15. Freire, *Pedagogy of the Oppressed,* p. 30.

16. Freire, *Pedagogy of the Oppressed,* p. 69.

17. Freire, *Pedagogy of the Oppressed,* p. 73.

18. Gayatri Chakravorty Spivak, "Can the Subaltern Speak?," in *Marxism and the Interpretation of Culture,* ed. Cary Nelson and Lawrence Grossberg (Urbana: University of Illinois Press, 1988), pp. 271–313.

19. Freire and Shor, *A Pedagogy for Liberation,* p. 93.

20. Peter McLaren, "Postmodernity and the Death of Politics: A Brazilian Reprieve," *Educational Theory, 36* (1986), p. 399.

21. When definitions of feminist pedagogy are attempted, they sometimes tend toward generalization and such a broad inclusiveness as to be of dubious usefulness. For example, Carolyn Shrewsbury characterizes feminist pedagogy as follows:

    > It does not automatically preclude any technique or approach. It does indicate the relationship that specific techniques have to educational goals. It is not limited to any specific subject matter but it does include a reflexive element that increases the feminist scholarship component involved in the teaching/learning of any subject matter. It has close ties with other liberatory pedagogies, but it cannot be subsumed under other pedagogical approaches. It is transformative, helping us revision the educational enterprise. But it can also be phased into a traditional teaching approach or another alternative pedagogical approach. (Shrewsbury, "What Is Feminist Pedagogy?," *Women's Studies Quarterly, 15,* Nos. 3–4 [1987], p. 12)

    Certain descriptions of feminist pedagogy show the influence of group dynamics and interractionist approaches. See, for example, Nancy Schniedewind, "Feminist Values: Guidelines for Teaching Methodology in Women's Studies," *Radical Teacher, 18,* 25–28. Methods used by feminist teachers include cooperation, shared leadership, and democratic process. Feminist teachers describe such techniques as keeping journals, soliciting students' responses to readings and to the classroom dynamics of a course, the use of role playing and theater games, the use of self-revelation on the part of the teacher, building leadership skills among students by requiring them to teach parts of a course, and contracting for grades. For accounts of classroom practice, see the articles in the special issue on feminist pedagogy of *Women's Studies Quarterly, 15,* Nos. 3–4 (1987); Culley and Portuges, *Gendered Subjects;* Charlotte Bunch and Sandra Pollack, eds., *Learning Our Way* (Trumansburg, NY: The Crossing Press, 1983); Gloria Hull, Patricia Bell Scott, and Barbara Smith, ed., *But Some of Us Are Brave* (Old Westbury, NY: The Feminist Press, 1982); and numerous articles in *Women's Studies Newsletter* and *Radical Teacher.*

22. Nancy Schniedewind, "Teaching Feminist Process," *Women's Studies Quarterly, 15,* Nos. 3–4 (1987), p. 29.

23. Linda Gordon, "A Socialist View of Women's Studies: A Reply to the Editorial, Volume 1, Number 1," *Signs, 1* (1975), p. 559.

24. A discussion of the relationship of the early women's liberation movement to the civil rights movement and the new left can be found in Sara Evans, *Personal Politics* (New York: Vintage Press, 1980). Based on extensive interviews as well as pamphlets and private documents, Evans shows the origins of both political goals and methods in the earlier male-dominated movement, particularly the model of Black student organizers and the Black church in the South.

25. While mid-nineteenth-century suffragists developed their ideas of human equality and justice through the abolitionist movement, by the late nineteenth century, White suffragists often demonstrated racist attitudes and employed racist strategies in their campaigns for suffrage. This offers another instructive parallel to the White feminist

movement of the 1960s. Here, once again, feminist claims emerged out of an anti-racist struggle for civil rights, but later too often took up the universalizing stance that the experiences and issues of White women represented the lives of all women. See bell hooks, *Ain't I a Woman?* (Boston: South End Press, 1981) and *Feminist Theory from Margin to Center* (Boston: South End Press, 1984) for powerful discussions of these issues.

26. Nancy Hawley as quoted in Evans, *Personal Politics,* p. 205.

27. Kathie Sarachild, "Consciousness Raising: A Radical Weapon," in *Feminist Revolution,* ed. Redstockings (New York: Random House, 1975).

28. Redstockings included a number of women who were influential in the women's movement; Shulamith Firestone, Rosalyn Baxandall, Ellen Willis, and Robin Morgan were among a number of other significant feminist writers and activists who participated.

29. Sarachild, "Consciousness Raising," p. 144.

30. Sarachild, "Consciousness Raising," p. 145.

31. Michele Russell, "Black-Eyed Blues Connection: From the Inside Out," in Bunch and Pollack, *Learning Our Way,* pp. 272–284.

32. Sarachild, "Consciousness Raising," p. 147.

33. William Hinton, *Fanshen* (New York: Vintage Books, 1966).

34. See Berenice Fisher, "Guilt and Shame in the Women's Movement: The Radical Ideal of Political Action and Its Meaning for Feminist Intellectuals," *Feminist Studies, 10* (1984), 185–212, for an extended discussion of the impact of the methods and goals of the civil rights movement on consciousness raising and the early women's liberation movement.

35. Sarachild, "Consciousness Raising," p. 145.

36. Sarachild, "Consciousness Raising," p. 147.

37. Irene Peslikis, "Resistances to Consciousness," in *Sisterhood Is Powerful,* ed. Robin Morgan (New York: Vintage Books, 1970), p. 339.

38. See, for example, Kathy McAfee and Myrna Wood, "Bread and Roses," in *Voices from Women's Liberation,* ed. Leslie Tanner (New York: New American Library, 1970) for an early socialist feminist analysis of the need to connect the women's movement with the class struggle.

39. Berenice Fisher, "What is Feminist Pedagogy?," *Radical Teacher, 18,* 20–25. See also bell hooks, "on self-recovery," in *talking back: thinking feminist, thinking black* (Boston: South End Press, 1989).

40. Marilyn Boxer, "For and about Women: The Theory and Practice of Women's Studies in the United States," in *Reconstructing the Academy: Women's Education and Women's Studies,* ed. Elizabeth Minnich, Jean O'Barr, and Rachel Rosenfeld (Chicago: University of Chicago Press, 1988), p. 71.

41. See Florence Howe, *Myths of Coeducation* (Bloomington: University of Indiana Press, 1984), for a collection of essays documenting this period.

42. Boxer estimates there were over 300 programs and 30,000 courses in women's studies given in 1982. See "For and about Women," p. 70.

43. The literature of feminist challenges to specific disciplines is by now immense. For general discussions of the impact of the new scholarship on women, see Ellen DuBois, Gail Kelly, Elizabeth Kennedy, Carolyn Korsmeyer, and Lillian Robinson, eds., *Feminist Scholarship: Kindling in the Groves of Academe* (Urbana: University of Illinois Press, 1985), and Christie Farnhum, ed., *The Impact of Feminist Research in the Academy* (Bloomington: Indiana University Press, 1987).

44. See, for example, Diana Fuss, *Essentially Speaking* (New York: Routledge, 1989); hooks, *talking back;* Britzman, *Practice Makes Practice.*

45. Susan Stanford Friedman, "Authority in the Feminist Classroom: A Contradiction in Terms?" in Culley and Portuges, *Gendered Subjects,* 203–208.

46. hooks, *talking back*, p. 29.
47. See Alison Jaggar, *Feminist Politics and Human Nature* (Sussex, Eng.: Harvester Press, 1983), for an excellent discussion of these perspectives.
48. Barbara Hillyer Davis, "Teaching the Feminist Minority," in Bunch and Pollack, *Learning Our Way,* p. 91.
49. See, for example, Evelyn Torton Beck, "Self-disclosure and the Commitment to Social Change," *Women's Studies International Forum, 6* (1983), 159–164.
50. Margo Culley and Catherine Portuges, "The Politics of Nurturance," in *Gendered Subjects,* p. 12. See also Margo Culley, "Anger and Authority in the Introductory Women's Studies Classroom," in *Gendered Subjects,* pp. 209–217.
51. See Davis, "Teaching the Feminist Minority," for a thoughtful discussion of the contradictory pressures on the feminist teacher both to nurture and challenge women students.
52. Friedman, "Authority in the Feminist Classroom," p. 207.
53. Fisher, "What is Feminist Pedagogy?" p. 22.
54. Fisher, "Guilt and Shame in the Women's Movement," p. 202.
55. Charlotte Bunch, "Not by Degrees: Feminist Theory and Education," in Bunch and Pollack, *Learning Our Way,* p. 156.
56. See Berenice Fisher, "Professing Feminism: Feminist Academics and the Women's Movement," *Psychology of Women Quarterly, 7* (1982), 55–69, for a thoughtful discussion of the difficulties of retaining an activist stance for feminists in the academy.
57. See Arlie Russell Hochschild, *The Managed Heart* (Berkeley: University of California Press, 1983), for a discussion of the social construction of emotions in contemporary society. Hochschild argues that emotion is a "biologically given sense . . . and a means by which we know about our relation to the world" (p. 219). At the same time she investigates the ways in which the emotions themselves are manipulated and constructed.
58. Berenice Fisher, "The Heart Has Its Reasons: Feeling, Thinking, and Community Building in Feminist Education," *Women's Studies Quarterly, 15,* Nos. 3–4 (1987), 48.
59. Lorde, *Sister Outsider,* p. 37.
60. Lorde, *Sister Outsider,* p. 34.
61. Lorde, *Sister Outsider,* p. 123.
62. Lorde, *Sister Outsider,* p. 58.
63. Lorde, *Sister Outsider,* p. 53.
64. Lorde, *Sister Outsider,* p. 100.
65. Adrienne Rich, "Taking Women Students Seriously," in *On Lies, Secrets, and Silence,* ed. Adrienne Rich (New York: W. W. Norton, 1979), p. 243.
66. Sarachild, "Consciousness Raising," p. 148.
67. Fuss, *Essentially Speaking,* p. 114.
68. Fuss, *Essentially Speaking,* p. 118.
69. Frigga Haug, *Female Sexualization* (London: Verso Press, 1987).
70. Haug, *Female Sexualization,* p. 41.
71. Sistren Collective with Honor Ford-Smith, *Lionheart Girl: Life Stories of Jamaican Women* (London: Woman's Press, 1986), p. 15.
72. Chris Weedon, *Feminist Practice and Poststructuralist Theory* (Oxford: Basil Blackwell, 1987), p. 33.
73. Jane Flax, "Postmodernism and Gender Relations in Feminist Theory," *Signs, 12* (1987), 621–643.
74. Donna Haraway, "A Manifesto for Cyborgs," *Socialist Review, 80* (1985), 72.
75. As representative, see Johnella Butler, "Toward a Pedagogy of Everywoman's Studies," in Culley and Portuges, *Gendered Subjects;* hooks, *talking back;* Hull, Scott, and Smith, *But Some of Us Are Brave;* Gloria Joseph and Jill Lewis, *Common Differences: Conflicts in Black and White Perspectives* (New York: Anchor Books, 1981); Chierrie Moraga and

Gloria Anzaldua, eds., *This Bridge Called My Back* (Watertown, MA: Persephone Press, 1981); Barbara Omolade, "A Black Feminist Pedagogy," *Women's Studies Quarterly, 15,* Nos. 3–4 (1987), 32–40; Russell, "Black-Eyed Blues Connection," pp. 272–284; Elizabeth Spellman, "Combatting the Marginalization of Black Women in the Classroom," in Culley and Portuges, *Gendered Subjects,* pp. 240–244.

76. Combahee River Collective, "Combahee River Collective River Statement," in *Home Girls,* ed. Barbara Smith (New York: Kitchen Table — Women of Color Press, 1983), p. 275.
77. Combahee River Collective, "Combahee River Collective Statement," p. 274.
78. Russell, "Black-Eyed Blues Connection," p. 155.
79. Omolade, "A Black Feminist Pedagogy," p. 39.
80. Combahee River Collective, "Combahee River Collective Statement," p. 272.
81. Juliet Mitchell, *Women: The Longest Revolution* (New York: Pantheon Books, 1984).
82. Biddy Martin and Chandra Mohanty, "Feminist Politics: What's Home Got to Do With It?" in *Feminist Studies/ Critical Studies,* ed. Teresa de Lauretis (Bloomington: University of Indiana Press, 1986), p. 208.
83. See, for example, Flax, "Postmodernism and Gender Relations in Feminist Theory"; Sandra Harding, *The Science Question in Feminism* (Ithaca: University of Cornell Press, 1986); Dorothy Smith, *The Everyday World as Problematic* (Boston: Northeastern University Press, 1987); Haraway, "A Manifesto for Cyborgs," *Socialist Review, 80* (1985), 64–107; Nancy Hartsock, *Money, Sex, and Power* (New York: Longman, 1983); Mary O'Brien, *The Politics of Reproduction* (Boston: Routledge & Kegan Paul, 1981); Irene Diamond and Lee Quinby, eds., *Feminism and Foucault* (Boston: Northeastern University Press, 1988); Linda Alcoff, "Cultural Feminism versus Post Structuralism: The Identity Crisis in Feminist Theory," *Signs, 13* (1988), 405–437; Special Issue on Feminism and Deconstruction, *Feminist Studies, 14,* No. 1 (1988); Judith Butler, *Gender Trouble* (New York: Routledge, 1990); Linda Nicholson, ed., *Feminism/Postmodernism* (New York: Routledge, 1990).
84. Fisher, "The Heart Has Its Reasons," p. 49.
85. Minnie Bruce Pratt, "Identity: Skin Blood Heart," in *Yours in Struggle,* ed. Elly Bulkin, Minnie Bruce Pratt, and Barbara Smith (Brooklyn, NY: Long Hand Press, 1984).
86. Martin and Mohanty, "What's Home Got to Do With It?"
87. Bernice Reagon, "Coalition Politics: Turning the Century," in Smith, *Home Girls,* pp. 356–369.

Interrupting Patriarchy:
Politics, Resistance, and Transformation
in the Feminist Classroom

MAGDA LEWIS

In this chapter, Magda Lewis investigates the psychological, social, and sexual dynamics of the feminist classroom as the women and men in her course struggle with the realities of violence against women and the negotiation strategies women use to succeed and survive in a patriarchal society. Lewis presents a feminist critique of patriarchy through her own feminist teaching practice within a context of both blatant and subtle forms of physical, social, emotional, and psychological violence against women. She analyzes students' resistance to such a critique, and self-consciously examines and questions the conditions under which her students make meaning of these events. Lewis shares some of the teaching strategies she has used to subvert the gendered status quo of her students' accounts of their experiences, perceptions, frustrations, and anger as they grapple with these issues. These stories illustrate the use of such instances as pedagogical moments of transformative power to lead students toward a more critical political perspective. Lewis concludes by suggesting a specific framework that articulates the terms of feminist teaching.

In Canada, the fall of 1989 marked a particularly hostile environment for women on university campuses. On my own campus, the events surrounding our "NO MEANS NO" campaign drew national attention. "NO MEANS NO" was an educational campaign organized by the Gender Issues Committee of the undergraduate student government (Alma Mater Society) aimed at alerting young women, particularly first-year women, to the forms and expressions of date rape. The reaction of a faction of the male students was to respond with a "sign campaign" that made explicit their belief that women's refusal of male sexual demands could appropriately be countered with violence ("No means tie me up") or with their own definitions of women's sexual deviance ("No means dyke"). To the extent that the signs were accompanied by active verbal threats and physical intimidation, many women experienced the threatening atmosphere as misogyny.

My campus was not the only one experiencing what appeared to be an increasing backlash to a feminist presence inside the academy. As women academics across and between campuses shared stories of violation, more and more examples of misogyny surfaced. Our isolation and small numbers (women still comprise a very small fraction of academic faculty) precluded any possibility of

Harvard Educational Review Vol. 60 No. 4 November 1990, 467–488.

collective action (Brodribb, 1987; McCormack, 1987). In the face of an academic community complicit in its complacency and unwilling to acknowledge its own oppressive practices born of the sexual subordination of women, we were atomized and held inside the private spaces of our own violations. And yet, despite the isolation of our struggles, we worked with our students to create an intellectually and emotionally supportive environment for them (Lewis, 1990a).

It was within this context that we witnessed with horror the spiraling momentum of woman-hating explode, in the early evening of December 6, 1989. Fourteen women at the Université de Montréal were massacred by a gun-wielding young man who had convinced himself that women, transposed in his own sad head into the phrase "you bunch of feminists," were the cause of his own personal misery.[1]

This incident focused, on several levels, my concerns about teaching and learning as a feminist in the academy. The historical context of our individual and collective experiences as intellectual women enabled me to see that what the media identified as the "idiosyncratic" madness of this young man actually reflected infinitely receding images of male power transformed into violence — a polished surface facing the mirror of masculine privilege. Because of our identification with a politic that makes explicit our critique of women's subordination as a function of masculine privilege, my students' and my own safety were in question. This was not the single act of a deranged mind, nor the outcome of peculiar conditions on that specific campus. That the events at the Université de Montréal could have happened on any campus in this country — indeed, any campus on this continent — became a tangible reality (Malette, 1990).

I am haunted by the image of young women — not unlike the women I teach — lined up against the wall, while their perplexed, perhaps helpless, male colleagues and male instructor vacated the classroom. I am haunted, too, by the words (reported in the media) of that young woman whose vain efforts to save herself and her women classmates were captured when she screamed at the gunman: "You have the wrong women; we are not feminists!"

The words "you have the wrong women; we are not feminists!" provide a backdrop for the question I raise: How might we bring about the social changes we desire without negating women's perspective on our reality, or turning it, yet one more time, into a self-perpetuated liability? More specifically, how might I create a feminist pedagogy that supports women's desire to wish well for ourselves when for many women the "good news" of the transformative powers of feminist consciousness turns into the "bad news" of social inequality and, therefore, a perspective and politics they want to resist. More than resistance, which, drawing on Willis (1977), I characterize as the struggles against social forms that are experienced as oppressive, transformation is the fusion of political perspective and practice. Transformation is the development of a critical perspective through which individuals can begin to see how social practices are organized to support certain interests, and the process whereby this understanding is then used as the basis for active political intervention directed toward social change with the intent to disempower relations of inequality.

In short, my agenda in this chapter is to understand the basis from which I might fashion a viable feminist pedagogy of transformation out of student resistance, not to patriarchic meaning-making, but to feminist politics.

Using my experiences in Foundations 490, in this chapter I continue to raise the dilemmas I face as a feminist teacher. I explore the possibilities and limits of feminist teaching and learning in the academy under conditions that directly contradict its intent (Lewis & Simon, 1986; Lewis, 1988b, 1989, 1990a). Foundations 490 is a sociology of education course I teach in the faculty of education at Queen's University. While it is not one of the core Women's Studies courses, it is cross-listed in the Women's Studies Programme Calendar. For this reason, the course often draws students from a wide range of disciplines. The specific title of the course, "Seminar in Social Class, Gender and Race in Education," is explicitly descriptive of the course focus. In the course outline I tell students that the theoretical framework we are using draws on critical and feminist theory and method. More specifically, the course proposes to "examine and develop a critical understanding of the implications for children's educational experiences of the effects of social class background, sex/gender differences and racial background." It also proposes to "locate school practices as part of the larger social context within which schools exist."

The course format is a seminar that incorporates class discussion around assigned readings and student presentations. The class presentation component requires students to articulate the social meaning of a cultural artifact or practice of their choice. Students examine how the artifact or practice reflects the social/cultural context out of which it has arisen. The purpose of the assignment is to help students develop their skills in raising questions about our culture, which they had previously taken as a given. My intention is also that, through the exercise, they might see differently how sexism, racism, class differentiation, homophobia, and so on, are embedded in concrete cultural products and social practices.

I begin the course with an introductory lecture that outlines to the students what I intend that we take up during the coming term and the perspective from which my analysis proceeds. By doing this I attempt to incorporate many aspects of women's lives articulated within feminist politics.

The course is attended by both female and male students, although women tend to outnumber the men four to one. This, in part, is accounted for by the fact that student enrollment in faculties of education is still largely skewed in favor of women, who comprise approximately 70 percent to 75 percent of the undergraduate teacher education complement. Because the majority of students in Foundations 490 are women, in this chapter I use the general designation "student" to refer to women or to the students in general. When I refer to the men in the classroom, I shall use the qualifier "male."

While in this chapter I explore the context of my teaching practice and the politics of the classroom, it is not my intention to offer prescriptive and generic feminist teaching strategies abstracted from the particular situations of feminist classrooms. Although it might be possible to employ suggestive approaches, we cannot artificially construct pedagogical moments in the classroom to serve as moments of transformation toward a critical political perspective. Nor can we predict how such moments will be responded to when they arise in particular situations, given the personal histories of the students and instructors involved.

Rather, I believe questions about the politics of feminist teaching have most specifically to do with how we identify those pedagogical moments whose transformative power lies precisely in the understandings we bring to the gendered context of the classroom. Ruth Pierson (1987) provides a clear and comprehensive definition of feminism, which frames the intent of my own teaching from a feminist perspective:

> One identifiable characteristic of feminism across an entire spectrum of varieties has been the pursuit of autonomy for women. Integral to this feminist pursuit of independent personhood is the critical awareness of a sex/gender system that relegates power and autonomy to men and dependence and subordination to women. Feminists start from an insistence on the importance of women and women's experience, but a woman-centered perspective alone does not constitute feminism. Before a woman-centered perspective becomes a feminist perspective, it has to have been politicized by the experience of women in pursuit of self-determination coming into conflict with a sex/gender system of male dominance. From a feminist perspective the sex/gender system appears to be a fundamental organizing principle of society and for that reason it becomes a primary object of analysis. (p. 203)

From this perspective I raise the psychological, social, and sexual dynamics of the feminist classroom as a site where, I believe, the political struggle over meaning must be seen as the focus of our pedagogical project. It is a context in which a serious intrusion of *feminist pedagogy* must concern itself, as Rachel Blau Du-Plessis (1985) suggests, not with urging our women students to "resent the treatment of [their] sex and plead for its rights" (p. 33) — a project that acts to reaffirm women's subordination and encourage our exploitation — but to examine and question self-consciously the conditions of our own meaning-making and to use it as the place from which to begin to work toward change.

In taking up the psychological, social, and sexual dynamics of the feminist classroom, in this chapter I propose to examine the violence/negotiation dichotomy environment as a feature of women's educational experience. In this context, I share the strategies I employ in specific instances as a feminist teacher to subvert the status quo of classroom interaction between women and men. Finally, in the conclusion I suggest a specific framework that articulates the terms of feminist teaching.

THEORETICAL FRAMEWORK

In the largely unchallenged practices of the school setting marked by patriarchic privilege (Corrigan, 1987), for women the dynamics of contestation born of knowledge are more complex than is often implied in the resistance literature. By paying close attention to practices in the classroom, forms of discourse, directions taken in discussion, the subtleties of body language, and so on, it is clear that, for women, a dichotomy between desire and threat is reproduced and experienced inside the classroom itself.

The salience of this dichotomy for women is suggested by Kathleen Rockhill (1987) in her powerful and moving article, "Literacy as Threat/Desire: Longing to be SOMEBODY," in which she articulates women's contradictory reality as an educational dilemma. For the women in Rockhill's study, the knowledge and power made potentially available through becoming literate contradictorily also repositioned them in such a way that it threatened familial, conjugal, and ulti-mately economic relations. Rockhill explains:

> It is common today for education to be ideologically dressed as the pathway to a new kind of romance for women, the romance of a "career," a profession, a mid-dle-class way of life; the image is one of a well-dressed woman doing "clean" work, important work. As such, it feeds her yearning, her desire, for a way out of the "working class" life she has known (Steedman, 1986). It is precisely because educa-tion holds out this promise for women that it also poses a threat to them in their everyday lives. This is especially true for women in heterosexual relationships when their men feel threatened by the images of power (independence and success) attached to education. (p. 315)

In the feminist classroom, the contradiction that women experience is com-pounded by the way in which feminist politics challenges the everyday lives they have learned to negotiate.

The complexities of student resistance to the intentions of schooling have been documented before, and indeed such accounts provide much of the data for the theoretical framework of critical pedagogy. Paul Willis's classic work, *Learning to Labour* (1977), influenced by the theoretical work of Bowles and Gintis, Althusser, Bourdieu and Passeron, and Gramsci, was one of the first. Willis's study dealt exclusively with the experiences of male students. He in-cluded women only in their relations as girl friends and mothers. In this context, it is interesting to note the irony of the title of the more recent book by Dale Spender and Elizabeth Sarah, *Learning to Lose* (1980), a study of the experiences of girls in school.

In its classic form, critical pedagogy emphasizes that student resistance to the experiences of institutionalized education is forged from the contradictions they perceive between the dominant discourse of school knowledge on the one hand and their own lived experiences of subordination and violation on the other. According to resistance theory, students struggle to mark themselves off against the dominant discourse of the school through the enactment of practices that reaffirm and validate their subjectivities as specifically classed, raced, and gen-dered social actors.

It is my explicit intent in the classroom to raise with students issues of social relations from a critical perspective. But I am also a feminist who has worked for many years in feminist politics across a variety of sites. My family life, my involvement with grassroots community organizations, and my intellectual work are informed in concrete ways by the politics of feminist analysis. By extension, the politics that informs my everyday life infuses my relations with students, generates the readings for the course, and suggests my classroom teaching style and practice. Yet my frustrations as a feminist teacher arise significantly from the extent to which critical thinking on transformative pedagogical practices fails to address the specifics of women's education as simultaneously a site of desire and threat.

Based on my own experiences, I know that a feminist perspective could offer understandings the students might develop and bring to bear on their own experiences (Lather, 1989). Yet I also realize that attending to feminist politics and cultural critique in the classroom requires difficult emotional work from them and from me. I know that new understandings are often experienced painfully, and that lives are transformed.

All of this has happened in Foundations 490. Yet, the forms through which such transformations have taken place are not those that I anticipated — or perhaps hoped for. As a teacher and a feminist I share the hope for the promise of education as a political project: that through the offer of a theoretical framework — analysis and critique — students would eagerly join in my enthusiasm to work for social change in their personal and public lives. Clearly there are times when women immediately embrace the intentions of feminist teaching because it helps them make a different sense of their experiences. But just as often students struggle with these new understandings as they explore the space between the public and theoretical agenda of the course and the privacy of their everyday lives, where complex negotiations across gender often take their most salient form.

In the academy, women find themselves inside institutions whose practices and intentions are historically designed to keep them outside its concrete and theoretical frames. For women students, negotiating masculine content and practices often means that they have to absorb as well as struggle to survive the violations of their subordination. My students often find more simple and, therefore, more powerful words through which to express my meaning. The legacy of the violations women experience in the academy are apparent in the following conversations:

I don't speak in class anymore. All this professor ever talked about was men, what they do, what they say, always just what's important to men. He, he, he is all I ever heard in class. He wasn't speaking my language. And whenever I tried to speak about what was important to me, whenever I tried to ask questions about how women fit into his scheme, all I got was a negative response. I always felt I was speaking from inside brackets, like walls I couldn't be heard past. I got tired of not being heard so I stopped speaking altogether.

I often tried to bring up examples of famous women in class because I thought it was important that people should acknowledge that women had done some things too. But no one ever knew who I was talking about. There was this assumption that if someone was a woman she couldn't possibly have done anything famous. The most important thing that happened to me in high school was that one of my history teachers had a picture of Agnes Mcphail pinned above the blackboard in the classroom. We never talked about it directly, but for me that became a symbol of a woman. Sometimes I got really disgusted in some of my classes, but I would think of that picture in that history class and that helped me to feel less alienated.

In history we never talked about what women did; in geography it was always what was important to men. The same in our English class, we hardly ever studied women authors. I won't even talk about math and science . . . I always felt that I didn't belong . . . sometimes the boys would make jokes about girls doing science experiments. They always thought they were going to do it better and it made me really nervous. Sometimes I didn't even try to do an experiment because I knew they would laugh if I got it wrong. Now I just *deaden* myself against it, so I don't hear it any more. But I feel really alienated. My experience now is one of total silence. Sometimes I even wish I didn't know what I know.

For me, as a feminist teacher, such statements are not only painful but revealing. The remarks suggest that the politics of my teaching should focus not on teaching women what we already know but on finding ways of helping all of us articulate the knowledge we gain with our experience.

As a beginning point I agree with the claim of Giroux and Simon (1988):

> We are not concerned with simply motivating students to learn, but rather *establishing the conditions of learning* that enable them to locate themselves in history and to interrogate the adequacy of that location as both a pedagogical and political question. (p. 3, emphasis added)

Yet a feminist pedagogy cannot stop here. For women, the cultural, political, and ultimately historical discourse of the everyday, the present, and the immediate are conditions of learning marked by the varied forms of patriarchic violence (Brookes, 1988; Belenkey, Clinchy, Goldberger, & Tarule, 1986; McMahan, 1986). Pedagogy, even radical pedagogy, does not easily translate into an education that includes women if we do not address the threat to women's survival and livelihood that a critique of patriarchy in its varied manifestations confronts.

The dynamics of the classroom context when students engage a feminist analysis present the most challenging aspects of feminist teaching (Lewis, 1988b). In what follows, I explore the psychological, social, and sexual aspects of this context.

PSYCHOLOGICAL DYNAMICS IN THE FEMINIST CLASSROOM

For women, tension in the feminist classroom is often organized around our historically produced nurturing capacity as a feature of our psychologically internalized role as caretakers (Lewis, 1988c). The following example is a case in point. Recently, in reference to a set of class readings dealing with peace education, my introductory presentation spoke to the connections between patriarchy, violence, and political economy. As I finished, one of the first students to speak was a young woman. She said, "As you were speaking I was wondering and worrying about how the men in the room were feeling. What you said made sense to me, but I felt uncomfortable about how the men took it." A couple of other women nodded their agreement. Such a protective posture on the part of women on behalf of men is a common drama played out in many classrooms.

Similar responses to feminist critique are not specific to mixed-gender classrooms. The absence of men in the classroom does not significantly diminish the psychological investment women are required to make in the emotional well-bring of men — an investment that goes well beyond the classroom into the private spaces of women's lives, which cannot easily be left at the classroom door. The response women bring to feminist politics/analyses arises from women's social/political location within patriarchic forms, which requires that men be the focus of women's attentions. Examples range from general claims that men are also isolated and contained by patriarchy in what is required of them within the terms of masculinity, to more specific references to personal family relations aimed at exempting intimate male relations from the general population of men. The sharing of household duties is often used as an example, although the articulation of details of this shared housework is often vague. Young women growing up in physically violent and sexually violating homes know a more brutal side of the caretaking imperative.[2]

Whether or not men are bodily present in the classroom, women carry the parameters of patriarchic meaning-making as a frame from within which we struggle to articulate our own interests. How women live this experience is not specific to mixed-gender classrooms. While it is my observation that the practice of a woman-as-caretaker ideology is more obvious in the presence of men, this ideology holds sway whether or not men are present, as long as women believe their interests to be served by maintaining existing relations.

This formulation is not intended to subsume the experiences of all women and men under seamless, hegemonic constructs articulated through dominant expressions of femininity/masculinity. I use Alison Jaggar's (1983) formulation of Gramsci's notion of hegemony: a concept "designed to explain how a dominant class maintains control by projecting its own particular way of seeing social reality so successfully that its view is accepted as common sense and as part of the natural order by those who in fact are subordinated to it" (p. 151). In this respect, hegemony is accomplished through an ongoing struggle over meaning not only against, but for the maintenance of, power. Lesbians and gay men experience the social constructs of femininity/masculinity differently than women and men whose emotional and psychic investment is in heterosexual relationships. However, especially in professional schools, where students' aspirations for future employment often govern their willingness to challenge the status quo, pressures to conform to the dominant social text are shared by lesbians and heterosexual women alike (Khayatt, 1987). Because lesbians and gay men often remain voiceless within such classroom dynamics, the relations between the women and men in the classroom remains a site that supports only practices that construct women's social acceptability as caretakers of men.

In the mixed-gender classroom, much of the caretaking takes the form of hard-to-describe body language displayed as a barely perceptible "moving toward"; a not-quite-visible extending of the hand; a protective stance accomplished through eye contact. However, as the young woman's question of concern has shown, just as often it is explicitly articulated. In the feminist classroom, such caretaking responses on the part of women toward men are ones that, as feminist teachers, we easily recognize and anticipate. We must choose words carefully and negotiate our analyses with the women students in ways that will not turn them away from the knowledge they carry in their experiences.

Following the young woman's comments, many of the men seemed to feel that what she said vindicated their feelings of discomfort with the way in which I was formulating the issues. Some of the men expressed this through verbal support of the woman's concern over their emotional well-being. They showed a strong inclination to redirect the discussion toward notions of world violence as a *human* and not a gendered problem. By doing so, the men attempted to reappropriate a speaking space for themselves, which they saw to be threatened by my analysis. Even more troublesome for me was the pleasure some of the men seemed to take in encouraging women to take up the caretaking on their behalf and in how the women seemed to be brought up against one another in the debate that followed. The question of whether or not feminist critique constituted a confrontational stance by women against men was the substance of the debate between the women and the men and among the women. Some of the men offered verbal support for women who agreed with them and a rebuttal of those who did not. However, the more subtle forms of pleasure-taking are difficult to describe. We do not have language that can adequately express the social meaning of the practice of relaxing back into one's chair, with a barely there smile on one's face while eyes are fixed on the object of negation. One of the reasons feminist films are a source of exceptionally powerful critique is because they can display how violation works at the level of the non-verbal (Lewis, 1990b). Yet such practices are unmistakable in their intent. The nonverbal is a social language that women — and all culturally marginal groups — have learned to read well and that does its sad work on women's emotions.

That such a dynamic should develop among the students was not a surprise. I know that, within the terms of patriarchy, women have had no choice but to care about the feelings of men. Women know that, historically, not caring has cost us our lives: intellectually, emotionally, socially, psychologically, and physically. I see this played out over and over again in my classes, and in every case it makes women recoil from saying what they really want to say and simultaneously leaves men reassured about their right to speak on behalf of us all.

For me, this dynamic presented a pedagogical dilemma. How could I question particularities of our present social organization, which requires women to work as caretakers of men not only in economic/material relations, but in emotional/psychological ones as well? Furthermore, how was I to do this in ways that did not reproduce the women's strong inclination to protect the men from what was *felt* to be an indictment of men in general and the men in the classroom in particular? Specifically, how could I help them focus on social organizational practices rather than on the man sitting next to them in the classroom?

I asked them to think of instances when we might expect men to reciprocate for women the kind of caretaking practices and ego support that women are expected to extend on behalf of men. Most specifically, I asked the women if they had ever been in the company of a male friend/partner/family member/stranger who, upon seeing our discomfort at the common public display of misogyny in such examples as billboards, had ever offered support for how uncomfortable and violated such displays must make us feel. By asking students to focus on the personal, I felt that it might be possible to reposition the women and men in a social configuration that did not take a gendered hierarchy and its attendant practices for granted. Not only the women, but the men as well, admitted that they had never had such an experience. More to the point, there was general agreement that the possibility had never even occurred to them.

Through our discussion, it became clear that as a collective social practice, for men, attentiveness to other than one's self is largely a matter of choice, whereas for women, it has been a socially and historically mandated condition of our acceptability as women. This provided, for some of the students in the class, a moment of critical reflection and transformation. It also offered a framework from which to envision a set of social relations not based fundamentally on inequality. For men such transformation often appears as a willingness to listen. Less eager to talk, they sometimes acknowledge that they can see themselves on the privileged side of the gender divide and admit that they had not previously given it a lot of thought. These acknowledgements are often fairly brief and to the point: "I had never thought of it that way" is a common response. Whether or not men carry their new understanding into their public and private lives outside the classroom is unclear. If they do, they have not shared it with me. For women, transformation often means a more active process. At times, younger women have asked to bring male friends to the class with them. More frequently, students have reported that they have asked their male friends or partners to read some of the course material. And some women have reported major changes in their family life, either in terms of renegotiated practices — mostly pertaining to household responsibilities — or in a decision to end a relationship. I do not want to suggest that every student in every class experiences these transformations. Progress is slow and often tentative as students struggle with the implications of their new understanding.

By shifting our focus from the topic of discussion (the political economy and masculine forms of world violence) and refocusing on the dynamics in the classroom at that moment, we made it possible to ask what cultural/political forms might articulate caretaking as a reciprocal process between women and men. This teaching strategy is central to my pedagogical agenda: identifying the moment when students might be most receptive to uncovering how they are invested in their own meaning-making practices.

SOCIAL DYNAMICS IN THE FEMINIST CLASSROOM

For many students, the social context of the feminist classroom is another sphere of tension. For the women students, the content and processes of feminist curricula and teaching can result in the classic version of consciousness raising. "Feminist method," says Catharine MacKinnon (1983), "is consciousness raising":

> the collective critical reconstitution of the meaning of women's social experience, as women live through it. . . . Consciousness raising . . . inquires into an intrinsically social situation, into that mixture of thought and materiality which is women's sexuality in the most generic sense. It approaches its world through a process that shares its determination: women's consciousness, not as individual or subjective ideas, but as a collective social being. . . . The process is transformative as well as perceptive, since thought and thing are inextricable and reciprocally constituting of women's oppression, just as the state of coercion and the state as legitimizing ideology are indistinguishable, and for the same reason. The pursuit of consciousness becomes a form of political practice. (p. 255)

Reading Catharine MacKinnon has convinced me that the politic of consciousness raising has earned a bad name precisely because it is a profoundly effective practice. There is a long history to the fear of women coming together and, in that space, sharing the personal stories that become metaphorical bases for generating a theory of women's subordination (Daly, 1978). The dominant forms of discourse are aimed hegemonically at preventing women from engaging in discussions that lead toward consciousness raising; the threat of social sanctions defuse the vitality of storytelling. Telling our stories of violation and subordination in the presence of those whose advantages are highlighted and challenged by such sharing, or doing so in the presence of those who hold the discursive power to subvert the act of consciousness raising as a feminist method is, for many women, a contradictory outcome of their experiences in the feminist classroom.

I believe the following exchange demonstrates this point well. Recently, a student was making a class presentation on the topic of violence against women. A few minutes after the beginning of her presentation, a frustrated young man demanded to know why we had to talk about women and men all the time, and why the presenter did not offer "the other side of the story." This example confirms other experiences indicating that students, particularly those who benefit from the present social arrangements, often find it difficult to engage in the self-reflection required to question the unequal and violent social relations in which we ourselves are social actors.

As a feature of classroom dynamics, the unpacking and uncovering of deeply submerged social practices of domination/entitlement experienced by the "other" as subordination/oppression, which we carry in and on our gendered bodies, in our verbal expressions, in the privilege (or lack of it) of having choice, can itself become another source for experiences of oppression. For women, as for other subordinate groups, it is the fact of "knowing" that is seen to be an act of insubordination; exposing that knowledge, speaking it in public space, claiming language through which to articulate our knowledge, refusing to believe that the dominant discourse speaks for all, as it speaks on behalf of patriarchic interests, is used as the justification for continued violation.

In part, patriarchy disempowers women by marginalizing their experiences of violation in an ongoing discourse that legitimates only those ways of making sense or the telling of only those kinds of stories that do not make men "look bad" (MacKinnon, 1987, p. 154). The use of language, for example, which exchanges "wife battering" with "family violence," as a way to redirect our focus away from masculine practices is a case in point.

One way male students sometimes wish to displace the sense women make of our experience is to refocus the discussion in directions that are less disquieting for them. In the instance mentioned above, I understood the young man's demand — the tone of his voice left no doubt that it was a demand — to be an attempt to redirect the discussion away from his own social identity as a male who, whether he acknowledges it or not, benefits from the culturally, legally, and politically encoded social relations of patriarchy (MacKinnon, 1987). Yet men can no more deny the embodiment of their masculine privilege than any of us can deny the embodiment of our entitlement if we are White, economically advantaged, heterosexual, able bodied, and carrying the valued assets of the privilege of Euro-American culture. As is suggested by Biddy Martin and Chandra Mohanty (1986), "the claim to a lack of identity or positionality is itself based on privilege, on a refusal to accept responsibility for one's implication in actual historical or social relations, on a denial that positionalities exist or that they matter, the denial of one's own personal history and the claim to a total separation from it" (p. 208). Furthermore, to the extent that sexism, racism, and social-class inequalities represent social systems within which we either appropriate or struggle against particular personal relations, those who embody positions of privilege are often not attracted to an articulation of their interests in the terms required by self-reflexivity.

On this occasion, I judged that, by providing for the possibility of self-reflexive critique, I might avert the tendency of such debates to degenerate into expressions of guilt and victimization that would destroy the creative potential of a feminist political discourse that speaks not only to women but to men as well. I also felt that how I presented my response was crucial. Whatever my response was, it had to be possible for women to see it as a model for how they might also take up similar challenges to their own meaning-making in ways other than to demand their right to do so — precisely the point of debate. My challenge was to create the possibility for students to be self-reflexive.

The young man's demand for the "other side" of the story about men's violence against women created the space I was looking for. In classrooms, as in other social/political spaces, women and men come together unequally (Lewis & Simon, 1986). In such a context, a pedagogical approach that fails to acknowledge how such inequality silences serves to reinforce the powerlessness of the powerless. I knew from my own experience that under such circumstances, asking women to "speak up" and intervene on their own behalf would have reproduced exactly that marginalization that the young man's demand was intended to create. Clearly, I needed to employ another strategy.

The power of teaching as dramatic performance cannot be discounted on this particular occasion. Following the question, I allowed a few moments of silence. In these few moments, as the question and the dynamics of the situation settled into our consciousness, the social history of the world was relived in the bodies of the women and men around the table. What is the "other side of the story" about violence against women! What could the women say? Faced with the demand to articulate their *reality in terms not of their own making,* the women visibly shrank into their chairs; their breathing became invisible (Rockhill, 1987a). In contrast, whether I imagined it or not, it seemed to me that the men sat more upright and "leaned into" the response that began to formulate in my head. It seemed clear to me that the young man's objections to the woman's presentation constructed women as objects of practices that were experienced by him as unproblematic; the threat of physical violence is not one that most men experience on a daily basis. By objectifying women through his question, he reinforced male privilege. I needed to find a way of repositioning us — women and men — in such a way that the young man had no options but to face his own social location as problematic.

The stage was set for dramatic performance. Reassuring the young man that indeed he was right, that "other sides" of issues need to be considered whenever possible, I wondered if *he* would perhaps be the one who could tell us about the "other side" of violence against women. My memory of this moment again focuses on the breath: the men's as it escaped their bodies and the women's as it replenished them.

Turning the question away from the women in the class created the self-reflexive space that I believed could truly challenge the men in the class to take up not women's subordination but their own positions of privilege. Given the social realities of violence against women, he was no more able to answer his own question than it might have been possible for the women to do so. At the same time, it remained for him to tell us why he couldn't answer his own question. He found himself speechless. This time the silence that followed reversed the order of privilege to name the social realities we live. The young man's failure to find a salient way of taking up the issue he had raised made it possible for the young woman to continue with her presentation without challenge to her fundamental right to do so.

The incident ended at this point and the class presentation proceeded. Reflecting on my own practice in this instance, I cannot deny that my politics embraced and supported the struggle for women's autonomy and self-determination. Working with women to create the space for our voice is fundamental to this politic. Whether the young man experienced transformation or was simply intimidated into silence was something that required sorting out. I was willing to let him undertake the hard work of doing so for himself. If I had silenced him, I could only hope that perhaps the experience would provide him with a deeper understanding of an experience women encounter every day. That the incident was experienced by the women in ways that signalled a moment of possibility for them is captured by a young woman who came over to where I was distractedly picking up my papers after the long three-hour class. She lightened the load of my exhaustion with the announcement that she wanted to be a sociologist and a feminist and would I tell her "how to become it." Both her naivete and mine embarrassed us into shared laughter; but then, such fleeting moments of embrace are sometimes all we have, it seems to me, to collect ourselves and move on. Such experiences reveal the feminist classroom as profoundly relevant to women's lives.

SEXUAL DYNAMICS IN THE FEMINIST CLASSROOM

Finally, the sexual dynamics of mixed-gender classrooms are complex and often contradictory. Particularly for younger women, at times still caught in the glare of sexual exploration and identification, the feminist classroom can feel threatening. The following example is a case in point.

Recently, during the introductory lecture I use as a way of framing the seminar session, I was addressing the educational concerns over the low number of women in mathematics and science programs. On this occasion, trying to concretize the issues for the students, I asked them to indicate, by a show of hands, which of them were preparing to be math and science teachers. A number of students raised their hands. As might be expected, many of those who raised their hands were men. However, a number of women also raised their hands. A "guffawed" and embarrassed laughter rose from the back corner of the room after a young man whispered a comment to a young woman who had raised her hand.

I do not generally make use of or support embarrassment as a pedagogical strategy. In this instance, however, I felt certain that I knew what the laughter was about and wanted to capture the moment as a concrete example of exactly the issues I was raising. I requested that the young man tell us what he had said.

He resisted; I insisted. The use of institutional power, I believe, should not always be viewed as counterproductive to our politics. Feminism is a politic that is both historical and contingent on existing social relations. I had no problem justifying the use of my institutional power to create the possibility for privilege to face itself and own its violation publicly. Using power to subjugate is quite different from using power to liberate. The young man complied. He told us that he had whispered to the young woman that perhaps she had had a sex change.

The assumed prerogative to pass such commentary on women's choices of career and life possibilities is not, of course, new to any of us. However, in the feminist classroom such commentary and attendant laughter become overtly political issues that can be taken up as instances of gender politics. I used the incident as an example of the kind of academic environment created for women when such interactions are not treated as problematic. In doing so, I was aware that both the women and the men experienced various degrees of discomfort. Many of the men and some of the women insisted that I was making too much of an innocent joke, while many of the women and none of the men, as far as I could tell, sat quietly with faces flushed. In thinking about how I approach my teaching, I can recall the salient details of this example to understand how gender politics can be transformed into sexual dynamics in the classroom. Not only gender, but sexuality is a deeply present organizing principle in the classroom and one that enters into the dynamics of how we come together as women and men in pursuit of shared meaning.

The production of shared meaning is one of the ways we experience deeply felt moments of psycho-sexual pleasure, whether across or within gender. Yet, in a patriarchic culture, women and men can find the articulation of shared meaning profoundly elusive, and the desire for pleasure in conflict with mutual understanding.

While women have always found support in separate women's communities, education cells, political movements, work, and so on, these sites of solidarity have usually existed outside of the dominant male culture — a culture of which, we cannot forget, women are also an integral part. Social, political, and economic relations are articulated through the personal/collective experience we have of the world. Feminist politics insist on using these experiences as the lens through which to look at the barely perceptible yet tenacious threads that hold the social forms and forces in place. For women who refuse subordination, who refuse to pretend that we don't know, standing against these social forces has not only economic and political consequences, but psycho/sexual ones as well. bell hooks (1989) comments:

> Sexism is unique. It is unlike other forms of domination — racism or classism — where the exploited and oppressed do not live in large numbers intimately with their oppressors or develop their primary love relationships (familial and/or romantic) with the individuals who oppress and dominate or share in the privileges attained by domination. . . . [For women] the context of these intimate relationships is also the site of domination and oppression. (p. 130)

This dynamic is seldom, if ever, talked about in the feminist classroom, and yet, it explains the conflicting emotional and analytic responses women have to the content of the course.

Exploring the sexual parameters of the conditions under which women are required to undertake their intellectual work is crucial. Finding examples is not hard; relating them is. It is with difficulty that I cite specific examples, and then only briefly, because of my own complex emotions associated with writing these words and having them stand starkly, darkly on the page to be read and reread; knowing that stories of violation violate at each retelling. These stories are not lightly told nor lightly received; they are often related in the privacy of my office. One woman's books disappeared (an event reminiscent of the one related in Janice Radway's *Reading the Romance,* 1984); another, alerted by the words, "maybe you should be reading this instead," had a copy of a pornographic magazine flung at her as she sat reading her course material; and yet another was told, as a "joke" at a social gathering, that to "celebrate" the completion of the course she would be "rewarded" by being "raped" so she could "get it out of her system" and return to her "old self." The monitoring and banning of what women read is shown in these examples to be closely associated with demands for women to conform to a particular version of male-defined sexuality. While the above may represent especially harsh examples, the antagonistic relationship drawn between women's desire for knowledge and our embodiment as sexually desirable human beings is an issue that lies always just below the surface in the classroom.

For many women, a feminist worldview is deeply incorporated at the level of everyday practice. Yet, we need to be aware that by requiring women to challenge masculine constructs — as I had done in the classroom example cited above — we also require them to break with the dominant phallocentric culture. While as feminist teachers we might believe that such a break may offer the only possibilities for the resolution of this conflict, we must be aware that for many women the concrete possibility of doing so is difficult to contemplate. As Claire Duchen, quoted in Rowbotham (1989), suggests, "the tailoring of desire to the logic of politics is not always possible or acceptable" (p. 85).

Feminist critique of phallocentric culture is at once fundamentally necessary for and profoundly disruptive of the possibilities for shared meaning across gender, leaving women vulnerable to what Sheila Radford-Hill (1986) has analyzed as the potential "betrayal" and "psychosexual rejection" of women by men (pp. 168–169), attended by more or less severe economic and political consequences. None of this dynamic escapes women's awareness. "The personal is political" is not just a useful organizing concept, it is also a set of material enactments that display and reflect back how the political is personal.

As Susan Griffin (1981) suggests, a woman knows that "over and over again culture tells her that men abandon women who speak too loudly, or who are too *present*" (p. 211). Coupled with the strong cultural message that "her survival in the world depends on her being able to find a man to marry" (p. 211), many young women in the feminist classroom find themselves caught in the double bind of needing to speak and to remain silent at the same time in order to guarantee some measure of survival. While the salience of this politic is more immediately obvious in the case of heterosexual women, woman-identified (Rich, 1986, p. 57) women who do not comply, at least minimally, with acceptable forms of sexual self-presentation do not escape the consequences of marginalization and exclusion. For all women in professional schools specifically, compliance with particular displays of femininity can mean the difference between having or not having a job.

As women and men struggle over establishing and articulating shared meanings, we need to notice the reality that, for many women, such struggles often take place in the context of deeply felt commitments reverberating with emotional psycho/sexual chords and attended by the material conditions of unequal power. While perhaps these relations are lived most deeply not in the classroom itself but in those private spaces lived out between women and men beyond the classroom, for women, course content can be instrumental in raising these relations as questions.

The following is an example of how one woman took up these struggles in her private life. After a particular encounter in the classroom regarding the issue of voice/discourse discussed in the context of who has the right to name whether or not a joke is funny, she wrote me the following note:

> The articles at this point in the course . . . have plunged me into the next phase of my feminist awareness, which is characterized by anger and a pervading sense of injustice. . . . The "feminist" anger that I feel is self-perpetuating. I get angry at the discrimination and stereotyping I run up against so I blame the patriarchal society I live in in particular, and men in general. Then I think about women who feel that feminism is unnecessary or obsolete and I get angry at that subset of women. Then I think about the good guys like Mike and Cam and I get angry because the patriarchal society biases the way I think about these men, simply because they're members of a particular gender (sex class?). Then I think about men who stereotype and discriminate against women and criticize us for being "overly sensitive" when we get uptight or even just point out or suggest humanistic egalitarian changes that are good and smart and I get REALLY angry because I realize that they're all a bunch of (expletives deleted) [sic]. . . . One of the most difficult aspects of this anger is that I become frustrated and impatient with people who can't see the problems or don't see the urgent need for solutions. (I am writing) a lot during this time because I often can't communicate orally with people who don't at least respect my feminist views.

hooks states that "feminist works that focus on strategies women can use to speak to males about male domination and change are not readily available, if they exist at all. Yet women have a deep longing to share feminist consciousness with the men in their lives (the 'good guys'), and together work at transforming their relationships." hooks goes on to say that "concern for this basic struggle should motivate feminist thinkers to talk and write more about how we relate to men and how we change and transform relationships with men characterized by domination" (p. 130).

Yet despite their desire genuinely to share the meanings they have drawn from their experiences, for young women in the feminist classrooms, phallocentric myth-making often collides with the theoretical agenda of the course. Phallocentric myths are those beliefs that continue to marginalize women through the process of naturalizing politically created gender inequalities: "Women are not in positions of decision and policymaking because they don't want to be"; "Everybody has equal opportunity to become school principal. Women choose not to be because they like teaching better"; "If abused and battered women don't leave their partners it is because they have deviant personalities"; "Women who are raped did something wrong"; "Boys are better at math, girls are better at reading"; "Women who do math are not really women"; "Jokes, sexually offensive to women, are funny"; "There are no women in history because they didn't do anything"; "Women like staying home with children"; "Men share equally in housework"; and so on. I have heard some version of all of these statements in the classroom. While the men might express a comfortable indignation at such beliefs, they don't often understand what practices are required of them to change how they live their lives. For example, one man recently told the class that he supports his wife's career by "baby-sitting" the children while she goes to work. It is precisely this imbalance of power that constructs the women's silence, suppressed behind embarrassed laughter.

The pedagogical implications of such gender relations in the feminist class-room must be taken seriously if we are to understand how and why women students might wish both to appropriate and yet resist feminist theoretical and political positions that aim to uncover the roots of our deeply misogynist culture and give legitimacy to women's desires and dreams of possibility. As feminist teachers we need to look closely at the psycho/sexual context within which we propose the feminist alternative and consider the substance of why women may genuinely wish to turn away from the possibilities it offers.

Women know through experience that the threat to our sexuality is a way of controlling our political activities. In her review of Spender (1982), Pierson (1983) points out that there is a long history to the process of displacing women's legitimate political and intellectual critique and struggles into distorted evaluations of women's sexuality as a form of social control hammered into place by the material conditions of women's lives. The meaning that patriarchy has assigned to the term "lesbian" has resulted in its use as a pejorative term to undermine the serious political work in which women as women have been engaged in resistance to a set of social relations marked by patriarchic domination. The misogyny of such a designation violates all women at all points of the heterosexual/lesbian continuum (Rich, 1986). Clearly "the regulation of speaking and silence" (Walkerdine, 1985) is not just achieved through concrete regulatory practices, but also through the emotional, psychic, and sexual sphere — articulated through the practices of patriarchic myth-making — that combine in our hearts and heads to silence us from within. Given the terms of such social conditions, it would be a surprise, indeed, if women did not feel the constraints of contradictory choices and conflicting interests.

The power of patriarchic social controls on women's sexuality does not escape even (or perhaps especially) very young women. For example, within a recent three-week period, two separate groups of elementary and high school students were invited to participate in different events sponsored by the faculty where I teach. The first was a forum on women and education, attended by 150 students, at which the guest speaker, Dale Spender, presented an address entitled "Young Women in Education: What Happens to Girls in Classrooms." Three weeks later, a dramatic presentation by a feminist acting troupe, The Company of Sirens, presented an upbeat production called *The Working People's Picture Show*, dealing with such issues as women in the work force, day care, unionism, and sexual harassment.[3] The question period that followed each event was telling. In each case the young women's concerns were well demonstrated by the almost identically phrased question aimed at the presenters, who were seen as the embodiment of feminist critique: "Are you married and do you have children?" I don't believe this was a theoretical question. For many young women, the concern about the compatibility of feminist politics with marriage and family is the concrete realization that making public what our feminist consciousness reveals about women's experiences of patriarchy can result in potential limits on desire. To the extent that any woman who displays autonomy and independent personhood is seen as a threat to male power and therefore subjected to male violence was reaffirmed by the massacre at the Université de Montréal. Such events are not lost on young women.

My response to the sexual dynamics in the classroom is to create a context that offers "space" and "safety," particularly to women students. Men in the feminist classroom often state that the course readings and class discussions feel threatening and that they experience various degrees of discomfort. I would like to understand more about these feelings of threat and discomfort — where do they come from, what do they fear? I am concerned that all students — women and men — have access to the analyses we take up in the class. I am also concerned that all students feel equally validated in doing the hard work toward a transformed consciousness. However, this work is different for women than it is for men. Women need space and safety so that they are free to speak in order to better understand and act against the violations they have experienced in a social/cultural setting that subordinates them in hurtful and violent ways. The consciousness around which men need to do hard work is the pain of their complicity in benefitting from the rewards of this same culture. I support men in doing this hard work. Personally, I have not seen many of them try. Those who have are strong and welcome allies.

The language of "space" and "safety" is not new to discussions of feminist teaching. However, I believe that it is not always clear what practices attend these abstractions. I believe, first, that women don't need to be taught what we already know: fundamentally, that women are exempted from a culture to which our productive and reproductive labor is essential. The power of phallocentrism may undermine our initiative, it may shake the foundations of our self-respect and self-worth, it may even force us into complicity with its violence. But it cannot prevent us from knowing. Nor do women need to be taught the language through which to speak what we know.

Rather, the challenge of feminist teaching is in finding ways to make speakable and legitimate the personal/political *investments* we all make in the meanings we ascribe to our historically contingent experiences. In this context, I raise with students the contradictory reality of women's lives, wherein one's interests, at the level of practice, lie both with the dominant group and against it. Through such discussion emerges the deeply paradoxical nature of the conditions of the subordinate in a hierarchical culture marked by gender, class, and race inequalities. Approaching women's lives from this perspective means that practices previously understood by students to be a function of choice can be seen as the result of a need to secure some measure of emotional, intellectual, and quite often physical survival (Wolfe, 1986, p. 58).

Pedagogy that is grounded in simple notions of false consciousness that articulates teaching as mediation or, worse, as a charitable act, does not support knowledge invested with the meanings students ascribe to their own experiences. This not only buries the complexity of human choices in an unproblematized notion of self-interest but, further, can only offer validating or supplementary educational options without transforming the conditions under which we learn (Lewis, 1989). By fusing women's emotional and concrete lives through feminist critique, it is possible to make problematic the conditions under which women learn, and perhaps to make a feminist political agenda viable in women's own lives wherein they can transcend the split between personal experience and social form.

CONCLUSION

What are the possibilities of doing feminist politics/pedagogy in the classroom? In answering this question I want to examine the potential for feminist teaching that does more than address the concerns of the already initiated. For me, the urgency of this issue arises from my own teaching. On one hand, the often chilling stories women students share with me and each other in the context of classroom relations point to their clear understanding of the politics of gender subordination. Within the confines of traditional academic practices, the politics of personal experience are often seen to be irrelevant. In contrast, the feminist classroom can be a deeply emotional experience for many women, offering the opportunity to claim relevance for the lives they live as the source of legitimate knowledge.

On the other hand, I also hear the young woman who speaks to me in anger, who derides me for being the bearer of "bad news," and who wants to believe that our oppression/subordination is something we create in our own heads. Given the context of violence within which students are being asked to embrace a feminist politic, their concerns about their emotional, intellectual, and, quite obviously, physical safety have to be recognized as crucial. For women, overt acts of violence, like the one that occurred at the Université de Montréal, are merely an extension of their daily experiences in the psychological/social/sexual spaces of the academy. Resistance to the emancipatory potential of a liberating politic indicates the extent of women's subordination. Thus, we cannot expect that students will readily appropriate a political stance that is truly counter-hegemonic, unless we also acknowledge the ways in which our feminist practice/politics *creates*, rather than ameliorates, feelings of threat: the threat of abandonment; the threat of having to struggle within unequal power relations; the threat of psychological/social/sexual, as well as economic and political marginality; the threat of retributive violence — threats lived in concrete embodied ways. Is it any wonder that many women desire to disassociate from "those" women whose critique of our social/cultural world seems to focus and condense male violence?

The challenge of feminist teaching lies for me in the specifics of how I approach the classroom. By reflecting on my own teaching, I fuse content and practice, politicizing them both through feminist theory and living them both concretely rather than treating them abstractly. To elaborate: as I reflect on my teaching, it is clear from the detailing of the examples I provide above that feminist teaching practices cannot be separated from the content of the curriculum. Specific political moments arise exactly because of the content of the course. As is suggested by Gayle MacDonald (1989), "the process by which teaching occurs in a feminist classroom is one which is very different from technique/pedagogy used in other settings" (p. 147). I want to extend this idea by suggesting that the "difference" MacDonald identifies in the feminist classroom is that, as students articulate their interests and investments through particular social practices, a dialectic develops between students and the curriculum in such a way that the classroom dynamics created by the topic of discussion reflect the social organization of gender inequality. Indeed, the irony is that feminist critique of social relations reproduces exactly the practices we are critiquing. When these practices are reproduced, so are the attendant violations, marginalizations, struggles, and transformation, which again lend themselves to be revisited by the critique of feminist politics.

An interesting case in point is the experience I have had on various occasions when I have presented some version of this argument at academic conferences. On each occasion, in responding to my presentation, some members of the audience tended to reproduce to some extent the practices that I take such great pains to critique in the text. The caretaking practices, the concern that men not feel unfairly marginalized or attacked, the willingness of men in the audience to speak unproblematically on behalf of women, and the dynamics of sexual marginalization have all played a part in the reception of my chapter-in-progress. My purpose here is not to suggest that every instance of critique of feminist social/cultural analysis is a display of phallocentric power or male privilege. Indeed, as feminist scholars we put our work forward in good faith and both invite and welcome articulate and substantive engagement of it (Ellsworth, 1989). My point is, rather, that responses to feminist critique often take forms that reproduce the gendered practices that I have described in this chapter.

The strategies I have employed in the classroom have been directed toward politicizing not only what we take up in the class as course content, but also the classroom dynamics that are generated by our topic and subsequent discussion. These practices included: shifting our focus from larger social issues to the dynamics in the classroom so that we might explore the relationship between the two; legitimating the meanings women bring to their experiences by turning challenges to these articulated meanings back on the questioner, thereby requiring the questioner to make different meanings sensible; disrupting the order of hierarchy regarding who can speak on whose behalf; requiring that men in the class own their social location by exploring the parameters of their own privilege rather than the limits on women of their oppression; providing opportunities for self-reflexive critique of unequal power relations; staying attentive to the political context of women's lives — those seemingly unconnected experiences made to seem livable by the tumble of daily life — in order to offer a vision of a future that women might embrace; attending to the ways in which women have been required historically to invest in particular and often contradictory practices in order to secure their own survival; and, finally, treating women's resistance to feminism as an active discourse of struggle derived from a complex set of meanings in which women's practices are invested.

The above suggestions are intended to be neither exhaustive nor prescriptive. Pedagogical moments arise in specific contexts: the social location of the teacher and students; the geographic and historical location of the institution in which they come together; the political climate within which they work; the personalities and personal profiles of the individuals in the classroom; the readings selected for the course; and the academic background of the students all come together in ways that create the specifics of the moment. It is not appropriate to think of what I have presented here as a "model" for feminist teaching. "Models" can only be restrictive and reductive because they cannot predict and thus cannot take into account the complexity of contingent and material realities. My intent, rather, has been to articulate how, at particular moments in my teaching, I made sense of those classroom dynamics that seemed to divide women and men across their inequalities in ways that reaffirmed women's subordination, and how making sense of those moments as politically rich allowed me to develop an interpretive framework for creating a counter-hegemony from my teaching practice. My hope is that through such shared struggles in the classroom, women might embrace for themselves the politics of autonomy and self-determination, rather than reject it as a liability.

NOTES

1. This article is dedicated to the fourteen women massacred at the Université de Montréal on December 6, 1989: Genevieve Bergeron, Helene Colgan, Nathalie Croteau, Barbara Diagneault, Anne-Marie Edward, Maud Haveirnick, Barbara Maria Klueznick, Maryse Laganiere, Maryse Leclair, Anne-Marie Lemay, Sonia Pelletier, Michele Richard, Annie St-Arneault, and Annie Turcotte.
2. I thank Barbara McDonald for providing me with a deeper understanding of this reality through the work we share.
3. The Company of Sirens, 176 Robert Street, Toronto, Ontario, Canada, M5S 2K3.

REFERENCES

Belenky, M. F., Clinchy, B. M., Goldberger, N. R., & Tarule, J. M. (1986). *Women's ways of knowing: The development of self, voice and mind*. New York: Basic Books.

Brodribb, S. (1987). Women's studies in Canada [Special issue]. *Resources for Feminist Research*.

Brookes, A-L. (1988). *Feminist pedagogy: A subject in/formation*. Unpublished doctoral dissertation, University of Toronto.

Childers, M. (1984). Women's studies: Sinking and swimming in the mainstream. *Women's Studies International Forum*, 7(3), 161–166.

Corrigan, P. (1987). In/forming schooling. In D. Livingston & contributors, *Critical pedagogy and cultural power* (pp. 17–40). Toronto: Garamond Press.

Daly, M. (1978). *Gyn/ecology: The metaethics of radical feminism*. Boston: Beacon Press.

DuPlessis, R. B. (1985). *Writing beyond the ending: Narrative strategies of twentieth-century women writers*. Bloomington: Indiana University Press.

Ellsworth, E. (1989). Why doesn't this feel empowering? Working through the repressive myths of critical pedagogy. *Harvard Educational Review, 59,* 297–324.

Giroux, H., & Simon, R. (1988). *Critical pedagogy and the politics of popular culture.* Unpublished manuscript.

Griffin, S. (1981). *Pornography and silence: Culture's revenge against nature.* New York: Harper & Row.

hooks, b. (1989). *talking back: thinking feminist, thinking black.* Boston: South End Press.

Jaggar, A. (1983). *Feminist politics and human nature.* Sussex, Eng.: Harvest Press.

Khayatt, D. M. (1987). *Gender role conformity in women teachers.* Unpublished doctoral dissertation, University of Toronto.

Lather, P. (1988a). Feminist perspectives on emancipatory research methodologies. *Women's Studies International Forum, 11,* 569–581.

Lewis, M. (1988b). *Without a word: Sources and themes for a feminist pedagogy.* Unpublished doctoral dissertation, University of Toronto.

Lewis, M. (1988c). The construction of femininity embraced in the work of caring for children: Caught between aspirations and reality. *Journal of Educational Thought, 22*(2A), 259–268.

Lewis, M. (1989). The challenge of feminist pedagogy. *Queen's Quarterly, 96,* 117–130.

Lewis, M. (1990a). *Solidarity work and feminist practice.* Paper presented at the annual meeting of the American Educational Research Association, Boston.

Lewis, M. (1990b). *Framing: Women and silence disrupting the hierarchy of discursive practices.* Paper presented at the annual meeting of the American Educational Research Association, Boston.

Lewis, M., & Simon, R. I. (1986). A discourse not intended for her: Learning and teaching within patriarchy. *Harvard Educational Review, 56,* 457–472.

MacDonald, G. (1989). Feminist teaching techniques for the committed but exhausted. *Atlantis, 15*(1), 145–152.

MacKinnon, C. A. (1983). Feminism, Marxism, method and the state: An agenda for theory. In E. Abel & E. Abel (Eds.), *The signs reader: Women, gender and scholarship* (pp. 227–256). Chicago: University of Chicago Press.

MacKinnon, C. (1987). *Feminism unmodified: Discourses of life and law.* Cambridge, MA: Harvard University Press.

Malette, L., & Chalouh, M. (Eds.). (1990). *Polytechnique, 6 Decémbre.* Montréal: Les Éditions du remue-ménage.

Martin, B., & Mohanty, C. T. (1986). Feminist politics: What's home got to do with it? In T. De Lauretis (Ed.), *Feminist studies/critical studies* (pp. 191–212). Bloomington: Indiana University Press.

McCormack, T. (1987). Feminism, women's studies and the new academic freedom. In J. Gaskell & A. McLaren (Eds.), *Women and education: A Canadian perspective* (pp. 289–303). Calgary: Detselig Enterprises.

McMahon, M. (1986). *A circuitous quest: Things that haunt me when I write.* Unpublished manuscript.

Pierson, R. R. (1983). Review of women of ideas and what men have done to them. *Resources for Feminist Research, 12*(2), 17–18.

Pierson, R. R. (1987). Two Marys and a Virginia: Historical moments in the development of a feminist perspective on education. In J. Gaskell & A. McLaren (Eds.), *Women and education: A Canadian perspective* (pp. 203–222). Calgary: Detselig Enterprises.

Radford-Hill, S. (1986). Considering feminism as a model for social change. In T. de Lauretis (Ed.), *Feminist studies/critical studies* (pp. 157–172). Bloomington: Indiana University press.

Radway, J. (1984). *Reading the romance: Women, patriarchy and popular literature.* Chapel Hill: University of North Carolina Press.

Rich, A. (1986). *Blood, bread and poetry.* New York: W. W. Norton.

Rockhill, K. (1987a). The chaos of subjectivity in the ordered halls of academe. *Canadian Women Studies, 8*(4).

Rockhill, K. (1987b). Literacy as threat/desire: Longing to be SOMEBODY. In J. Gaskell & A. McLaren (Eds.), *Women and education: A Canadian perspective* (pp. 315–331). Calgary: Detselig Enterprises.

Rowbotham, S. (1989). To be or not to be: The dilemmas of mothering. *Feminist Review, 31*, 82–93.

Spender, D. (1982). *Women of ideas and what men have done to them.* London: Routledge & Kegan Paul.

Spender, D., & Sarah, E. (Eds.). (1980). *Learning to lose: Sexism and education.* London: Women's Press.

Walkerdine, V. (1985). On the regulation of speaking and silence: Subjectivity, class and gender in contemporary schooling. In C. Steedman, C. Urwin, & V. Walkerdine (Eds.), *Language, gender and childhood* (pp. 203–241). London: Routledge & Kegan Paul.

Williamson, J. (1981/1982). How does girl number twenty understand ideology? *Screen Education, 40*, 80–87.

Willis, P. (1977). *Learning to labour: How working class kids get working class jobs.* New York: Columbia University Press.

Wolfe, A. (1986). Inauthentic democracy: A critique of public life in modern liberal society. *Studies in Political Economy, 21*, 57–81.

I wish to thank Gayle MacDonald, Barbara McDonald, Elizabeth Ellsworth, and Roberta Lamb for making helpful comments on earlier drafts of this chapter.

Nobody Mean More to Me Than You[1]
and the Future Life of Willie Jordan

JUNE JORDAN

Progressive teachers often face the problem of making education in the schools relevant to life outside of the schools. They are confronted regularly with the challenge of introducing controversial subject matter that often forces students to examine critically their values and worldviews, and their positions in this society. In this chapter, June Jordan describes the experiences in her undergraduate course on Black English in which both she and her students mounted the charge of making education and schooling truly relevant and useful when they decided to mobilize themselves on behalf of a Black classmate whose unarmed brother had been killed by White police officers in Brooklyn, New York. In 1988, the Editors decided to include this article from a book by June Jordan in HER's Special Issue on Race, Racism, and American Education. We have decided to reprint it a second time because of its relevance to the themes of this book.

Black English is not exactly a linguistic buffalo; as children, most of the thirty-five million African Americans living in the United States depend on this language for our discovery of the world. But then we approach our maturity inside a larger social body that will not support our efforts to become anything other than the clones of those who are neither our mothers nor our fathers. We begin to grow up in a house where every true mirror shows us the face of somebody who does not belong there, whose walk and whose talk will never look or sound "right," because that house was meant to shelter a family that is alien and hostile to us. As we learn our way around this environment, either we hide our original word habits, or we completely surrender our own voice, hoping to please those who will never respect anyone different from themselves: Black English is not exactly a linguistic buffalo, but we should understand its status as an endangered species, as a perishing, irreplaceable system of community intelligence, or we should expect its extinction, and, along with that, the extinguishing of much that constitutes our own proud, and singular, identity.

What we casually call "English" less and less defers to England and its "gentlemen." "English" is no longer a specific matter of geography or an element of class privilege; more than thirty-three countries use this tool as a means of "intranational communication."[2] Countries as disparate as Zimbabwe and Malaysia,

Originally published in *On Call: Political Essays* by June Jordan (Boston: South End Press, 1985).

Harvard Educational Review   Vol. 58   No. 3   August 1988, 363–374.

or Israel and Uganda, use it as their non-native currency of convenience. Obviously, this tool, this "English," cannot function inside thirty-three discrete societies on the basis of rules and values absolutely determined somewhere else, in a thirty-fourth other country, for example.

In addition to that staggering congeries of non-native users of English, there are five countries, or 333,746,000 people, for whom this thing called "English" serves as a native tongue.[3] Approximately 10 percent of these native speakers of "English" are African-American citizens of the United States. I cite these numbers and varieties of human beings dependent on "English" in order, quickly, to suggest how strange and how tenuous is any concept of "Standard English." Obviously, numerous forms of English now operate inside a natural, an uncontrollable, continuum of development. I would suppose "the standard" for English in Malaysia is not the same as "the standard" in Zimbabwe. I know that standard forms of English for Black people in this country do not copy that of Whites. And, in fact, the structural differences between these two kinds of English have intensified, becoming more Black, or less White, despite the expected homogenizing effects of television and other mass media.[4]

Nonetheless, White standards of English persist, supreme and unquestioned, in these United States. Despite our multilingual population, and despite the deepening Black and White cleavage within that conglomerate, White standards control our official and popular judgments of verbal proficiency and correct, or incorrect, language skills, including speech. In contrast to India, where at least fourteen languages coexist as legitimate Indian languages, in contrast to Nicaragua, where all citizens are legally entitled to formal school instruction in their regional or tribal languages, compulsory education in America compels accommodation to exclusively White forms of "English." White English, in America, is "Standard English."

This story begins two years ago. I was teaching a new course, "In Search of the Invisible Black Woman," and my rather large class seemed evenly divided among young Black women and men. Five or six White students also sat in attendance. With unexpected speed and enthusiasm we had moved through historical narratives of the nineteenth century to literature by and about Black women, in the twentieth. I had assigned the first forty pages of Alice Walker's *The Color Purple,* and I came eagerly to class that morning:

"So!" I exclaimed, aloud. "What did you think? How did you like it?"

The students studied their hands, or the floor. There was no response. The tense, resistant feeling in the room fairly astounded me.

At last, one student, a young woman still not meeting my eyes, muttered something in my direction:

"What did you say?" I prompted her.

"Why she have them talk so funny. It don't sound right."

"You mean the language?"

Another student lifted his head: "It don't look right, neither. I couldn't hardly read it."

At this, several students dumped on the book. Just about unanimously, their criticisms targeted the language. I listened to what they wanted to say and silently marvelled at the similarities between their casual speech patterns and Alice Walker's written version of Black English.

But I decided against pointing to these identical traits of syntax; I wanted not to make them self-conscious about their own spoken language — not while they clearly felt it was "wrong." Instead I decided to swallow my astonishment. Here was a negative Black reaction to a prize-winning accomplishment of Black literature that White readers across the country had selected as a best seller. Black rejection was aimed at the one irreducibly black element of Walker's work: the language — Celie's Black English. I wrote the opening lines of *The Color Purple* on the blackboard and asked the students to help me translate these sentences into Standard English:

You better not never tell nobody but God. It'd kill your mammy.

Dear God,
   I am fourteen years old. I have always been a good girl. Maybe you can give me a sign letting me know what is happening to me.
   Last spring after Little Lucious come I heard them fussing. He was pulling on her arm. She say it too soon, Fonso. I aint well. Finally he leave her alone. A week go by, he pulling on her arm again. She say, Naw, I ain't gonna. Can't you see I'm already half dead, an all of the children.[5]

Our process of translation exploded with hilarity and even hysterical, shocked laughter: The Black writer, Alice Walker, knew what she was doing! If rudimentary criteria for good fiction include the manipulation of language so that the syntax and diction of sentences will tell you the identity of speakers, the probable age and sex and class of speakers, and even the locale — urban/rural/southern/western — then Walker had written, perfectly. This is the translation into Standard English that our class produced:

Absolutely, one should never confide in anybody besides God. Your secrets could prove devastating to your mother.

Dear God,
   I am fourteen years old. I have always been good. But now, could you help me to understand what is happening to me?
   Last spring, after my little brother, Lucious, was born, I heard my parents fighting. My father kept pulling at my mother's arm. But she told him, "It's too soon for sex, Alfonso. I am still not feeling well." Finally, my father left her alone. A week went by, and then he began bothering my mother again: Pulling her arm. She told him, "No, I won't! Can't you see I'm already exhausted from all of these children?"

(Our favorite line was "It's too soon for sex, Alfonso.")
Once we could stop laughing, once we could stop our exponentially wild improvisations on the theme of Translated Black English, the students pushed to explain their own negative first reactions to their spoken language on the printed page. I thought it was probably akin to the shock of seeing yourself in a photograph for the first time. Most of the students had never before seen a written facsimile of the way they talk. None of the students had ever learned how to read and write their own verbal system of communication: Black English. Alternatively, this fact began to baffle or else bemuse and then infuriate my

students. Why not? Was it too late? Could they learn how to do it, now? And, ultimately, the final test question, the one testing my sincerity: Could I teach them? Because I had never taught anyone Black English and, as far as I knew, no one, anywhere in the United States, had ever offered such a course, the best I could say was "I'll try."

* * *

He looked like a wrestler.

He sat dead center in the packed room and, every time our eyes met, he quickly nodded his head as though anxious to reassure, and encourage me.

Short, with strikingly broad shoulders and long arms, he spoke with a surprisingly high, soft voice that matched the soft bright movement of his eyes. His name was Willie Jordan. He would have seemed even more unlikely in the context of Contemporary Women's Poetry, except that ten or twelve other Black men were taking the course, as well. Still, Willie was conspicuous. His extreme fitness, the muscular density of his presence underscored the riveted, gentle attention that he gave to anything anyone said. Generally, he did not join the loud and rowdy dialogue flying back and forth, but there could be no doubt about his interest in our discussions. And, when he stood to present an argument he'd prepared, overnight, that nervous smile of his vanished and an irregular stammering replaced it, as he spoke with visceral sincerity, word by word.

That was how I met Willie Jordan. It was in between "In Search of the Invisible Black Women" and "The Art of Black English." I was waiting for department approval and I supposed that Willie might be, so to speak, killing time until he, too, could study Black English. But Willie really did want to explore contemporary women's poetry and, to that end, volunteered for extra research and never missed a class.

Towards the end of that semester, Willie approached me for an independent study project on South Africa. It would commence the next semester. I thought Willie's writing needed the kind of improvement only intense practice will yield. I knew his intelligence was outstanding. But he'd wholeheartedly opted for "Standard English" at a rather late age, and the results were stilted and frequently polysyllabic, simply for the sake of having more syllables. Willie's unnatural formality of language seemed to me consistent with the formality of his research into South African apartheid. As he projected his studies, he would have little time, indeed, for newspapers. Instead, more than 90 percent of his research would mean saturation in strictly historical, if not archival, material. I was certainly interested. It would be tricky to guide him into a more confident and spontaneous relationship both with language and apartheid. It was going to be wonderful to see what happened when he could catch up with himself, entirely, and talk back to the world.

September 1984: Breezy fall weather and much excitement! My class, "The Art of Black English," was full to the limit of the fire laws. And in Independent Study, Willie Jordan showed up weekly, fifteen minutes early for each of our sessions. I was pretty happy altogether to be teaching!

I remember an early class when a young brother, replete with his ever-present porkpie hat, raised his hand and then told us that most of what he'd heard was "all right" except it was "too clean." "The brothers on the street," he continued, "they mix it up more. Like 'fuck' and 'motherfuck.' Or like 'shit.'" He waited. I waited. Then all of us laughed a good while, and we got into a brawl about "correct" and "realistic" Black English that led to Rule 1.

Rule 1: Black English is about a whole lot more than mothafuckin.

As a criterion, we decided, "realistic" could take you anywhere you want to go. Artful places. Angry places. Eloquent and sweetalkin places. Polemical places. Church. And the local Bar & Grill. We were checking out a language, not a mood or a scene or one guy's forgettable mouthing off.

It was hard. For most of the students, learning Black English required a fall-back to patterns and rhythms of speech that many of their parents had beaten out of them. I mean *beaten*. And, in a majority of cases, correct Black English could be achieved only by striving for *incorrect* Standard English, something they were still pushing at, quite uncertainly. This state of affairs led to Rule 2.

Rule 2: If it's wrong in Standard English it's probably right in Black English, or, at least, you're hot.

It was hard. Roommates and family members ridiculed their studies, or remained incredulous, "You *studying* that shit? At school?" But we were beginning to feel the companionship of pioneers. And we decided that we needed another rule that would establish each one of us as equally important to our success. This was Rule 3.

Rule 3: If it don't sound like something that come out somebody mouth then it don't sound right. If it don't sound right then it ain't hardly right. Period.

This rule produced two weeks of compositions in which the students agonizingly tried to spell the sound of the Black English sentence they wanted to convey. But Black English is, preeminently, an oral/spoken means of communication. *And spelling don't talk.* So we needed Rule 4.

Rule 4: Forget about the spelling. Let the syntax carry you.

Once we arrived at Rule 4 we started to fly, because syntax, the structure of an idea, leads you to the world view of the speaker and reveals her values. The syntax of a sentence equals the structure of your consciousness. If we insisted that the language of Black English adheres to a distinctive Black syntax, then we were postulating a profound difference between White and Black people, *per se.* Was it a difference to prize or to obliterate?

There are three qualities of Black English — the presence of life, voice, and clarity — that intensify to a distinctive Black value system that we became excited about and self-consciously tried to maintain.

1. Black English has been produced by a pre-technocratic, if not anti-technological, culture. More, our culture has been constantly threatened by annihilation or, at least, the swallowed blurring of assimilation. Therefore, our

language is a system constructed by people constantly needing to insist that we exist, that we are present. Our language devolves from a culture that abhors all abstraction, or anything tending to obscure or delete the fact of the human being who is here and now/the truth of the person who is speaking or listening. Consequently, *there is no passive voice construction possible in Black English.* For example, you cannot say, "Black English is being eliminated." You must say, instead, "White people eliminating Black English." The assumption of the presence of life governs all of Black English. Therefore, overwhelmingly, *all action takes place in the language of the present indicative.* And every sentence assumes the living and active participation of at least two human beings, the speaker and the listener.

2. A primary consequence of the person-centered values of Black English is the delivery of voice. If you speak or write Black English, your ideas will necessarily possess that otherwise elusive attribute, *voice.*

3. One main benefit following from the person-centered values of Black English is that of *clarity.* If your idea, your sentence, assumes the presence of at least two living and active people, you will make it understandable, because the motivation behind every sentence is the wish to say something real to somebody real.

As the weeks piled up, translation from Standard English into Black English or vice versa occupied a hefty part of our course work. For example:

Standard English (hereafter S.E.): "In considering the idea of studying Black English those questioned suggested — "

(What's the subject? Where's the person? Is anybody alive in here, in that idea?"

Black English (hereafter B.E.): "I been asking people what you think about somebody studying Black English and they answer me like this:"

But there were interesting limits. You cannot "translate" instances of Standard English preoccupied with abstraction or with nothing/nobody evidently alive into Black English. That would warp the language into uses antithetical to the guiding perspective of its community of users. Rather you must first change those Standard English sentences, themselves, into ideas consistent with the person-centered assumptions of Black English.

GUIDELINES FOR BLACK ENGLISH

1. Minimal number of words for every idea: This is the source for the aphoristic and/or poetic force of the language; eliminate every possible word.

2. Clarity: If the sentence is not clear it's not Black English.

3. Eliminate use of the verb *to be* whenever possible. This leads to the deployment of more descriptive and, therefore, more precise verbs.

4. Use *be* or *been* only when you want to describe a chronic, ongoing state of things.
   He *be* at the office, by 9. (He is always at the office by 9.)
   He *been* with her since forever.

5. Zero copula: Always eliminate the verb *to be* whenever it could combine with another verb in Standard English.

   S.E.: She is going out with him.

   B.E.: She going out with him.

6. Eliminate *do* as in:

   S.E.: What do you think? What do you want?

   B.E.: What you think? What you want?

Rules number 3, 4, 5, and 6 provide for the use of the minimal number of verbs per idea, and, therefore, greater accuracy in the choice of verb.

7. In general, if you wish to say something really positive, try to formulate the idea using emphatic negative structure.

   S.E.: He's fabulous.

   B.E.: He bad.

8. Use double or triple negatives for dramatic emphasis.

   S.E.: Tina Turner sings out of this world.

   B.E.: Ain nobody sing like Tina.

9. Never use the *-ed* suffix to indicate the past tense of a verb.

   S.E.: She closed the door.

   B.E.: She close the door. Or, she have close the door.

10. Regardless of intentional verb time, only use the third person singular, present indicative, for use of the verb *to have,* as an auxiliary.

    S.E.: He had his wallet then he lost it.

    B.E.: He have him wallet then he lose it.

    S.E.: We had seen that movie.

    B.E.: We seen that movie. Or, we have see that movie.

11. Observe a minimal inflection of verbs. Particularly, never change from the first person singular forms to the third person singular.

    S.E.: Present Tense Forms: He goes to the store.

    B.E.: He go to the store.

    S.E.: Past Tense Forms: He went to the store.

    B.E.: He go to the store. Or, he gone to the store. Or, he been to the store.

12. The possessive case scarcely ever appears in Black English. Never use an apostrophe ('s) construction. If you wander into a possessive case component of an idea, then keep logically consistent: *ours, his, theirs, mines.* But, most likely, if you bump into such a component, you have wandered outside the underlying world view of Black English.

    S.E.: He will take their car tomorrow.

    B.E.: He taking they car tomorrow.

13. Plurality: Logical consistency, continued: If the modifier indicates plurality then the noun remains in the singular case.

    S.E.: He ate twelve doughnuts.

    B.E.: He eat twelve doughnut.

    S.E.: She has many books.

    B.E.: She have many book.

14. Listen for, or invent, special Black English forms of the past tense, such as: "He losted it. That what she felted." If they are clear and readily understood, then use them.

15. Do not hesitate to play with words, sometimes inventing them: e.g. "astro-potomous" means huge like a hippo plus astronomical and, therefore, signifies real big.

16. In Black English, unless you keenly want to underscore the past tense nature of an action, stay in the present tense and rely on the overall context of your ideas for the conveyance of time and sequence.

17. Never use the suffix -*ly* form of an adverb in Black English.
    S.E.: The rain came down rather quickly.
    B.E.: The rain come down pretty quick.

18. Never use the indefinite article *an* in Black English.
    S.E.: He wanted to ride an elephant.
    B.E.: He wanted to ride him a elephant.

19. Invariant syntax: in correct Black English it is possible to formulate an imperative, an interrogative, and a simple declarative idea with the same syntax:
    B.E.: You going to the store?
    You going to the store.
    You going to the store!

Where was Willie Jordan? We'd reached the mid-term of the semester. Students had formulated Black English guidelines, by consensus, and they were now writing with remarkable beauty, purpose, and enjoyment:

I ain hardly speakin for everybody but myself so understan that. (Kim Parks)

Samples from student writings:

Janie have a great big old hole inside her. Tea Cake the only thing that fit that hole. . . .

That pear tree beautiful to Janie, especial when bees fiddlin with the blossomin pear there growin large and lovely. But personal speakin, the love she get from starin at that tree ain the love what starin back at her in them relationship. (Monica Morris)

Love a big theme in, *They Eye Was Watching God.* Love show people new corners inside theyself. It pull out good stuff and stuff back bad stuff . . . Joe worship the doing uh his own hand and need other people to worship him too. But he ain't think about Janie that she a person and ought to live like anybody common do. Queen life not for Janie. (Monica Morris)

In both life and writin, Black womens have varietous experience of love that be cold like a iceberg or fiery like a inferno. Passion got for the other partner involve, man or women, seems as shallow, ankle-deep water or the most profoundest abyss. (Constance Evans)

Family love another bond that ain't never break under no pressure. (Constance Evans)

You know it really cold/When the friend you/Always get out the fire/Act like they don't know you/When you in the heat. (Constance Evans)

Big classroom discussion bout love at this time. I never take no class where us have any long arguin for and against for two or three day. New to me and great. I find the class time talkin a million time more interestin than detail bout the book. (Kathy Esseks)

As these examples suggest, Black English no longer limited the students, in any way. In fact, one of them, Philip Garfield, would shortly "translate" a pivotal scene from Ibsen's *A Doll's House,* as his final term paper:

Nora: I didn't gived no shit. I thinked you a asshole back then, too, you make it so hard for me save mines husband life.

Krogstad: Girl, it clear you ain't any idea what you done. You done exact what I once done, and I losed my reputation over it.

Nora: You asks me believe you once act brave save you wife like?

Krogstad: Law care less why you done it.

Nora: Law must suck.

Krogstad: Suck or no, if I wants, judge screw you wid dis paper.

Nora: No way, man. (Philip Garfield)

But where was Willie? Compulsively punctual, and always thoroughly prepared with neat typed compositions, he had disappeared. He failed to show up for our regularly scheduled conference, and I received neither a note nor a phone call of explanation. A whole week went by. I wondered if Willie had finally been captured by the extremely current happenings in South Africa: passage of a new constitution that did not enfranchise the Black majority, and militant Black South African reaction to that affront. I wondered if he'd been hurt, somewhere. I wondered if the serious workload of weekly readings and writings had over-whelmed him and changed his mind about independent study. Where was Willie Jordan?

One week after the first conference that Willie missed, he called: "Hello, Professor Jordan? This is Willie. I'm sorry I wasn't there last week. But something has come up and I'm pretty upset. I'm sorry but I really can't deal right now."

I asked Willie to drop by my office and just let me see that he was okay. He agreed to do that. When I saw him I knew something hideous had happened. Something had hurt him and scared him to the marrow. He was all agitated and stammering and terse and incoherent. At last, his sadly jumbled account let me surmise as follows: Brooklyn police had murdered his unarmed, twenty-five-year-old brother, Reggie Jordan. Neither Willie nor his elderly parents knew what to do about it. Nobody from the press was interested. His folks had no money. Police ran his family around and around, to no point. And Reggie was really dead. And Willie wanted to fight, but he felt helpless.

With Willie's permission I began to try to secure legal counsel for the Jordan family. Unfortunately, Black victims of police violence are truly numerous, while the resources available to prosecute their killers are truly scarce. A friend of mine at the Center for Constitutional Rights estimated that just the preparatory costs for bringing the cops into court normally approaches $180,000. Unless the execution of Reggie Jordan became a major community cause for organizing and protest, his murder would simply become a statistical item.

Again, with Willie's permission, I contacted every newspaper and media person I could think of. But the Bastone feature article in *The Village Voice* was the only result from that canvassing.

Again, with Willie's permission, I presented the case to my class in Black English. We had talked about the politics of language. We had talked about love and sex and child abuse and men and women. But the murder of Reggie Jordan broke like a hurricane across the room.

There are few "issues" as endemic to Black life as police violence. Most of the students knew and respected and liked Jordan. Many of them came from the very neighborhood where the murder had occurred. All of the students had known somebody close to them who had been killed by police, or had known frightening moments of gratuitous confrontation with the cops. They wanted to do everything at once to avenge death. Number One: They decided to compose a personal statement of condolence to Willie Jordan and his family, written in Black English. Number Two: They decided to compose individual messages to the police, in Black English. These should be prefaced by an explanatory paragraph composed by the entire group. Number Three: These individual messages, with their lead paragraph, should be sent to *Newsday*.

The morning after we agreed on these objectives, one of the young women students appeared with an unidentified visitor, who sat through the class, smiling in a peculiar, comfortable way.

Now we had to make more tactical decisions. Because we wanted the messages published, and because we thought it imperative that our outrage be known by the police, the tactical question was this: Should the opening, group paragraph be written in Black English or Standard English?

I have seldom been privy to a discussion with so much heart at the dead heat of it. I will never forget the eloquence, the sudden haltings of speech, the fierce struggle against tears, the furious throwaway, and useless explosions that this question elicited.

That one question contained several others, each of them extraordinarily painful to even contemplate. How best to serve the memory of Reggie Jordan? Should we use the language of the killer — Standard English — in order to make our ideas acceptable to those controlling the killers? But wouldn't what we had to say be rejected, summarily, if we said it in our own language, the language of the victim, Reggie Jordan? But if we sought to express ourselves by abandoning our language wouldn't that mean our suicide on top of Reggie's murder? But if we expressed ourselves in our own language wouldn't that be suicidal to the wish to communicate with those who, evidently, did not give a damn about us/Reggie/police violence in the Black community?

At the end of one of the longest, most difficult hours of my own life, the students voted, unanimously, to preface their individual messages with a paragraph composed in the language of Reggie Jordan. "*At least we don't give up nothing else. At least we stick to the truth: Be who we been. And stay all the way with Reggie.*"

It was heartbreaking to proceed, from that point. Everyone in the room realized that our decision in favor of Black English had doomed our writings, even as the distinctive reality of our Black lives always has doomed our efforts to "be who we been" in this country.

I went to the blackboard and took down this paragraph dictated by the class:

YOU COPS!

WE THE BROTHER AND SISTER OF WILLIE JORDAN, A FELLOW STONY BROOK STUDENT WHO THE BROTHER OF THE DEAD REGGIE JORDAN. REGGIE, LIKE MANY BROTHER AND SISTER, HE A VICTIM OF BRUTAL RACIST POLICE, OCTOBER 25, 1984. US APPALL, FED UP, BECAUSE THAT ANOTHER SENSELESS DEATH WHAT OCCUR IN OUR COMMUNITY. THIS WHAT WE FEEL, THIS, FROM OUR HEART, FOR WE AIN'T STAYIN' SILENT NO MORE:

With the completion of this introduction, nobody said anything. I asked for comments. At this invitation, the unidentified visitor, a young Black man, ceaselessly smiling, raised his hand. He was, it so happens, a rookie cop. He had just joined the force in September and, he said, he thought he should clarify a few things. So he came forward and sprawled easily into a posture of barroom, or fireside, nostalgia:

"See," Officer Charles enlightened us, "Most times when you out on the street and something come down you do one of two things. Over-react or under-react. Now, if you under-react then you can get yourself kilt. And if you over-react then maybe you kill somebody. Fortunately it's about nine times out of ten and you will over-react. So the brother got kilt. And I'm sorry about that, believe me. But what you have to understand is what kilt him: Over-reaction. That's all. Now you talk about Black people and White police but see, now, I'm a cop myself. And (big smile) I'm Black. And just a couple months ago I was on the other side. But it's the same for me. You a cop, you the ultimate authority: the Ultimate Authority. And you on the street, most of the time you can only do one of two things: over-react or under-react. That's all it is with the brother. Over-reaction. Didn't have nothing to do with race."

That morning Officer Charles had the good fortune to escape without being boiled alive. But barely. And I remember the pride of his smile when I read about the fate of Black policemen and other collaborators in South Africa. I remember him, and I remember the shock and palpable feeling of shame that filled the room. It was as though that foolish, and deadly, young man had just relieved himself of his foolish, and deadly, explanation, face to face with the grief of Reggie Jordan's father and Reggie Jordan's mother. Class ended quietly. I copied the paragraph from the blackboard, collected the individual messages and left to type them up.

Newsday rejected the piece.

The Village Voice could not find room in their "Letters" section to print the individual messages from the students to the police.

None of the TV news reporters picked up the story.

Nobody raised $180,000 to prosecute the murder of Reggie Jordan.
Reggie Jordan is really dead.

I asked Willie Jordan to write an essay pulling together everything important to him from that semester. He was still deeply beside himself with frustration and amazement and loss. This is what he wrote, unedited, and in its entirety:

> "Throughout the course of this semester I have been researching the effects of oppression and exploitation along racial lines in South Africa and its neighboring countries. I have become aware of South African police brutalization of native Africans beyond the extent of the law, even though the laws themselves are catalyst affliction upon Black men, women and children. Many Africans die each year as a result of the deliberate use of police force to protect the white power structure.

> Social control agents in South Africa, such as policemen, are also used to force compliance among citizens through both overt and covert tactics. It is not uncommon to find bold-faced coercion and cold-blooded killings of Blacks by South African police for undetermined and/or inadequate reasons. Perhaps the truth is that the only reasons for this heinous treatment of Blacks rests in racial differences. We should also understand that what is conveyed through the media is not always accurate and may sometimes be construed as the tip of the iceberg at best.

> I recently received a painful reminder that racism, poverty, and the abuse of power are global problems which are by no means unique to South Africa. On October 25, 1984 at approximately 3:00 p.m. my brother, Mr. Reginald Jordan, was shot and killed by two New York City policemen from the 75th precinct in the East New York section of Brooklyn. His life ended at the age of twenty-five. Even up to this current point in time the Police Department has failed to provide my family, which consists of five brothers, eight sisters, and two parents, with a plausible reason for Reggie's death. Out of the many stories that were given to my family by the Police Department, not one of them seems to hold water. In fact, I honestly believe that the Police Department's assessment of my brother's murder is nothing short of ABSOLUTE BULLSHIT, and thus far no evidence had been produced to alter perception of the situation.

> Furthermore, I believe that one of three cases may have occurred in this incident. First, Reggie's death may have been the desired outcome of the police officer's action, in which case the killing was premeditated. Or, it was a case of mistaken identity, which clarifies the fact that the two officers who killed my brother and their commanding parties are all grossly incompetent. Or, both of the above cases are correct, i.e., Reggie's murderers intended to kill him and the Police Department behaved insubordinately.

> Part of the argument of the officers who shot Reggie was that he had attacked one of them and took his gun. This was their major claim. They also said that only one of them had actually shot Reggie. The facts, however, speak for themselves. According to the Death Certificate and autopsy report, Reggie was shot eight times from point-blank range. The Doctor who performed the autopsy told me himself that two bullets entered the side of my brother's head, four bullets were sprayed into his back, and two bullets struck him in the back of his legs. It is obvious that unnecessary force was used by the police and that it is extremely difficult to shoot someone in his back when he is attacking or approaching you.

> After experiencing a situation like this and researching South Africa I believe that to a large degree, justice may only exist as rhetoric. I find it difficult to talk of true justice when the oppression of my people both at home and abroad attests to the fact that inequality and injustice are serious problems whereby Blacks and Third

World people are perpetually short-changed by society. Something has to be done about the way in which this world is set up. Although it is a difficult task, we do have the power to make a change."

— Willie J. Jordan Jr.
EGL 487, Section 58, November 14, 1984

It is my privilege to dedicate this book to the future life of Willie J. Jordan Jr. August 8, 1985.

NOTES

1. Black English aphorisms crafted by Monica Morris, a Junior at S.U.N.Y., Stony Brook, October 1984.
2. "English Is Spreading, But What Is English." A presentation by Professor S. N. Sridhar, Department of Linguistics, S.U.N.Y., Stony Brook, New York, April 9, 1985: Dean's Convocation Among the Disciplines.
3. Sridhar, "English Is Spreading."
4. "Report on Study by Linguists at the University of Pennsylvania," *New York Times*, March 15, 1985, p. 14.
5. Alice Walker, *The Color Purple* (New York: Harcourt Brace Jovanovich, 1982), p. 11.

Talking about Race, Learning about Racism: The Application of Racial Identity Development Theory in the Classroom

BEVERLY DANIEL TATUM

The inclusion of race-related content in college courses often generates emotional responses in students that range from guilt and shame to anger and despair. The discomfort associated with these emotions can lead students to resist the learning process. Based on her experience teaching a course on the psychology of racism and an application of racial identity development theory, Beverly Daniel Tatum identifies three major sources of student resistance to talking about race and learning about racism, as well as some strategies for overcoming this resistance.

As many educational institutions struggle to become more multicultural in terms of their students, faculty, and staff, they also begin to examine issues of cultural representation within their curriculum. Text examination has evoked a growing number of courses that give specific consideration to the effect of variables such as race, class, and gender on human experience — an important trend that is reflected and supported by the increasing availability of resource manuals for the modification of course content (Bronstein & Quina, 1988; Hull, Scott, & Smith, 1982; Schuster & Van Dyne, 1985).

Unfortunately, less attention has been given to the issues of process that inevitably emerge in the classroom when attention is focused on race, class, and/or gender. It is very difficult to talk about these concepts in a meaningful way without also talking and learning about racism, classism, and sexism.[1] The introduction of these issues of oppression often generates powerful emotional responses in students that range from guilt and shame to anger and despair. If not addressed, these emotional responses can result in student resistance to oppression-related content areas. Such resistance can ultimately interfere with the cognitive understanding and mastery of the material. This resistance and potential interference is particularly common when specifically addressing issues of race and racism. Yet, when students are given the opportunity to explore race-related material in a classroom where both their affective and intellectual responses are acknowledged and addressed, their level of understanding is greatly enhanced.

This chapter seeks to provide a framework for understanding students' psychological responses to race-related content and the student resistance that can result, as well as some strategies for overcoming this resistance. It is informed

Harvard Educational Review   Vol. 62   No. 1   Spring 1992, 1–24.

by more than a decade of experience as an African-American woman engaged in teaching an undergraduate course on the psychology of racism, by thematic analyses of student journals and essays written for the racism class, and by an understanding and application of racial identity development theory (Helms, 1990).

SETTING THE CONTEXT

As a clinical psychologist with a research interest in racial identity development among African-American youth raised in predominantly White communities, I began teaching about racism quite fortuitously. In 1980, while I was a part-time lecturer in the Black Studies department of a large public university, I was invited to teach a course called Group Exploration of Racism (Black Studies 2). A requirement for Black Studies majors, the course had to be offered, yet the instructor who regularly taught the course was no longer affiliated with the institution. Armed with a folder full of handouts, old syllabi that the previous instructor left behind, a copy of *White Awareness: Handbook for Anti-racism Training* (Katz, 1978), and my own clinical skills as a group facilitator, I constructed a course that seemed to meet the goals already outlined in the course catalogue. Designed "to provide students with an understanding of the psychological causes and emotional reality of racism as it appears in everyday life," the course incorporated the use of lectures, readings, simulation exercises, group research projects, and extensive class discussion to help students explore the psychological impact of racism on both the oppressor and the oppressed.

Though my first efforts were tentative, the results were powerful. The students in my class, most of whom were White, repeatedly described the course in their evaluations as one of the most valuable educational experiences of their college careers. I was convinced that helping students understand the ways in which racism operates in their own lives, and what they could do about it, was a social responsibility that I should accept. The freedom to institute the course in the curriculum of the psychology departments in which I would eventually teach became a personal condition of employment. I have successfully introduced the course in each new educational setting I have been in since leaving that university.

Since 1980, I have taught the course (now called the Psychology of Racism) eighteen times, at three different institutions. Although each of these schools is very different — a large public university, a small state college, and a private, elite women's college — the challenges of teaching about racism in each setting have been more similar than different.

In all of the settings, class size has been limited to thirty students (averaging twenty-four). Though typically predominantly White and female (even in coeducational settings), the class make-up has always been mixed in terms of both race and gender. The students of color who have taken the course include Asians and Latinos/as, but most frequently the students of color have been Black. Though most students have described themselves as middle class, all socioeconomic backgrounds (ranging from very poor to very wealthy) have been represented over the years.

The course has necessarily evolved in response to my own deepening awareness of the psychological legacy of racism and my expanding awareness of other forms of oppression, although the basic format has remained the same. Our weekly three-hour class meeting is held in a room with movable chairs, arranged in a circle. The physical structure communicates an important premise of the course — that I expect the students to speak with each other as well as with me.

My other expectations (timely completion of assignments, regular class attendance) are clearly communicated in our first class meeting, along with the assumptions and guidelines for discussion that I rely upon to guide our work together. Because the assumptions and guidelines are so central to the process of talking and learning about racism, it may be useful to outline them here.

Working Assumptions

1. Racism, defined as a "system of advantage based on race" (see Wellman, 1977), is a pervasive aspect of U.S. socialization. It is virtually impossible to live in contemporary U.S. society and not be exposed to some aspect of the personal, cultural, and/or institutional manifestations of racism in our society. It is also assumed that, as a result, all of us have received some misinformation about those groups disadvantaged by racism.

2. Prejudice, defined as a "preconceived judgment or opinion, often based on limited information," is clearly distinguished from racism (see Katz, 1978). I assume that all of us may have prejudices as a result of the various cultural stereotypes to which we have been exposed. Even when these preconceived ideas have positive associations (such as "Asian students are good in math"), they have negative effects because they deny a person's individuality. These attitudes may influence the individual behaviors of people of color as well as of Whites, and may affect intergroup as well as intragroup interaction. However, a distinction must be made between the negative racial attitudes held by individuals of color and White individuals, because it is only the attitudes of Whites that routinely carry with them the social power inherent in the systematic cultural reinforcement and institutionalization of those racial prejudices. To distinguish the prejudices of students of color from the racism of White students is *not* to say that the former is acceptable and the latter is not; both are clearly problematic. The distinction is important, however, to identify the power differential between members of dominant and subordinate groups.

3. In the context of U.S. society, the system of advantage clearly operates to benefit Whites as a group. However, it is assumed that racism, like other forms of oppression, hurts members of the privileged group as well as those targeted by racism. While the impact of racism on Whites is clearly different from its impact on people of color, racism has negative ramifications for everyone. For example, some White students might remember the pain of having lost important relationships because Black friends were not allowed to visit their homes. Others may express sadness at having been denied access to a broad range of experiences because of social segregation. These individuals often attribute the discomfort or fear they now experience in racially mixed settings to the cultural limitations of their youth.

4. Because of the prejudice and racism inherent in our environments when we were children, I assume that we cannot be blamed for learning what we were

taught (intentionally or unintentionally). Yet as adults, we have a responsibility to try to identify and interrupt the cycle of oppression. When we recognize that we have been misinformed, we have a responsibility to seek out more accurate information and to adjust our behavior accordingly.

5. It is assumed that change, both individual and institutional, is possible. Understanding and unlearning prejudice and racism is a lifelong process that may have begun prior to enrolling in this class, and which will surely continue after the course is over. Each of us may be at a different point in that process, and I assume that we will have mutual respect for each other, regardless of where we perceive one another to be.

To facilitate further our work together, I ask students to honor the following guidelines for our discussion. Specifically, I ask students to demonstrate their respect for one another by honoring the confidentiality of the group. So that students may feel free to ask potentially awkward or embarrassing questions, or share race-related experiences, I ask that students refrain from making personal attributions when discussing the course content with their friends. I also discourage the use of "zaps," overt or covert put-downs often used as comic relief when someone is feeling anxious about the content of the discussion. Finally, students are asked to speak from their own experience, to say, for example, "I think . . ." or "In my experience, I have found . . ." rather than generalizing their experience to others, as in "People say. . .".

Many students are reassured by the climate of safety that is created by these guidelines and find comfort in the nonblaming assumptions I outline for the class. Nevertheless, my experience has been that most students, regardless of their class and ethnic background, still find racism a difficult topic to discuss, as is revealed by these journal comments written after the first class meeting (all names are pseudonyms):

> The class is called Psychology of Racism, the atmosphere is friendly and open, yet I feel very closed in. I feel guilt and doubt well up inside me. (Tiffany, a White woman)

> Class has started on a good note thus far. The class seems rather large and disturbs me. In a class of this nature, I expect there will be many painful and emotional moments. (Linda, an Asian woman)

> I am a little nervous that as one of the few students of color in the class people are going to be looking at me for answers, or whatever other reasons. The thought of this inhibits me a great deal. (Louise, an African-American woman)

> I had never thought about my social position as being totally dominant. There wasn't one area in which I wasn't in the dominant group. . . . I first felt embarrassed. . . . Through association alone I felt in many ways responsible for the unequal condition existing in the world. This made me feel like shrinking in a hole in a class where I was surrounded by 27 women and 2 men, one of whom was Black and the other was Jewish. I felt that all these people would be justified in venting their anger upon me. After a short period, I realized that no one in the room was attacking or even blaming me for the conditions that exist. (Carl, a White man)

Even though most of my students voluntarily enroll in the course as an elective, their anxiety and subsequent resistance to learning about racism quickly emerge.

SOURCES OF RESISTANCE

In predominantly White college classrooms, I have experienced at least three major sources of student resistance to talking and learning about race and racism. They can be readily identified as the following:

1. Race is considered a taboo topic for discussion, especially in racially mixed settings.
2. Many students, regardless of racial-group membership, have been socialized to think of the United States as a just society.
3. Many students, particularly White students, initially deny any personal prejudice, recognizing the impact of racism on other people's lives, but failing to acknowledge its impact on their own.

Race as a Taboo Topic

The first source of resistance, race as a taboo topic, is an essential obstacle to overcome if class discussion is to begin at all. Although many students are interested in the topic, they are often most interested in hearing other people talk about it, afraid to break the taboo themselves.

One source of this self-consciousness can be seen in the early childhood experiences of many students. It is known that children as young as three years old notice racial differences (see Phinney & Rotheram, 1987). Certainly preschoolers talk about what they see. Unfortunately, they often do so in ways that make adults uncomfortable. Imagine the following scenario: A White child in a public place points to a dark-skinned African-American child and says loudly, "Why is that boy Black?" The embarrassed parent quickly responds, "Sh! Don't say that." The child is only attempting to make sense of a new observation (Derman-Sparks, Higa, & Sparks, 1980), yet the parent's attempt to silence the perplexed child sends a message that this observation is not okay to talk about. White children quickly become aware that their questions about race raise adult anxiety, and as a result, they learn not to ask questions.

When asked to reflect on their earliest race-related memories and the feelings associated with them, both White students and students of color often report feelings of confusion, anxiety, and/or fear. Students of color often have early memories of name-calling or other negative interactions with other children, and sometimes with adults. They also report having had questions that went both unasked and unanswered. In addition, many students have had uncomfortable interchanges around race-related topics as adults. When asked at the beginning of the semester, "How many of you have had difficult, perhaps heated conversations with someone on a race-related topic?" routinely almost everyone in the class raises his or her hand. It should come as no surprise then that students often approach the topic of race and/or racism with both curiosity and trepidation.

The Myth of the Meritocracy

The second source of student resistance to be discussed here is rooted in students' belief that the United States is a just society, a meritocracy where individual efforts are fairly rewarded. While some students (particularly students of color) may already have become disillusioned with that notion of the United States, the majority of my students who have experienced at least the personal success of college acceptance still have faith in this notion. To the extent that these students acknowledge that racism exists, they tend to view it as an individual phenomenon, rooted in the attitudes of the "Archie Bunkers" of the world or located only in particular parts of the country.

After several class meetings, Karen, a White woman, acknowledged this attitude in her journal:

> At one point in my life — the beginning of this class — I actually perceived America to be a relatively racist free society. I thought that the people who were racist or subjected to racist stereotypes were found only in small pockets of the U.S., such as the South. As I've come to realize, racism (or at least racially orientated stereotypes) is rampant.

An understanding of racism as a system of advantage presents a serious challenge to the notion of the United States as a just society where rewards are based solely on one's merit. Such a challenge often creates discomfort in students. The old adage "ignorance is bliss" seems to hold true in this case; students are not necessarily eager to recognize the painful reality of racism.

One common response to the discomfort is to engage in denial of what they are learning. White students in particular may question the accuracy or currency of statistical information regarding the prevalence of discrimination (housing, employment, access to health care, and so on). More qualitative data, such as autobiographical accounts of experiences with racism, may be challenged on the basis of their subjectivity.

It should be pointed out that the basic assumption that the United States is a just society for all is only one of many basic assumptions that might be challenged in the learning process. Another example can be seen in an interchange between two White students following a discussion about cultural racism, in which the omission or distortion of historical information about people of color was offered as an example of the cultural transmission of racism.

"Yeah, I just found out that Cleopatra was actually a Black woman."

"What?"

The first student went on to explain her newly learned information. Finally, the second student exclaimed in disbelief, "That can't be true. Cleopatra was beautiful!" This new information and her own deeply ingrained assumptions about who is beautiful and who is not were too incongruous to allow her to assimilate the information at that moment.

If outright denial of information is not possible, then withdrawal may be. Physical withdrawal in the form of absenteeism is one possible result; it is for precisely this reason that class attendance is mandatory. The reduction in the completion of reading and/or written assignments is another form of withdrawal. I have found this response to be so common that I now alert students to this possibility at the beginning of the semester. Knowing that this response is a common one seems to help students stay engaged, even when they experience the desire to withdraw.

Following an absence in the fifth week of the semester, one White student wrote, "I think I've hit the point you talked about, the point where you don't want to hear any more about racism. I sometimes begin to get the feeling we are all hypersensitive." (Two weeks later she wrote, "Class is getting better. I think I am beginning to get over my hump.")

Perhaps not surprisingly, this response can be found in both White students and students of color. Students of color often enter a discussion of racism with some awareness of the issue, based on personal experiences. However, even these students find that they did not have a full understanding of the widespread impact of racism in our society. For students who are targeted by racism, an increased awareness of the impact in and on their lives is painful, and often generates anger.

Four weeks into the semester, Louise, an African-American woman, wrote in her journal about her own heightened sensitivity:

> Many times in class I feel uncomfortable when White students use the term Black because even if they aren't aware of it they say it with all or at least a lot of the negative connotations they've been taught goes along with Black. Sometimes it just causes a stinging feeling inside of me. Sometimes I get real tired of hearing White people talk about the conditions of Black people. I think it's an important thing for them to talk about, but still I don't always like being around when they do it. I also get tired of hearing them talk about how hard it is for them, though I under-stand it, and most times I am very willing to listen and be open, but sometimes I can't. Right now I can't.

For White students, advantaged by racism, a heightened awareness of it often generates painful feelings of guilt. The following responses are typical:

> After reading the article about privilege, I felt very guilty. (Rachel, a White woman)

> Questions of racism are so full of anger and pain. When I think of all the pain White people have caused people of color, I get a feeling of guilt. How could someone like myself care so much about the color of someone's skin that they would do them harm? (Terri, a White woman)

White students also sometimes express a sense of betrayal when they realize the gaps in their own education about racism. After seeing the first episode of the documentary series "Eyes on the Prize," Chris, a White man, wrote:

> I never knew it was really that bad just 35 years ago. Why didn't I learn this in elementary or high school? Could it be that the White people of America want to forget this injustice? . . . I will never forget that movie for as long as I live. It was like a big slap in the face.

Barbara, a White woman, also felt anger and embarrassment in response to her own previous lack of information about the internment of Japanese Ameri-cans during World War II. She wrote:

> I feel so stupid because I never even knew that these existed. I never knew that the Japanese were treated so poorly. I am becoming angry and upset about all of the things that I do not know. I have been so sheltered. My parents never wanted to let me know about the bad things that have happened in the world. After I saw the movie (*Mitsuye and Nellie*), I even called them up to ask them why they never told

me this. . . . I am angry at them too for not teaching me and exposing me to the complete picture of my country.

Avoiding the subject matter is one way to avoid these uncomfortable feelings.

"I'm Not Racist, But . . ."

A third source of student resistance (particularly among White students) is the initial denial of any personal connection to racism. When asked why they have decided to enroll in a course on racism, White students typically explain their interest in the topic with such disclaimers as, "I'm not racist myself, but I know people who are, and I want to understand them better."

Because of their position as the targets of racism, students of color do not typically focus on their own prejudices or lack of them. Instead they usually express a desire to understand why racism exists, and how they have been affected by it.

However, as all students gain a better grasp of what racism is and its many manifestations in U.S. society, they inevitably start to recognize its legacy within themselves. Beliefs, attitudes, and actions based on racial stereotypes begin to be remembered and are newly observed by White students. Students of color as well often recognize negative attitudes they may have internalized about their own racial group or that they have believed about others. Those who previously thought themselves immune to the effects of growing up in a racist society often find themselves reliving uncomfortable feelings of guilt or anger.

After taping her own responses to a questionnaire on racial attitudes, Barbara, a White woman previously quoted, wrote:

> I always want to think of myself as open to all races. Yet when I did the interview to myself, I found that I did respond differently to the same questions about different races. No one could ever have told me that I would have. I would have denied it. But I found that I did respond differently even though I didn't want to. This really upset me. I was angry with myself because I thought I was not prejudiced and yet the stereotypes that I had created had an impact on the answers that I gave even though I didn't want it to happen.

The new self-awareness, represented here by Barbara's journal entry, changes the classroom dynamic. One common result is that some White students, once perhaps active participants in class discussion, now hesitate to continue their participation for fear that their newly recognized racism will be revealed to others.

> Today I did feel guilty, and like I had to watch what I was saying (make it good enough), I guess to prove I'm really *not* prejudiced. From the conversations the first day, I guess this is a normal enough reaction, but I certainly never expected it in me. (Joanne, a White woman)

This withdrawal on the part of White students is often paralleled by an increase in participation by students of color who are seeking an outlet for what are often feelings of anger. The withdrawal of some previously vocal White students from the classroom exchange, however, is sometimes interpreted by students of color as indifference. This perceived indifference often serves to fuel the anger and frustration that many students of color experience, as awareness of their own oppression is heightened. For example, Robert, an African-American man, wrote:

> I really wish the White students would talk more. When I read these articles, it makes me so mad and I really want to know what the White kids think. Don't they care?

Sonia, a Latina, described the classroom tension from another perspective:

> I would like to comment that at many points in the discussions I have felt uncomfortable and sometimes even angry with people. I guess I am at the stage where I am tired of listening to Whites feel guilty and watch their eyes fill up with tears. I do understand that everyone is at their own stage of development and I even tell myself every Tuesday that these people have come to this class by choice. Some days I am just more tolerant than others. . . . It takes courage to say things in that room with so many women of color present. It also takes courage for the women of color to say things about Whites.

What seems to be happening in the classroom at such moments is a collision of developmental processes that can be inherently useful for the racial identity development of the individuals involved. Nevertheless, the interaction may be perceived as problematic to instructors and students who are unfamiliar with the process. Although space does not allow for an exhaustive discussion of racial identity development theory, a brief explication of it here will provide additional clarity regarding the classroom dynamics when issues of race are discussed. It will also provide a theoretical framework for the strategies for dealing with student resistance that will be discussed at the conclusion of this chapter.

STAGES OF RACIAL IDENTITY DEVELOPMENT

Racial identity and racial identity development theory are defined by Janet Helms (1990) as

> a sense of group or collective identity based on one's *perception* that he or she shares a common racial heritage with a particular racial group. . . . Racial identity development theory concerns the psychological implications of racial-group membership, that is belief systems that evolve in reaction to perceived differential racial-group membership. (p. 3)

It is assumed that in a society where racial-group membership is emphasized, the development of a racial identity will occur in some form in everyone. Given the dominant/subordinate relationship of Whites and people of color in this society, however, it is not surprising that this developmental process will unfold in different ways. For purposes of this discussion, William Cross's (1971, 1978) model of Black identity development will be described along with Helms's (1990) model of White racial identity development theory. While the identity development of other students (Asian, Latino/a, Native American) is not included in this particular theoretical formulation, there is evidence to suggest that the process for these oppressed groups is similar to that described for African Americans (Highlen et al., 1988; Phinney, 1990).[2] In each case, it is assumed that a positive sense of one's self as a member of one's group (which is not based on any assumed superiority) is important for psychological health.

Black Racial Identity Development

According to Cross's (1971, 1978, 1991) model of Black racial identity development, there are five stages in the process, identified as Preencounter, Encounter, Immersion/Emersion, Internalization, and Internalization-Commitment. In the first stage of Preencounter, the African American has absorbed many of the beliefs and values of the dominant White culture, including the notion that "White is right" and "Black is wrong." Though the internalization of negative Black Stereotypes may be outside of his or her conscious awareness, the individual seeks to assimilate and be accepted by Whites, and actively or passively distances him/herself from other Blacks.[3]

Louise, an African-American woman previously quoted, captured the essence of this stage in the following description of herself at an earlier time:

> For a long time it seemed as if I didn't remember my background, and I guess in some ways I didn't. I was never taught to be proud of my African heritage. Like we talked about in class, I went through a very long stage of identifying with my oppressors. Wanting to be like, live like, and be accepted by them. Even to the point of hating my own race and myself for being a part of it. Now I am ashamed that I ever was ashamed. I lost so much of myself in my denial of and refusal to accept my people.

In order to maintain psychological comfort at this stage of development, Helms writes:

> The person must maintain the fiction that race and racial indoctrination have nothing to do with how he or she lives life. It is probably the case that the Preencounter person is bombarded on a regular basis with information that he or she cannot really be a member of the "in" racial group, but relies on denial to selectively screen such information from awareness. (1990, p. 23)

This de-emphasis on one's racial-group membership may allow the individual to think that race has not been or will not be a relevant factor in one's own achievement, and may contribute to the belief in a U.S. meritocracy that is often a part of a Preencounter worldview.

Movement into the Encounter phase is typically precipitated by an event or series of events that forces the individual to acknowledge the impact of racism in one's life. For example, instances of social rejection by White friends or colleagues (or reading new personally relevant information about racism) may lead the individual to the conclusion that many Whites will not view him or her as an equal. Faced with the reality that he or she cannot truly be White, the individual is forced to focus on his or her identity as a member of a group targeted by racism.

Brenda, a Korean-American student, described her own experience of this process as a result of her participation in the racism course:

> I feel that because of this class, I have become much more aware of racism that exists around. Because of my awareness of racism, I am now bothered by acts and behaviors that might not have bothered me in the past. Before when racial comments were said around me I would somehow ignore it and pretend that nothing was said. By ignoring comments such as these, I was protecting myself. It became sort of a defense mechanism. I never realized I did this, until I was confronted with

stories that were found in our reading, by other people of color, who also ignored comments that bothered them. In realizing that there is racism out in the world and that there are comments concerning race that are directed towards me, I feel as if I have reached the first step. I also think I have reached the second step, because I am now bothered and irritated by such comments. I no longer ignore them, but now confront them.

The Immersion/Emersion stage is characterized by the simultaneous desire to surround oneself with visible symbols of one's racial identity and an active avoidance of symbols of Whiteness. As Thomas Parham describes, "At this stage, everything of value in life must be Black or relevant to Blackness. This stage is also characterized by a tendency to denigrate White people, simultaneously glorifying Black people. . . ." (1989, p. 190). The previously described anger that emerges in class among African-American students and other students of color in the process of learning about racism may be seen as part of the transition through these stages.

As individuals enter the Immersion stage, they actively seek out opportunities to explore aspects of their own history and culture with the support of peers from their own racial background. Typically, White-focused anger dissipates during this phase because so much of the person's energy is directed toward his or her own group- and self-exploration. The result of this exploration is an emerging security in a newly defined and affirmed sense of self.

Sharon, another African-American woman, described herself at the beginning of the semester as angry, seemingly in the Encounter stage of development. She wrote after our class meeting:

> Another point that I must put down is that before I entered class today I was angry about the way Black people have been treated in this country. I don't think I will easily overcome that and I basically feel justified in my feelings.

At the end of the semester, Sharon had joined with two other Black students in the class to work on their final class project. She observed that the three of them had planned their project to focus on Black people specifically, suggesting movement into the Immersion stage of racial identity development. She wrote:

> We are concerned about the well-being of our own people. They cannot be well if they have this pinned-up hatred for their own people. This internalized racism is something that we all felt, at various times, needed to be talked about. This semester it has really been important to me, and I believe Gordon [a Black classmate], too.

The emergence from this stage marks the beginning of Internalization. Secure in one's own sense of racial identity, there is less need to assert the "Blacker than thou" attitude often characteristic of the Immersion stage (Parham, 1989). In general, "pro-Black attitudes become more expansive, open, and less defensive" (Cross, 1971, p. 24). While still maintaining his or her connections with Black peers, the internalized individual is willing to establish meaningful relationships with Whites who acknowledge and are respectful of his or her self-definition. The individual is also ready to build coalitions with members of other oppressed groups. At the end of the semester, Brenda, a Korean American, concluded that she had in fact internalized a positive sense of racial identity. The process she described parallels the stages described by Cross:

sponses of White students to race-related content are characteristic of the transition from the Contact to the Disintegration stage of development.

Helms (1990) describes another response to the discomfort of Disintegration, which involves attempts to change significant others' attitudes toward African Americans and other people of color. However, as she points out,

> due to the racial naivete with which this approach may be undertaken and the person's ambivalent racial identification, this dissonance-reducing strategy is likely to be met with rejection by Whites as well as Blacks. (p. 59)

In fact, this response is also frequently observed among White students who have an opportunity to talk with friends and family during holiday visits. Suddenly they are noticing the racist content of jokes or comments of their friends and relatives and will try to confront them, often only to find that their efforts are, at best, ignored or dismissed as a "phase," or, at worst, greeted with open hostility.

Carl, a White male previously quoted, wrote at length about this dilemma:

> I realized that it was possible to simply go through life totally oblivious to the entire situation or, even if one realizes it, one can totally repress it. It is easy to fade into the woodwork, run with the rest of society, and never have to deal with these problems. So many people I know from home are like this. They have simply accepted what society has taught them with little, if any, question. My father is a prime example of this. . . . It has caused much friction in our relationship, and he often tells me as a father he has failed in raising me correctly. Most of my high school friends will never deal with these issues and propagate them on to their own children. It's easy to see how the cycle continues. I don't think I could ever justify within myself simply turning my back on the problem. I finally realized that my position in all of these dominant groups gives me power to make change occur. . . . It is an unfortunate result often though that I feel alienated from friends and family. It's often played off as a mere stage that I'm going through. I obviously can't tell if it's merely a stage, but I know that they say this to take the attention off of the truth of what I'm saying. By belittling me, they take the power out of my argument. It's very depressing that being compassionate and considerate are seen as only phases that people go through. I don't want it to be a phase for me, but as obvious as this may sound, I look at my environment and often wonder how it will not be.

The societal pressure to accept the status quo may lead the individual from Disintegration to Reintegration. At this point the desire to be accepted by one's own racial group, in which the overt or covert belief in White superiority is so prevalent, may lead to a reshaping of the person's belief system to be more congruent with an acceptance of racism. The guilt and anxiety associated with Disintegration may be redirected in the form of fear and anger directed toward people of color (particularly Blacks), who are now blamed as the source of discomfort.

Connie, a White woman of Italian ancestry, in many ways exemplified the progression from the Contact stage to Reintegration, a process she herself described seven weeks into the semester. After reading about the stages of White identity development, she wrote:

> I think mostly I can find myself in the disintegration stage of development. . . .
> There was a time when I never considered myself a color. I never described myself

as a "White, Italian female" until I got to college and noticed that people of color always described themselves by their color/race. While taking this class, I have begun to understand that being White makes a difference. I never thought about it before but there are many privileges to being White. In my personal life, I cannot say that I have ever felt that I have had the advantage over a Black person, but I am aware that my race has the advantage.

I am feeling really guilty lately about that. I find myself thinking: "I didn't mean to be White, I really didn't mean it." I am starting to feel angry towards my race for ever using this advantage towards personal gains. But at the same time I resent the minority groups. I mean, it's not our fault that society has deemed us "superior." I don't feel any better than a Black person. But it really doesn't matter because I am a member of the dominant race. . . . I can't help it . . . and I sometimes get angry and feel like I'm being attacked.

I guess my anger toward a minority group would enter me into the next stage of Reintegration, where I am once again starting to blame the victim. This is all very trying for me and it has been on my mind a lot. I really would like to be able to reach the last stage, autonomy, where I can accept being White without hostility and anger. That is really hard to do.

Helms (1990) suggests that it is relatively easy for Whites to become stuck at the Reintegration stage of development, particularly if avoidance of people of color is possible. However, if there is a catalyst for continued self-examination, the person "begins to question her or his previous definition of Whiteness and the justifiability of racism in any of its forms. . . ." (p. 61). In my experience, continued participation in a course on racism provides the catalyst for this deeper self-examination.

This process was again exemplified by Connie. At the end of the semester, she listened to her own taped interview of her racial attributes that she had recorded at the beginning of the semester. She wrote:

Oh wow! I could not believe some of the things that I said. I was obviously in different stages of the White identity development. As I listened and got more and more disgusted with myself when I was at the Reintegration stage, I tried to remind myself that these are stages that all (most) White people go through when dealing with notions of racism. I can remember clearly the resentment I had for people of color. I feel the one thing I enjoyed from listening to my interview was noticing how much I have changed. I think I am finally out of the Reintegration stage. I am beginning to make a conscious effort to seek out information about people of color and accept their criticism. . . . I still feel guilty about the feeling I had about people of color and I always feel bad about being privileged as a result of racism. But I am glad that I have reached what I feel is the Pseudo-Independent stage of White identity development.

The information-seeking that Connie describes often marks the onset of the Pseudo-Independent stage. At this stage, the individual is abandoning beliefs in White superiority, but may still behave in ways that unintentionally perpetuate the system. Looking to those targeted by racism to help him or her understand racism, the White person often tries to disavow his or her own Whiteness through active affiliation with Blacks, for example. The individual experiences a sense of alienation from other Whites who have not yet begun to examine their own racism, yet may also experience rejection from Blacks or other people of color who are suspicious of his or her motives. Students of color moving from the Encounter to the Immersion phase of their own racial identity development may be particularly unreceptive to the White person's attempts to connect with them.

Uncomfortable with his or her own Whiteness, yet unable to be truly anything else, the individual may begin searching for a new, more comfortable way to be White. This search is characteristic of the Immersion/Emersion stage of development. Just as the Black student seeks to redefine positively what it means to be of American ancestry in the United States through immersion in accurate information about one's culture and history, the White individual seeks to replace racially related myths and stereotypes with accurate information about what it means and has meant to be White in U.S. society (Helms, 1990). Learning about Whites who have been antiracist allies to people of color is a very important part of this process.

After reading articles written by antiracist activists describing their own process of unlearning racism, White students often comment on how helpful it is to know that others have experienced similar feelings and have found ways to resist the racism in their environments.[5] For example, Joanne, a White woman who initially experienced a lot of guilt, wrote:

> This article helped me out in many ways. I've been feeling helpless and frustrated. I know there are all these terrible things going on and I want to be able to do something. . . . Anyway this article helped me realize, again, that others feel this way, and gave me some positive ideas to resolve my dominant class guilt and shame.

Finally, reading the biographies and autobiographies of White individuals who have embarked on a similar process of identity development (such as Barnard, 1987) provides White students with important models for change.

Learning about White antiracists can also provide students of color with a sense of hope that they can have White allies. After hearing a White antiracist activist address the class, Sonia, a Latina who had written about her impatience with expressions of White guilt, wrote:

> I don't know when I have been more impressed by anyone. She filled me with hope for the future. She made me believe that there are good people in the world and that Whites suffer too and want to change things.

For White students, the internalization of a newly defined sense of oneself as White is the primary task of the Autonomy stage. The positive feelings associated with this redefinition energize the person's efforts to confront racism and oppression in his or her daily life. Alliances with people of color can be more easily forged at this stage of development than previously because the person's antiracist behaviors and attitudes will be more consistently expressed. While Autonomy might be described as "racial self-actualization, . . . it is best to think of it as an ongoing process . . . wherein the person is continually open to new information and new ways of thinking about racial and cultural variables" (Helms, 1990, p. 66).

Annette, a White woman, described herself in the Autonomy stage, but talked at length about the circular process she felt she had been engaged in during the semester:

> If people as racist as C. P. Ellis (a former Klansman) can change, I think anyone can change. If that makes me idealistic, fine. I do not think my expecting society

to change is naive anymore because I now *know* exactly what I want. To be naive means a lack of knowledge that allows me to accept myself both as a White person and as an idealist. This class showed me that these two are not mutually exclusive but are an integral part of me that I cannot deny. I realize now that through most of this class I was trying to deny both of them.

While I was not accepting society's racism, I was accepting society's telling me as a White person, there was nothing I could do to change racism. So, I told myself I was being naive and tried to suppress my desire to change society. This is what made me so frustrated — while I saw society's racism through examples in the readings and the media, I kept telling myself there was nothing I could do. Listening to my tape, I think I was already in the Autonomy stage when I started this class. I then seemed to decide that being White, I also had to be racist which is when I became frustrated and went back to the Disintegration stage. I was frustrated because I was not only telling myself there was nothing I could do but I also was assuming society's racism was my own which made me feel like I did not want to be White. Actually, it was not being White that I was disavowing but being racist. I think I have now returned to the Autonomy stage and am much more secure in my position there. I accept my Whiteness now as just a part of me as is my idealism. I will no longer disavow these characteristics as I have realized I can be proud of both of them. In turn, I can now truly accept other people for their unique characteristics and not by the labels society has given them as I can accept myself that way.

While I thought the main ideas that I learned in this class were that White people need to be educated to end racism and everyone should be treated as human beings, I really had already incorporated these ideas into my thoughts. What I learned from this class is being White does not mean being racist and being idealistic does not mean being naive. I really did not have to form new ideas about people of color; I had to form them about myself — and I did.

IMPLICATIONS FOR CLASSROOM TEACHING

Although movement through all the stages of racial identity development will not necessarily occur for each student within the course of a semester (or even four years of college), it is certainly common to witness beginning transformations in classes with race-related content. An awareness of the existence of this process has helped me to implement strategies to facilitate positive student development, as well as to improve interracial dialogue within the classroom.

Four strategies for reducing student resistance and promoting student development that I have found useful are the following:

1. the creation of a safe classroom atmosphere by establishing clear guidelines for discussion;
2. the creation of opportunities for self-generated knowledge;
3. the provision of an appropriate developmental model that students can use as a framework for understanding their own process;
4. the exploration of strategies the empower students as change agents.

Creating a Safe Climate

As was discussed earlier, making the classroom a safe space for discussion is essential for overcoming students' fears about breaking the race taboo, and will also reduce later anxieties about exposing one's own internalized racism. Establishing the guidelines of confidentiality, mutual respect, "no zaps," and speaking from one's own experience on the first day of class is a necessary step in the process.

Students respond very positively to these ground rules, and do try to honor them. While the rules do not totally eliminate anxiety, they clearly communicate to students that there is a safety net for the discussion. Students are also encouraged to direct their comments and questions to each other rather than always focusing their attention on me as the instructor, and to learn each other's names rather than referring to each other as "he," "she," or "the person in the red sweater" when responding to each other.[6]

The Power of Self-Generated Knowledge

The creation of opportunities for self-generated knowledge on the part of students is a powerful tool for reducing the initial stage of denial that many students experience. While it may seem easy for some students to challenge the validity of what they read or what the instructor says, it is harder to deny what they have seen with their own eyes. Students can be given hands-on assignments outside of class to facilitate this process.

For example, after reading *Portraits of White Racism* (Wellman, 1977), some students expressed the belief that the attitudes expressed by the White interviewees in the book were no longer commonly held attitudes. Students were then asked to use the same interview protocol used in the book (with some revision) to interview a White adult of their choice. When students reported on these interviews in class, their own observation of the similarity between those they had interviewed and those they had read about was more convincing than anything I might have said.

After doing her interview, Patty, a usually quiet White student, wrote:

> I think I learned a lot from it and that I'm finally getting a better grip on the idea of racism. I think that was why I participated so much in class. I really felt like I knew what I was talking about.

Other examples of creating opportunities for self-generated knowledge include assigning students the task of visiting grocery stores in neighborhoods of differing racial composition to compare the cost and quality of goods and services available at the two locations, and to observe the interactions between the shoppers and the store personnel. For White students, one of the most powerful assignments of this type has been to go apartment hunting with an African-American student and to experience housing discrimination firsthand. While one concern with such an assignment is the effect it will have on the student(s) of color involved, I have found that those Black students who choose this assignment rather than another are typically eager to have their White classmates experience the reality of racism, and thus participate quite willingly in the process.

Naming the Problem

The emotional responses that students have to talking and learning about racism are quite predictable and related to their own racial identity development. Unfortunately, students typically do not know this; thus they consider their own guilt, shame, embarrassment, or anger an uncomfortable experience that they alone are having. Informing students at the beginning of the semester that these feelings may be part of the learning process is ethically necessary (in the sense of informed consent), and helps to normalize the students' experience. Knowing in advance that a desire to withdraw from classroom discussion or not to complete assignments is a common response helps students to remain engaged when they reach that point. As Alice, a White woman, wrote at the end of the semester:

> You were so right in saying in the beginning how we would grow tired of racism (I did in October) but then it would get so good! I have *loved* the class once I passed that point.

In addition, sharing the model of racial identity development with students gives them a useful framework for understanding each other's processes as well as their own. This cognitive framework does not necessarily prevent the collision of developmental processes previously described, but it does allow students to be less frightened by it when it occurs. If, for example, White students understand the stages of racial identity development for students of color, they are less likely to personalize or feel threatened by an African-American student's anger.

Connie, a White student who initially expressed a lot of resentment at the way students of color tended to congregate in the college cafeteria, was much more understanding of this behavior after she learned about racial identity development theory. She wrote:

> I learned a lot from reading the article about the stages of development in the model of oppressed people. As a White person going through my stages of identity development, I do not take time to think about the struggle people of color go through to reach a stage of complete understanding. I am glad that I know about the stages because now I can understand people of color's behavior in certain situations. For example, when people of color stay to themselves and appear to be in a clique, it is not because they are being rude as I originally thought. Rather they are engaged perhaps in the Immersion stage.

Mary, another White student, wrote:

> I found the entire Cross model of racial identity development very enlightening. I knew that there were stages of racial identity development before I entered this class. I did not know what they were, or what they really entailed. After reading through this article I found myself saying, "Oh. That explains why she reacted this way to this incident instead of how she would have a year ago." Clearly this person has entered a different stage and is working through different problems from a new viewpoint. Thankfully, the model provides a degree of hope that people will not always be angry, and will not always be separatists, etc. Although I'm not really sure about that.

Conversely, when students of color understand the stages of White racial identity development, they can be more tolerant or appreciative of a White student's struggle with guilt, for example. After reading about the stages of White identity development, Sonia, a Latina previously quoted, wrote:

> This article was the one that made me feel that my own prejudices were showing. I never knew that Whites went through an identity development of their own.

155

She later told me outside of class that she found it much easier to listen to some of the things White students said because she could understand their potentially offensive comments as part of a developmental stage.

Sharon, an African-American woman, also found that an understanding of the respective stages of racial identity development helped her to understand some of the interactions she had had with White students since coming to college. She wrote:

> There is a lot of clash that occurs between Black and White people at college which is best explained by their respective stages of development. Unfortunately schools have not helped to alleviate these problems earlier in life.

In a course on the psychology of racism, it is easy to build in the provision of this information as part of the course content. For instructors teaching courses with race-related content in other fields, it may seem less natural to do so. However, the inclusion of articles on racial identity development and/or class discussion of these issues in conjunction with the other strategies that have been suggested can improve student receptivity to the course content in important ways, making it a very useful investment of class time. Because the stages describe kinds of behavior that many people have commonly observed in themselves, as well as in their own intraracial and interracial interactions, my experience has been that most students grasp the basic conceptual framework fairly easily, even if they do not have a background in psychology.

Empowering Students as Change Agents

Heightening students' awareness of racism without also developing an awareness of the possibility of change is a prescription for despair. I consider it unethical to do one without the other. Exploring strategies to empower students as change agents is thus a necessary part of the process of talking about race and learning about racism. As was previously mentioned, students find it very helpful to read about and hear from individuals who have been effective change agents. Newspaper and magazine articles, as well as biographical or autobiographical essays or book excerpts, are often important sources for this information.

I also ask students to work in small groups to develop an action plan of their own for interrupting racism. While I do not consider it appropriate to require students to engage in antiracist activity (since I believe this should be a personal choice the student makes for him/herself), students are required to think about the possibility. Guidelines are provided (see Katz, 1978), and the plans that they develop over several weeks are presented at the end of the semester. Students are generally impressed with each other's good ideas, and, in fact, they often do go on to implement their projects.

Joanne, a White student who initially struggled with feelings of guilt, wrote:

> I thought that hearing others' ideas for action plans was interesting and informative. It really helps me realize (reminds me) the many choices and avenues there are once I decided to be an ally. Not only did I develop my own concrete way to be an ally, I have found many other ways that I, as a college student, can be an active anti-racist. It was really empowering.

Another way all students can be empowered is by offering them the opportunity to consciously observe their own development. The taped exercise to which some of the previously quoted students have referred is an example of one way to provide this opportunity. At the beginning of the semester, students are given an interview guide with many open-ended questions concerning racial attitudes and opinions. They are asked to interview themselves on tape as a way of recording their own ideas for future reference. Though the tapes are collected, students are assured that no one (including me) will listen to them. The tapes are returned near the end of the semester, and students are asked to listen to their own tapes and use their understanding of racial identity development to discuss it in essay form.

The resulting essays are often remarkable and underscore the psychological importance of giving students the chance to examine racial issues in the classroom. The following was written by Elaine, a White woman:

> Another common theme that was apparent in the tape was that, for the most part, I was aware of my own ignorance and was embarrassed because of it. I wanted to know more about the oppression of people in the country so that I could do something about it. Since I have been here, I have begun to be actively resistant to racism. I have been able to confront my grandparents and some old friends from high school when they make racist comments. Taking this psychology of racism class is another step toward active resistance to racism. I am trying to educate myself so that I have a knowledge base to work from.
>
> When the tape was made, I was just beginning to be active and just beginning to be educated. I think I am now starting to move into the redefinition stage. I am starting to feel ok about being White. Some of my guilt is dissipating, and I do not feel as ignorant as I used to be. I think I have an understanding of racism; how it effects [*sic*] myself, and how it effects this country. Because of this I think I can be more active in doing something about it.

In the words of Louise, a Black female student:

> One of the greatest things I learned from this semester in general is that the world is not only Black and White, nor is the United States. I learned a lot about my own erasure of many American ethnic groups. . . . I am in the (immersion) stage of my identity development. I think I am also dangling a little in the (encounter) stage. I say this because a lot of my energies are still directed toward White people. I began writing a poem two days ago and it was directed to White racism. However, I have also become more Black-identified. I am reaching to the strength in Afro-American heritage. I am learning more about the heritage and history of Afro-American culture. Knowledge = strength and strength = power.

While some students are clearly more self-reflective and articulate about their own process than others, most students experience the opportunity to talk and learn about these issues as a transforming process. In my experience, even those students who are frustrated by aspects of the course find themselves changed by it. One such student wrote in her final journal entry:

> What I felt to be a major hindrance to me was the amount of people. Despite the philosophy, I really never felt at ease enough to speak openly about the feelings I have and kind of watched the class pull farther and farther apart as the semester

went on. . . . I think that it was your attitude that kept me intrigued by the topics we were studying despite my frustrations with the class time. I really feel as though I made some significant moves in my understanding of other people's positions in our world as well as of my feelings of racism, and I feel very good about them. I feel like this class has moved me in the right direction. I'm on a roll I think, because I've been introduced to so much.

Facilitating student development in this way is a challenging and complex task, but the results are clearly worth the effort.

IMPLICATIONS FOR THE INSTITUTION

What are the institutional implications for an understanding of racial identity development theory beyond the classroom? How can this framework be used to address the pressing issues of increasing diversity and decreasing racial tensions on college campuses? How can providing opportunities in the curriculum to talk about race and learn about racism affect the recruitment and retention of students of color specifically, especially when the majority of the students enrolled are White?

The fact is, educating White students about race and racism changes attitudes in ways that go beyond the classroom boundaries. As White students move through their own stages of identity development, they take their friends with them by engaging them in dialogue. They share the articles they have read with roommates, and involve them in their projects. An example of this involvement can be seen in the following journal entry, written by Larry, a White man:

> Here it is our fifth week of class and more and more I am becoming aware of the racism around me. Our second project made things clearer, because while watching T.V. I picked up many kinds of discrimination and stereotyping. Since the project was over, I still find myself watching these shows and picking up bits and pieces every show I watch. Even my friends will be watching a show and they will say, "Hey, Larry, put that in your paper." Since they know I am taking this class, they are looking out for these things. They are also watching what they say around me for fear that I will use them as an example. For example, one of my friends has this fascination with making fun of Jewish people. Before I would listen to his comments and take them in stride, but now I confront him about his comments.

The heightened awareness of the White students enrolled in the class has a ripple effect in their peer group, which helps to create a climate in which students of color and other targeted groups (Jewish students, for example) might feel more comfortable. It is likely that White students who have had the opportunity to learn about racism in a supportive atmosphere will be better able to be allies to students of color in extracurricular settings, like student government meetings and other organizational settings, where students of color often feel isolated and unheard.

At the same time, students of color who have had the opportunity to examine the ways in which racism may have affected their own lives are able to give voice to their own experience, and to validate it rather than be demoralized by it. An understanding of internalized oppression can help students of color recognize the ways in which they may have unknowingly participated in their own victimization, or the victimization of others. They may be able to move beyond victimization to empowerment, and share their learning with others, as Sharon, a previously quoted Black woman, planned to do.

Campus communities with an understanding of racial identity development could become more supportive of special-interest groups, such as the Black Student Union or the Asian Student Alliance, because they would recognize them not as "separatist" but as important outlets for students of color who may be at the Encounter or Immersion stage of racial identity development. Not only could speakers of color be sought out to add diversity to campus programming, but Whites who had made a commitment to unlearning their own racism could be offered as models to those White students looking for new ways to understand their own Whiteness, and to students of color looking for allies.

It has become painfully clear on many college campuses across the United States that we cannot have successfully multiracial campuses without talking about race and learning about racism. Providing a forum where this discussion can take place safely over a semester, a time period that allows personal and group development to unfold in ways that day-long or weekend programs do not, may be among the most proactive learning opportunities an institution can provide.

NOTES

1. A similar point could be made about other issues of oppression, such as anti-Semitism, homophobia and heterosexism, ageism, and so on.
2. While similar models of racial identity development exist, Cross and Helms are referenced here because they are among the most frequently cited writers on Black racial identity development and on White racial identity development, respectively. For a discussion of the commonalities between these and other identity development models, see Phinney (1989, 1990) and Helms (1990).
3. Both Parham (1989) and Phinney (1989) suggest that a preference for the dominant group is not always a characteristic of this stage. For example, children raised in households and communities with explicitly positive Afrocentric attitudes may absorb a pro-Black perspective, which then serves as the starting point for their own exploration of racial identity.
4. After being introduced to this model and Helms's model of White identity development, students are encouraged to think about how the models might apply to their own experience or the experiences of people they know. As is reflected in the cited journal entries, some students resonate to the theories quite readily, easily seeing their own process of growth reflected in them. Other students are sometimes puzzled because they feel as though their own process varies from these models, and may ask if it is possible to "skip" a particular stage, for example. Such questions provide a useful departure point for discussing the limitations of stage theories in general, and the potential variations in experience that make questions of racial identity development so complex.
5. Examples of useful articles include essays by McIntosh (1988), Lester (1987), and Braden (1987). Each of these combines autobiographical material, as well as a conceptual framework for understanding some aspect of racism that students find very helpful. Bowser and Hunt's (1981) edited book, *Impacts of Racism on Whites,* though less autobiographical in nature, is also a valuable resource.

6. Class size has a direct bearing on my ability to create safety in the classroom. Dividing the class into pairs or small groups of five or six students to discuss initial reactions to a particular article or film helps to increase participation, both in the small groups and later in the large group discussions.

REFERENCES

Barnard, H. F. (Ed.). (1987). *Outside the magic circle: The autobiography of Virginia Foster Durr.* New York: Simon & Schuster. (Original work published in 1985 by University of Alabama Press)

Bowser, B. P., & Hunt, R. G. (1981). *Impacts of racism on whites.* Beverly Hills: Sage.

Braden, A. (1987, April–May). Undoing racism: Lessons for the peace movement. *The Nonviolent Activist,* pp. 3–6.

Bronstein, P. A., & Quina, K. (Eds.). (1988). *Teaching a psychology of people: Resources for gender and sociocultural awareness.* Washington, DC: American Psychological Association.

Cross, W. E., Jr. (1971). The Negro to black conversion experience: Toward a psychology of black liberation. *Black World, 20*(9), 13–27.

Cross, W. E., Jr. (1978). The Cross and Thomas models of psychological nigrescence. *Journal of Black Psychology, 5*(1), 13–19.

Cross, W. E., Jr. (1991). *Shades of black: Diversity in African-American identity.* Philadelphia: Temple University Press.

Cross, W. E., Jr., Parham, T. A., & Helms, J. E. (1991). The stages of black identity development: Nigrescence models. In R. Jones (Ed.), *Black psychology* (3rd ed., pp. 319–338). San Francisco: Cobb and Henry.

Derman-Sparks, L., Higa, C. T., & Sparks, B. (1980). Children, race and racism: How race awareness develops. *Interracial Books for Children Bulletin, 11*(3/4), 3–15.

Helms, J. E. (Ed.). (1990). *Black and white racial identity: Theory, research and practice.* Westport, CT: Greenwood Press.

Highlen, P. S., Reynolds, A. L., Adams, E. M., Hanley, T. C., Myers, L. J., Cox, C., & Speight, S. (1988, August 13). *Self-identity development model of oppressed people: Inclusive model for all?* Paper presented at the American Psychological Association Convention, Atlanta.

Hull, G. T., Scott, P. B., & Smith, B. (Eds.). (1982). *All the women are white, all the blacks are men, but some of us are brave: Black women's studies.* Old Westbury, NY: Feminist Press.

Katz, J. H. (1978). *White awareness: Handbook for anti-racism training.* Norman: University of Oklahoma Press.

Lester, J. (1987). *What happens to the mythmakers when the myths are found to be untrue?* Unpublished paper, Equity Institute, Emeryville, CA.

McIntosh, P. (1988). *White privilege and male privilege: A personal account of coming to see correspondences through work in women's studies.* Working paper, Wellesley College Center for Research on Women, Wellesley, MA.

McIntosh, P. (1989, July/August). White privilege: Unpacking the invisible knapsack. *Peace and Freedom,* pp. 10–12.

Parham, T. A. (1989). Cycles of psychological nigrescence. *The Counseling Psychologist, 17*(2), 187–226.

Phinney, J. (1989). Stages of ethnic identity in minority group adolescents. *Journal of Early Adolescence, 9,* 34–39.

Phinney, J. (1990). Ethnic identity in adolescents and adults: Review of research. *Psychological Bulletin, 198*(3), 499–514.

Phinney, J. S., & Rotheram, J. M. (Eds.). (1987). *Children's ethnic socialization: Pluralism and development.* Newbury Park, CA: Sage.

Schuster, M. R., & Van Dyne, S. R. (Eds.). (1985). *Women's place in the academy: Transforming the liberal arts curriculum.* Totowa, NJ: Rowman & Allenheld.

Wellman, D. (1977). *Portraits of white racism.* New York: Cambridge University Press.

Basic Writing:
Moving the Voices on the Margin
to the Center

ANNE J. HERRINGTON
MARCIA CURTIS

Reacting to what many considered a racially motivated conflict on the UMass/Amherst campus in 1986, Anne Herrington and Marcia Curtis felt compelled to reconstruct their Basic Writing course to give voice to minority students who were usually kept on the fringes — "marginalized" — academically and socially within the university. They aimed to create a curriculum that reflected an accurate image of the university's students, to affirm the diversity of the student body rather than deny it. They changed their reading list to include predominantly non-White authors and encouraged students to engage in a dialogue with those authors while reflecting in writing on their own experience of marginalization. By raising students' consciousness and by encouraging students to speak out through their writings, Herrington and Curtis contributed to the acceptance and respect their students demanded — to validate the voices on the margin — as they accomplished their academic aims for the course.

In October 1986, the Basic Writing course at the University of Massachusetts, Amherst, was radically altered by a baseball game — that is, by the Boston Red Sox's World Series loss to the New York Mets and the conflict it precipitated. Beginning among a handful of Boston and New York fans, the melee eventually involved some twelve hundred to three thousand students who took sides along racial lines, leaving some to argue whether this was indeed a racial confrontation or just a particularly ugly sports brawl.

While faculty, administrators, and some townspeople continued to haggle over the definition of the conflict that erupted that fall night, African-American and other minority students who took part in the demonstrations that followed were clear. Although the altercation occurred in a dormitory complex on the margins of the campus, its cause, as well as its resolution, lay at the University's core. African-American, Latino, and Asian speakers — both male and female — took the stage with their common demands: that their voices be heard not just when racial violence shook the campus, but throughout all aspects of the college's operation; that minority authors be included in heretofore predominantly all-White reading lists; that minority teachers and scholars be recruited into still

Harvard Educational Review   Vol. 60   No. 4   November 1990, 489–496.

predominantly White male faculties; that minority culture and knowledge be represented in American education as it is truly present in American life.

In the weeks that followed, the University of Massachusetts administration was pressed to respond. The Chancellor appointed Frederick Hurst, a commissioner with the Massachusetts Commission Against Discrimination, to investigate the October brawl and recommend actions to improve the climate on campus. His report suggested, among other things, that the university develop educational programs to maximize the awareness of racial issues on campus and in society at large; that it review minority programs, focusing especially on the recruitment and retention of African-American students, faculty, and staff; and that it extend these recommendations to include other "marginalized" groups in a continuing effort to interrupt all manifestations of prejudice within the university.

Independent of Commissioner Hurst's investigation, a number of us in the Freshman Writing Program were moved to review our curricula. Two of us — White, middle-class women — recognized almost immediately that in the silence of our Basic Writing curriculum we had been complicit in marginalizing our students' voices, despite our conscious efforts to construct a "student-centered" course. Basic Writing is a preparatory course required of approximately 5 percent of our first-year students who, on the basis of a placement essay, we judge to be inadequately prepared to enter our main first-year writing course, College Writing. Basic Writing, which is run as a workshop, has students work through a process of brainstorming, drafting, and revising each written piece. Until 1986, students had written almost exclusively from personal experience, without a reader or any text other than the students' writing. We had an increasing sense that our curriculum, while helping students develop confidence as writers, did not adequately address the problems they faced when called upon to read and write in other university classes. We felt that they were too likely to face a text passively, since they did not have the strategies or self-assurance to assimilate the text and make it the basis on which to develop their own ideas in writing. Consequently, for some time we had been considering broadening the student-centered workshop focus to a reading-based writing course, following in general the propositions presented by Bartholomae and Petrosky in *Facts, Artifacts and Counterfacts* (1986).

It was the minority student demonstrators, however, who set before us that fall day the full requirements of any curriculum meant to help writers move confidently and thoughtfully through private meaning-making to significant communication with others. Indeed, our Basic Writing sections are some of the most ethnically, racially, and linguistically diverse classes at the university. Our writers are on the so-called "margin" both academically and socially: academically, as students in Basic Writing, and socially, as citizens of color in a predominantly White, Anglo-European, English-speaking institution traditionally unreceptive to their cultural and linguistic heritages. Hearing the student demonstrators speak out for themselves so forcefully and eloquently convinced us of our appropriateness of capitalizing on this diversity by affirming it in our classrooms, as we are doing now, instead of tacitly denying it, as we had been doing before. Rather than having our curriculum be an image of the university, we decided to construct it in the image of our students. We reasoned that by reflecting their varied cultural heritages, instead of ours alone, we could accomplish both the traditional "academic" aims of a basic writing course and new, equally important personal and social aims as well.

We now believe that by relieving students of the burden of double marginalization, we can teach our students better. By bringing their varied cultures and life experiences from the margin into the center of the course — a relatively easy task — we can help them cross that academic boundary or, perhaps more accurately, we can begin to erode this false boundary and the institutionally constructed impediment to education it represents. As we will show, we can set the stage to learn a great deal from our students, and to let them learn from one another.

Our personal-social aim — bringing our students' cultures in from the margin to the center — is accomplished by focusing the course on texts that reflect their experiences and speak to them. Our academic aim is met when, as active thinkers and writers, our students can, in turn, formulate their own ideas and use their own voices in active, albeit silent, dialogue with the texts before them. As teachers, we make the choice of whether to help or hinder students in meeting these aims every time we design a reading list: J. D. Salinger or African-American novelist John Edgar Wideman; Jonathan Swift or Mexican-American writer Richard Rodríguez; George Orwell or Asian-American novelist Maxine Hong Kingston. From each pairing, we have chosen the latter author, and have selected readings that deal with the acculturation process that occurs as groups and individuals fight to accommodate new ways while preserving old identities. Now, we believe, instead of representing the traditional Anglo-American canon, our reading list better represents the diverse identities comprising our student body and the challenges they face daily. The full reading list is shown in Table 1.

We make the same choice again when we decide on instructional methods: do we confront them with an Anglo-American "classic" upon which to model their "own" writing or encourage them to enter a truly interactive dialogue with the author before them? More specifically, in the course we provide a reading process that relies on writing as a guide for exploring ideas as well as a means of communicating them. The guided exploratory writings — done during and after the reading process — encourage students to see themselves as equal to the "professional" author, two kindred voices of equal authority. For example, one guided writing asks them to select what strikes them as significant: "Imagine Maxine Hong Kingston is a member of your peer response group and explain to her what you believe to be the single most important detail of her essay 'Parents.'" Another asks them to consider multiple interpretations: "Imagine you are a member of Richard Rodríguez's family, or another member of your own, and explain what you believe his central dilemma in *Hunger of Memory* to be." Or we might ask them to identify vexing questions — "Write down everything that strikes you as significant, whether interesting, familiar or just plain puzzling" — in order to finally settle on their own angle of interest to write about for an audience.

We hope that these readings and the students' writings will stir them to reflect on their own histories while at the same time recognizing the bonds they share with others. We also hope the combined reading and writing process will lead them through initial personal reaction into ideas of wider appeal by helping them make the fundamental connection between private and social, self and other. But, most important, we hope to create a setting that enables students to recognize "minority" voices, including their own, as voices of authority proclaiming important and powerful messages.

Here are some of our students' messages, ones we think relevant to teachers of reading and writing. All are commenting on Richard Rodríguez's often excerpted and anthologized memoir "Aria," from his autobiography *Hunger of Memory*, which chronicles the entry of a young Chicano into mainstream American academic life. Of all our minority-authored texts, this is one frequently used in college writing classes in the United States and mentioned in professional journals (Bartholomae & Petrosky, 1986; Dean, 1989; Roemer, 1987). Because of that very familiarity, we use it again here in this chapter to demonstrate the eloquence with which "marginalized" students can argue their positions on "home ground."

The first passage is by Ron Showell, an African-American student in one of our Basic Writing classes. Identifying with Rodríguez's situation as "an alien in gringo society," he sees the issue not just as one for immigrants who do not speak English, but as one for Black native Americans as well. As he argues in his essay "Smoldering," the central problem is that "the dominant group displaces individual members who become Americanized from their own cultures." In this essay, Showell uses Rodríguez's memoir as a starting point to tell his own story, from which he derives the force of his argument. This was written midway through the semester. Earlier, Showell had chosen to read and write on Richard Wright's *Black Boy*. In that writing, Showell spoke of Blacks in the third person and made no personal references. Here, as you can see, he chooses to write his own "aria":

> I, too, like Rodríguez, had experienced disconcerting confusion attending school. In fifth and sixth grades I was bused from a predominantly black school to a solely white middle class school. . . . For the first time, I started questioning, realizing, or maybe understanding I was different, but being different meant conforming. Unconsciously, I began changing my attitude, wanting blue eyes, blond hair, a stunning car, a home, and plenty of moolah. Still, I slapped five and spoke the black idiom but a metamorphosis was happening. I was losing my culture, my individual distinctiveness.

As a child in an integrated school, Showell felt the pressure to adopt a White, middle-class culture in order to be accepted. And, as he says, the pressure is still there today. But according to Showell, and in contrast to Rodríguez, the pressure is to be partly resisted, partly accommodated. For individuals of marginalized and dominated groups, Showell writes, the challenge is to find some

> workable balance between his or her individual culture and white American values. . . . If one concentrates solely on individualism, power, dominance, and control, he or she may achieve success at the cost of being alienated from one's own culture. On the other hand, if one completely ignores those values that will allow progress into the mainstream, he or she will reduce their available range of options, smoldering in the melting pot of the multitudes.

TABLE I
Basic Writing Reading List

Over the course of the semester, each student is to select and read two books from the following list:

Chute, Carolyn. *The Beans of Egypt, Maine*. New York: Warner Books, 1985.
Curran, Mary Doyle. *The Parish and the Hill*. New York: The Feminist Press at CUNY, 1986.
Dorris, Michael. *A Yellow Raft in Blue Water*. New York: Warner Books, 1987.
Erdrich, Louise. *Love Medicine*. New York: Bantam Books, 1984.
Fricke, Aaron. *Reflections of a Rock Lobster*. Boston: Alyson Publications, 1981.
Hayslip, Le Ly. *When Heaven and Earth Changed Places*. New York: Penguin Books, 1990.
Kingston, Maxine Hong. *China Men*. New York: Ballantine Books, 1981.
Laye, Camara. *The Dark Child: The Autobiography of an African Boy*. New York: Hill & Wang, 1989.
Marshall, Paule. *Brown Girl, Brownstones*. New York: The Feminist Press at CUNY, 1981.
Rivera, Edward. *Family Installments: Memories of Growing up Hispanic*. New York: Penguin Books, 1988.
Rodríguez, Richard. *Hunger of Memory: The Education of Richard Rodríguez*. New York: Bantam Books, 1988.
Tan, Amy. *The Joy Luck Club*. New York: Ivy Books, 1989.
Wideman, John Edgar. *Brothers and Keepers*. New York: Penguin Books, 1984.
Wright, Richard. *Black Boy*. New York: Harper & Row, 1989.

Students keep reading journals as they read the books, and one of the major writing assignments is based on their reading. Four to five other short readings are used in class.

The costs are great: alienation from one's own culture or "suffering at the whims of the middle class and the very rich." But there is no sense of powerlessness in Showell's forceful articulation of his dilemma.

Two other Basic Writing students — Puerto Rican women — also identified with Rodríguez. Both share a common language with Rodríguez and as a result identified with him. Both women also challenged Rodríguez. The first is Rebecca Grajales, a young woman who grew up in the United States and went through bilingual education here. In working out her reactions to Rodríguez, she recognizes that she "felt more and more disgusted with Richard but also with myself" for having accepted the label he refused:

> When I started reading *Hunger of Memory* by Richard Rodríguez I decided to have an open mind. I had heard from friends that he was a[n] insensitive, selfish, ignorant writer. The reason for [these] accusations I did not know, but, as I read further along I felt more and more disgusted with Richard but also with myself. I felt this way because at points when I was reading I (literally) hated Richard but at (many) other points I agreed with him.
>
> Richard did not like to be labeled a minority student and I do not like to be labeled as a minority student either. We, as Americans, fight racism and prejudice every day. We want our children to be able to feel (not only have) the freedom to do anything they want. But even though we want this we go and have ourselves labeled as a "minority" or "minority students." This labeling, to me is just another (nicer) way of telling us: "Hey, you are not equal with the white American."

Like Showell and Rodríguez, Grajales feels the pressure of the dominant White culture. She identifies with Rodríguez for not liking to be labeled a minority student, but she also renames the "minority" label for what it is — another means of oppression and reminder of separation. Still, she was angry with Rodríguez because he turned his back on his family and culture and consequently lost the necessary balance, as Showell argues, for true personal as well as cultural survival.

The other woman, Arlene Ayala, lives in Puerto Rico and because of that may feel the pressure of being a minority to a lesser extent than Grajales, Showell, or Rodríguez, all of whom grew up in mainland, mainstream United States. In a way, Ayala's message is an extension of Grajales's and a complement to Showell's. In contrast to Showell, who uses Rodríguez as an occasion to tell his own story, Ayala takes on Rodríguez directly and with authority. She tells us that as individuals, particularly ones in marginalized groups, we should not accept or succumb to the pressures that would label us as minority or inferior:

> After reading the book *Hunger of Memory*, I felt the need to tell Richard Rodríguez and all the people like him that they are wrong. There is no need for forgetting your culture, your language or your family in order to be successful in life or just to feel that you belong to a place. What you become of yourself . . . determines where you are going to be standing in life.

Ayala follows this observation with a direct quote from *Hunger of Memory*, upon which she then comments:

> *Only when I was able to think of myself as an American, no longer an alien in gringo society, could I seek the rights and opportunities necessary for full public individuality.*

> This quotation provides a good description of Richard, a persona whose major objective has been to be a "public person" in a "gringo society": In other words, being one of them no matter what it cost, a person who is ashamed of his nationality, his language, and even of his family. . . . Richard thinks that all these things make him disadvantaged, that in order to be successful he has to cast them aside. This is not true. What makes Richard disadvantaged is his sense of inferiority. . . . I'm Hispanic, but unlike Richard I feel proud of it.

Interestingly, in standing up to Rodríguez, Ayala turns to the young gay autobiographer Aaron Fricke for identification and support: "Aaron Fricke's story should be a lesson to all of us, including Rodríguez," she writes. "It should make us think, not if being gay is right or wrong, no, that's not the point. The point is that we should stand up for what we think is right."

How do English-speaking Anglo-Americans fare in this sort of curriculum, which gives authority to "other" voices and places the voices of their ancestry, for the first time, on the cultural margin? Some do encounter some difficulty. For example, one young Anglo-American woman could not reach across the margin on which she now found herself. She seemed unable to form any sort of empathy or sympathy with the "foreign" writers she encountered, and her own writings, which focused consistently on difference, conveyed a not-so-subtle sense of anger and frustration. Her response to "Aria," based on her senior high trip to Spain, enumerated the benefits of "Knowing a Second Language," not the least of which was being able to tell the begging children of Madrid "*¡No me* *moleste!*" ("Don't bother me!") and "*¿Por que no trabajas?*" ("Why don't you get a job?") in two languages. And when she concluded her essay — "I would love to speak Spanish fluently, but unlike Richard Rodríguez, I would never . . . let myself lose my native language" — she tells us pretty emphatically that there are boundaries of identity and identification she's simply not ready to cross. We did not penalize her for her reluctance, nor did we prevent her from expressing her frustration. In fact, we believe there was/is a lesson for her and for us in her resistance and the emotions it expressed. We believe it was demonstrating precisely what many marginalized students must feel every day in traditional courses. And we hope she actually was experiencing, however unwillingly, an identification with marginalized people that she might be able to reflect upon later.

This young woman was one of the few — and, from our observations, there are very few — mainstream students who resist entering, even imaginatively, the world of non-mainstream writers. Most enter willingly, as did one young White male from rural Massachusetts. He is a year-round resident of one of the more isolated areas of Martha's Vineyard. Interestingly, he identified himself to his university advisor as coming from a different culture. So although apparently from the dominant group, he perceives himself, at least in the university context, in some ways as "other." In reading "Aria," though, this student did not so much identify with the "others" — whom he perceived to be immigrants who do not speak English — as he did come to understand their experiences for the first time and sympathize with them. As he writes in "Language as a Barrier":

> It's almost as if young immigrant children were from broken homes, because they are unsure as to where they belong, in the American society, or in their Native environment. Reading Richard Rodríguez's *The Hunger of Memory* has given me some understanding of what people go through when they don't know how to speak English.

For this student, understanding also came from discussions in class with other students whose primary languages were Chinese and Spanish. His reading and discussions led him to conclude not only that immigrants should learn English, but also that it's important to know one's home language and traditions; further, that "Americans should learn about the different cultures that come into the United States."

There have been other Anglo students for whom entrance was awkward, a bit fumbling and incomplete. And there have been some students — both marginalized and mainstream — for whom entrance has been too precipitous, and ultimately silencing. Prompted by a reading to disclose in free-writing or early draft an especially disturbing moment of exclusion or abuse, they have pulled back from further disclosure, unwilling or unable to turn their private expression into public discourse. Their silence, in itself, is a message we need to respect. It informs us of the grave importance of the situation recalled; it informs us also of the dangers these students sense in the situation we have provided for its recollection. To force disclosure would only validate their distrust of us; by respecting their silence, on the other hand, we affirm our trust in them.

Showell, Grajales, and even Rodríguez are reminding us of the pressure they have felt to suppress their own culture and be displaced from who they are. They are also expressing their rightful anger at a White mainstream culture — that's many of us — that has been the agent of that displacement, and which has labeled them as minority and inferior. Showell, Grajales, and Ayala are saying to any who have felt that pressure: Resist it — move to the center and with pride affirm your self and culture, whether it be Hispanic, African-American, gay, African, or Indian. For, as Basic Writer Maritza Vélez urges,

> it's not necessary to quit all this to triumph. . . . Quitting your family and your own culture, I think you quit yourself and your own roots. I think you have to be proud about all this because it talks about who you are.

What, then, is their message to us, predominantly White teachers, especially in predominantly White institutions? They are implicitly calling on us to consider our role in creating and perpetuating the pressures that make it difficult for them to affirm themselves. While we have to recognize the social-political reality that some groups in the United States are marginalized, we, too, need to resist that marginalization in our classrooms. That means, most importantly, moving our students to the center by inviting in and listening to their family and cultural histories and recognizing the authority of their ideas and writing. Through the writings our students offer us and the readings we provide for them, we can contribute to the sort of multicultural acceptance and respect our students are calling for. Our experience in our Basic Writing course tells us that when we do that we also have more success in accomplishing our academic aims for the course.

And this, after all, is our aim — not to force self-disclosure, but to validate voices from the margin — voices, both heard and unheard, that have for too long and too often been excluded from curricula. And we do this by making these voices the center of our readings, in a classroom in which we strive to create an environment that encourages reflection, not confrontation, and encourages us all to listen to and respect one another. We should aim to do no less.

REFERENCES

Bartholomae, D., & Petrosky, A. (1986). *Facts, artifacts and counterfacts.* Upper Montclair, NJ: Boynton.

Dean, T. (1989). Multicultural classrooms, monocultural teachers. *College Composition and Communication, 40,* 23–37.

Roemer, M. G. (1987). Which reader's response? *College English, 49,* 911–921.

Teaching Undergraduates about AIDS:
An Action-Oriented Approach

KIMBERLY CHRISTENSEN

Since 1981, over 182,000 Americans have died from AIDS. More than 1.5 million others are infected with HIV, the virus believed to cause AIDS. Schools and colleges across the country have responded to the AIDS epidemic by providing a variety of education and risk-reduction programs for their students. In this article, Kimberly Christensen describes the content and pedagogy of an action-oriented, semester-long undergraduate course she taught on AIDS at the State University of New York College at Purchase in the spring of 1990. It is her view that educators must not only teach risk-reduction behavior, but also explore the deeper causes of the AIDS epidemic: the social forces that grant differential access to information, health care, and social services for people of different race, gender, sexual orientation, and social class. Furthermore, she suggests that successful AIDS educational efforts should also be designed to help students combat their pervasive feelings of powerlessness by actively involving them in efforts to end the AIDS crisis. In this article, Christensen provides a critique and evaluation of the content and pedagogy of the course, shares her students' reactions to the class, and makes suggestions for designing similar courses.

Ten years into the AIDS epidemic, there are few, if any, college campuses that have not been touched directly or indirectly by this crisis. Students, faculty, and administrators across the country have responded to the threat of AIDS with a variety of educational programs, ranging from guest speakers, to safer-sex workshops, to the distribution of condoms.

Located a half hour from New York City, the epicenter of the AIDS epidemic, the State University of New York's College at Purchase had been significantly affected by AIDS. We had lost a colleague, a professor of anthropology, to AIDS-related complications in 1988. There were consistent reports of HIV-positive students being harassed by fellow students. Finally, a confidential survey of our campus revealed that, although a large percentage of our student body — particularly gay and bisexual students — was aware of AIDS, only a small percentage of our sexually active students of any sexual orientation was taking precautions to protect themselves from the disease (Fastje, 1990).

In the fall of 1987, a colleague and I proposed at the general faculty meeting that a student/faculty/staff AIDS Task Force be established to educate all segments of the campus community about the epidemic. The faculty meeting unanimously approved the proposal. Since that time, two faculty members and I have consistently participated in Task Force activities, along with several staff mem-

Harvard Educational Review   Vol. 61   No. 3   August 1991, 337–356.

bers from the Student Affairs and Campus Life offices and about a half-dozen enthusiastic students. Activities of the AIDS Task Force have included workshops at freshmen orientation, condom and pamphlet distribution in the campus center and dining halls, and a day-long teach-in on AIDS. We also set up VCRs in heavily traveled centers on campus, and played AIDS awareness and prevention videos during lunch hour and dinnertime.[1] We have installed condom vending machines in many campus locations, along with racks of AIDS information pamphlets. We prepared a 90-minute "road show" on AIDS, which visited classes at the request of faculty members. Finally, I prepared an annotated bibliography on the medical, political, and social aspects of the AIDS crisis, which was widely distributed to faculty members.

There is some evidence that the efforts of the AIDS Task Force have been successful. On their own initiative, students have formed support groups for HIV-positive people and for friends and lovers of HIV-positive people. The student newspaper now regularly prints information on AIDS and AIDS prevention, and for a time even carried a regular column on AIDS. Finally, the atmosphere on campus regarding HIV-positive people and People With AIDS (PWAs) has changed significantly. In a previous semester, two students felt comfortable enough to be interviewed openly as HIV-positive people for the campus paper; to date they have suffered no negative repercussions.

Despite these successes, I felt that our AIDS education efforts on campus were inadequate. In particular, given the sporadic nature of AIDS Task Force discussions with students, it was difficult to convey more than the most superficial knowledge, or to build up enough trust with the students to discuss their complicated feelings around AIDS. For these reasons, I decided in the spring of 1990 to design and teach a full-credit course on the political, economic, and ethical issues raised by the AIDS crisis.

Having lost a dear friend to AIDS, I have been involved in the AIDS activist movement (ACT UP/New York) for over three-and-a-half years. ACT UP is a diverse group of people, many of whom have lost friends or family to AIDS or are themselves HIV infected. Our goals are to increase public awareness of the AIDS crisis, to increase public and private funding for AIDS research, and to combat discrimination against those who are HIV infected. ACT UP's tactics include letter-writing and phone-calling campaigns to public officials; producing and distributing bilingual pamphlets, T-shirts, videos, and other popular AIDS education materials; and demonstrating against government officials and institutions whose policies on AIDS exacerbate the epidemic. ACT UP has had some notable successes. These include the implementation of a "parallel track program" whereby HIV-infected people can get access to experimental AIDS drugs earlier in the process of FDA approval; the high school condom-distribution plan recently adopted in New York City, which began as a project of the ACT UP "Youth Brigade"; and a recent ruling by a New York City criminal court that the distribution of clean needles to drug addicts may be justified in order to stop the spread of HIV.[2] But our efforts to convince our public officials on a federal level to make AIDS a top health priority, to mount a "Manhattan Project" against AIDS, have been less than successful.

Through my own work with ACT UP, I have learned a tremendous amount about AIDS, not only about the medical and technical aspects of the disease, but also about its political and economic context. With the death of my friend, I experienced the sense of powerlessness and horror that often accompany losing someone to AIDS. I also learned that acting to prevent the spread of this disease and working to speed a cure can help one to cope with that sense of loss and powerlessness.

It was this sense of empowerment and commitment that I wished to share with my students. I wanted to create an atmosphere in the classroom in which students would not only feel free to confront and change their own risk behaviors, but would also become actively involved in the fight against AIDS. I wanted them to begin to understand both the viral and societal origins of the AIDS crisis. I wanted students to understand that confronting the AIDS crisis involves more than condom use; that is, that it also involves addressing the structural inequalities and laissez-faire public policies that have allowed this epidemic to assume crisis proportions in the United States and abroad. The rapid spread of AIDS in the Untied States is symptomatic of many deeper problems in our society, including the persistence of racism and heterosexism, an economy that does not provide jobs or adequate income for many of its citizens, an increasingly inadequate health care delivery and finance system, and a "war on drugs" that does little to address the real roots of the drug crisis.[3]

STRUCTURE OF THE COURSE

In the spring of 1990, I offered a sophomore-level elective course, "AIDS: Political, Economic, and Ethical Issues." John Leppo, a male staff member from the Campus Life office, served as my unofficial teaching assistant. My choice of a male TA turned out to be a real boon to the course, since the young men in the class found it much easier to talk to him than to me about safer sex and related issues. I highly recommend mixed-sex teams for teaching courses of this nature.

The course enrolled over sixty students from the school's fine arts and liberal arts programs. African Americans and Latino/as were more heavily represented than in the student population as a whole, and we had approximately a half-dozen older (aged 35–55) students from the local community. Two of these older students were devout Roman Catholic women, whose views on sexual matters were much more conservative than those of the younger students. The class also included several members of the Gay, Lesbian, and Bisexual Union (GLBU), which made for some rather lively discussions. But although the students expressed their widely divergent views, these discussions never became mean-spirited, and actually took on a friendly, teasing quality by the end of the semester. For example, a GLBU member said to one of the older women, "Victoria, I'm about to say something very gay; you may want to block your ears!" Victoria laughed, and made a show of covering her ears with her hands.

I believe that there were several reasons for this tolerant attitude among the students. First, whatever their differences, every student in the class had an earnest desire to learn about and help to end the AIDS crisis. That common commitment, of which I reminded them frequently, saw us through many potentially divisive situations. Second, while moderating and guiding class discussions, I tried very hard to let every student have his or her "say," even if I disagreed strongly with his or her position. Students were free to complain loudly about others' opinions, but they knew that they would never be "jumped on" by the teacher for expressing an unpopular view. The one exception was if a student put forth medically incorrect information; then I would correct the misinformation but allow the discussion to proceed. Third, I believe that journals kept by the students (described in the next section) also helped to "let off steam" about their classmates, thus reducing the level of tension in the classroom. For instance, one of the older women wrote more than twenty pages in her journal about how she felt her religious views were not being taken seriously by the younger students, and how this reminded her of the anti-Catholic bigotry she had faced as a young girl. Similarly, one of the gay male students wrote extensively about how the older woman's homophobia reminded him of his mother's similar attitudes, and how dealing with this fellow student brought up the pain he felt at being kicked out of his parents' house for being gay. In both cases, having an outlet for their feelings allowed the students to deal with each other in a respectful manner.

The Journal

Two ongoing assignments helped establish an atmosphere of reflection and activism in the class: the journal and the service project. My experience in teaching women's studies had convinced me that the journals were an effective way to deal with emotionally charged material. Keeping a weekly log gave students an outlet to express and work through their fears, confusions, and other difficult feelings about the material being covered in class, and about the AIDS crisis in general. I also gave students specific questions to respond to in their journals: for example, "Discuss your reaction to Paul and Roger's gay relationship in *Borrowed Time*" (Monette, 1988) or, "Discuss your reaction to the AIDS-prevention needle-exchange program in Tacoma, Washington" or, "Do you believe that Larry Kramer is justified in using the analogy of the Holocaust to describe the AIDS epidemic? Explain."

The journals not only helped students express themselves, which some did beautifully, through poetry and artwork, they also gave me instant feedback about students' reactions to the class material. While many of the students who had taken Women's Studies and other classes with me were familiar with the process of journal-keeping, a few students had trouble getting started, as the following entry indicates:

> After a week of failing to find the "key" to this journal-writing process, some dread at some false starts, I have to begin now. I have not kept a journal in the past seven years . . . because I am embarrassed by the sound of my own "voice." . . . I shudder to think that I am the person such writing contains. . . . So if I am embarrassed when confronting (privately) my own naivete and stupidity, documenting this for others to stumble upon is even more difficult.

I encouraged students who were having trouble starting this assignment to consider using forms of self-expression other than plain prose in their journals;

for example one woman who had a "writer's block about AIDS" turned in a journal consisting almost entirely of powerful pen-and-ink sketches representing her feelings about the disease.

When asked to evaluate the helpfulness of the journal in a confidential survey seen only by myself and my teaching assistant, the students rated it highly: an average of 4.3 on a 5-point scale. Many also made comments such as, "It forced me to think! (Damn it!)" and, "When being educated about AIDS, I think I really liked the journal. It helped me express my emotions towards AIDS, which is ultimately just as important as lectures."

The Service Project

To establish and maintain the action orientation of the class, I also required each student to participate in a service project. The students were allowed considerable latitude in designing and implementing their projects. The only requirements were that the student spend at least one hour per week on the project, and that the project contribute in some way to ending the AIDS crisis. To help the students develop these projects and make contacts in the community, I distributed a list of "AIDS Resources" on the first day of class.[4] I also invited representatives from several local AIDS service and activist organizations to give brief presentations about their activities during the first few class sessions.

The variety and creativity the students displayed in their AIDS service projects exceeded my wildest expectations. Rarely during my teaching career have I been as moved as I was by the commitment and courage demonstrated by my students in these projects. Some of the students who took the course now volunteer on a weekly basis with the "AIDS orphan" baby-holding program in Harlem Hospital. Twenty students from the class wrote, choreographed, directed, and performed a professional-caliber theater production about AIDS; their *Divided We Fall: An AIDS Collective* moved me and most of the audience to tears.[5] These same students, some of whom have graduated, are currently making plans to present their production in high schools around New York City. Other students have become AIDS "buddies," and still others are making audio tapes for PWAs who have lost their sight. Half a dozen students organized a successful benefit concert for Community Research Initiative, a local community-based AIDS research program. And during the last class session, one student "came out" as HIV-positive to his classmates; he has since organized AIDS education workshops in his high school, and he recently wrote a piece as an openly HIV-positive person for the school newspaper.

My students were as enthusiastic about the usefulness of the service project as they were about the journal; they rated it 4.4 on a 5-point scale. Their evaluations included comments like, "On a scale of one to five, a ten!" and, "I really enjoyed our service project. It made me feel like I was actively doing something. As my first 'project' concerning AIDS, it was an ice breaker. I want to be more involved now" and, "The service project was AMAZING!"

I believe that allowing the students to design their own projects was a critical factor in the success of this component of the course. Students who were not emotionally ready to be buddies to PWAs, or who did not possess the public-speaking skills to lead AIDS-education workshops, could make posters for AIDS fundraisers or audio-tapes for blind PWAs. Each student was allowed to choose his or her own comfortable level of involvement with PWAs, and with service and activist organizations. In my opinion, a large number of options and a high degree of flexibility are critical aspects of any required service projects.

CONTENT AND PEDAGOGY

I divided the course content into three basic sections. In order of presentation, these were:

Awareness/Risk Assessment   The purpose of this section was to help students overcome their fears of PWAs as "the other," and to help them to recognize and change their own risk behaviors. Coming to terms with AIDS on an emotional level was, in my opinion, absolutely necessary for the students. Having already begun to deal with their fears, anger, and other feelings allowed them to concentrate on the biomedical, political, and other aspects of the crisis. Several students told me that connecting to the personal reality of AIDS in this section also motivated them to "plow through" what was sometimes rather tedious and difficult biomedical material.

Biomedical   In this section, students were introduced to the basic vocabulary of HIV infection and opportunistic infections, and were encouraged to learn about current treatment options. Having a basic understanding of the process of HIV infection and of the major treatment modalities was necessary for them to comprehend some of the controversies in the social/political section of the course; for example, an understanding of how HIV infects cells is a necessary precondition for comprehending debates over the FDA's approval or non-approval of various experimental AIDS treatments (see Eigo et al., 1988).

Social/Political   Activities and lectures in this section taught students to analyze AIDS in terms of racism, heterosexism, and other domestic and international forces that have contributed to the spread of this crisis worldwide, and which have impeded progress towards a cure.

Since student involvement was crucial to the success of the course, I used participatory pedagogy as much as possible. Some lectures were needed to introduce very basic concepts and to give us some common vocabulary with which to discuss the epidemic. For example, during the first week I gave a short lecture focused on the medical definition of AIDS, the common opportunistic infections found in male and female PWAs, the epidemiology of HIV infection here and abroad, and the socioeconomic context of the AIDS crisis. The required readings (see the references) also helped the students gain basic biological and social/political information. The following are some of the assigned readings and pedagogical techniques I found useful in the three sections of the course.

Awareness/Risk Assessment

— *The Names Exercise*
I began the first class of the semester by listing on the blackboard the names of my friends and acquaintances who had died of AIDS, and I invited the students to add names to the list. I was surprised when the students, most of them in their

teens, filled up the blackboard with names. We then dedicated the class to the memory of those who had died and to those struggling to live with AIDS.

— *Personal Risk-Assessment Exercise*
For the risk-assessment exercise, I passed out file cards and instructed the students to complete the following statements anonymously:

1. I am/am not (choose one) at risk for AIDS because . . .

2. I do/do not (choose one) practice safer sex because . . .

3. Some of the myths of AIDS transmission which I have heard from other students are: . . .

4. I have the following questions about AIDS: . . .

I collected and shuffled the cards and randomly passed them back to the students. I read the questions aloud and asked students to volunteer to read the answers on the cards they were holding. The entire class then commented on these anonymous answers and on each other's knowledge of AIDS. I intervened only when medically incorrect information was being given. I found this exercise to be a powerful pedagogical device for students; it forced them to confront their own risk behaviors and to see that they too could be at risk for AIDS. I would recommend that anyone who is interested in developing AIDS education curricula consider using a similar exercise.

These two exercises enabled me to see that as educators, sharing our experiences with AIDS with our students can encourage them to come to terms with the disease. However, it is only after we have confronted our own fears and anxieties about AIDS that we can help our students to confront theirs.

— *Guest Lectures*
Two early guest lectures were crucial in establishing the tone for the class: one by a mother who had lost her son to AIDS and another by a PWA.

Local chapters of Parents and Friends of Lesbians and Gays (PFLAG) are an excellent source of well-informed, committed speakers about AIDS. A mother of an AIDS patient from the New York City PFLAG spoke honestly and movingly to our class about her and her husband's struggle to understand and accept their son's being gay, and about his battle to live as fully as possible from the time of his AIDS diagnosis to his death.

A PWA friend of mine from ACT UP/New York also visited the class early in the semester. He spoke to the class honestly and with humor about a whole range of experiences common to many PWAs: fear and pain about his medical condition, the frustration of dealing with the medical and social service bureaucracies, and the strength he has gained from his activist work on behalf of PWAs. Many students told me later that they "turned a corner" after his visit: AIDS was no longer an overwhelming and abstract fear; while still frightening, it had become a real disease being fought by someone they had met.

— *Required Readings*
The first reading assignment in this section was Paul Monette's *Borrowed Time: An AIDS Memoir* (1988). Monette's book is a moving personal account of the

death of his lover, Roger, from AIDS, in October of 1986. I assigned this book both to draw students into the emotional reality of AIDS and to force them to confront and deal with any homophobia they might feel.[6] The students were as moved as I was by Monette's work. One man in the class had lost his lover to AIDS two years earlier, and had spoken about it to only a few people. He wrote:

> Often I found myself remembering intimately the feelings Monette was relating, reliving my experiences with the treatments and the doctors, the denial and the mask of unfounded hopes. So much feeling which I have repressed for so long now beginning to surface. Wednesday, Thursday, Friday were crying days. . . . The first night when I started the book, I could not sleep. All curled up in my bed though I wasn't cold, I cried till I fell asleep, crying for Paul Monette and his lover, crying for S. and myself.

One of the older women in the class wrote:

> I am now close to the end of *Borrowed Time.* I no longer see the two gay men. I see two people so desperately [*sic*] in love. So pathetically in love. It is heart wrenching. The more Paul clings to Roger, the more I want to take my husband in my arms just for the comfort and the feeling of security. Death must come to all of us, but — why must it be so painful to some? . . . to take away some of life's most precious gifts ever so slowly. Energy, sight, dignity.

Many of the students in the class, a significant number of whom were from low-income families, said that they sometimes felt "distanced" from the story by Roger and Paul's obvious and ostentatious wealth (e.g., the references to "the Jag," and their ability to afford experimental treatments and 24-hour nursing care). Nonetheless, the class rated the book highly, 4.0 on a 5-point scale, and all but three students recommended that it be required reading the next time I taught the course.

The second book in this section was Randy Shilts's *And the Band Played On* (1987). I had ambivalent feelings about assigning Shilts, due to his sensational descriptions of gay male life. But I also felt that his documentation of government and media apathy in the early years of the AIDS crisis was crucial. The students' feelings about the book mirrored my own. One young women wrote:

> I've been trudging my way through Shilts's *And the Band Played On;* for the same reason, I have a lot of trouble getting through it. Much of what he said was valid (i.e., the government's [lack of] response to AIDS etc.) but I could have lived without all the gossip.

Another simply said: "*And the Band Played On,* and on, and on, and on . . .".

Shilts's book was the one item on the reading list that the students recommended against using in the next class. When I teach the class again, I plan to use instead Bruce Nussbaum's *Good Intentions: How Big Business and the Medical Establishment Are Corrupting the Fight Against AIDS* (1990). Nussbaum, a writer for *Business Week,* makes many of the same points about government and corrupt management, but does so without "all the gossip."[7]

Other readings for this section included *Making It: A Woman's Guide to Sex in the Age of AIDS* (Patton & Kelly, 1988), which was an invaluable addition to the safer-sex role-play exercise (see below), and several articles on the personal experience of being HIV-positive or having AIDS, which I copied from *The Body*

Positive (Slocum, 1989), *The PWA Newsline,* and other sources. Since two of the primary texts for this section, Monette and Shilts, focused on gay White men, I concentrated on finding articles by and about women and/or people of color (see, for example, Pearson, 1990; Rieder & Ruppelt, 1988; Terson, 1989; Whitmore, 1988).

— *Safer-Sex Materials and the Role-Play Exercise*
Two exercises facilitated class discussion of the sometimes difficult subject of safer sex. First, my teaching assistant and I collected every unusual and humorous safer-sex material we could find, including fluorescent-green condoms, chocolate-flavored lubricant, and red-white-and-blue dental dams. The hilarity that erupted in class when we produced these items helped break the ice and begin a serious discussion of the obstacles to practicing safer sex.[8]

For the role-play exercise, I divided the class into three groups and asked them to break down into pairs. I then announced that the pairs within these three groups would play the roles of heterosexual couples, gay male couples, and lesbian couples. Their assignment was to negotiate safer sex, with one partner trying to convince the other, who thought that protection was unnecessary. After ten minutes, the convincer and the "convincee" switched roles and repeated the negotiations. Three volunteer couples, one from each sexual orientation group, were then asked to replay their negotiations before the class.

This exercise, predictably, brought gales of giggles from the students, but the discussion it generated was very enlightening. The students unanimously agreed that the subject of AIDS and safer sex should be broached before one gets into a potential sexual situation. By the time they were in the situation I had set up for the role play (back in the apartment alone together), rational discourse was very difficult. I believe this role play makes an important point, and I plan to continue to use it in future classes.

Most of the students also realized that they had trouble actually saying the words required to negotiate safer sex. As one woman put it, "If you ask him to put 'whazit' on his 'thingee,' you're not going to get very far." The difficulty these students — most of whom were sexually active — had in vocalizing simple anatomical words like "penis," "vagina," and "semen" illuminated the sexual shame that still lurks below the surface of our so-called sexually liberated culture, shame that greatly complicates safer-sex negotiations.

The reactions to the roles of convincee and convincer differed significantly by gender and by sexual orientation. Several of the heterosexual men said that they felt they were being "accused" of being gay, bisexual, or IV drug users when women raised the issue of AIDS and condom use. A few heterosexual women said they felt they were being accused of promiscuity when a male partner raised the issue. Women of all sexual orientations said that fear of abandonment, of losing the relationship, was the major reason they "gave in" and had unsafe sex. But one heterosexual woman stated that negotiations about safer sex were a good "test" of a relationship; if a man did not respect her enough to protect her health, then he was not worth worrying about!

We also discussed strategies that could be used on partners who were reluctant to use protection. These included bringing up the experience of a friend who had contracted HIV or died of AIDS, inundating the reluctant partner with pamphlets and other AIDS information, and, in a tight spot, claiming to have a medical or birth-control problem that requires the use of condoms. One woman suggested, "Tell him you forgot to take your pill or that you have a yeast infection. Then you have a *real* discussion with him in the morning!" One last strategy, which was semi-seriously proposed was "blaming it on the teacher" — that is, telling the reluctant partner, "I'm taking this AIDS class, and the prof says it's important to practice safer sex." (I assured the students that I would be happy to act as their excuse for safer sex, though I was not sure how much weight this would carry in the heat of passion!)

Biomedical

Two colleagues of mine from the biology department opened this section of the course with a guest lecture on the basic biology of the immune system and of the HIV infection. Their lectures built on the material covered in the assigned readings, taken from *The Science of AIDS: Readings from Scientific American* (1984).[9]

Due to the difficult nature of this material, I spent several class sessions recapitulating and answering their questions. I found reviewing questions in small groups helpful, particularly if science majors were divided among the groups. Also useful was the popularly written section on HIV infection found in the *Treatment Decisions Handbook* (Bohne, Cunningham, Engbretson, Fornataro, & Harrington, 1989) published by ACT UP's Treatment and Data Committee.

One scene from the students' production *Divided We Fall* also made me consider using art to reinforce learning of the basic biomedical material. The dancers wore T-shirts, each one labelled as either a component of the immune system (e.g., T4 cell or macrophage, two types of white blood cells vulnerable to HIV infection), or as a component of the HIV virus (e.g., gp-120, a surface protein of HIV, central to the cell infection process).[10] The beautifully choreographed piece visually demonstrated the process of HIV infection of an immune system cell and subsequent viral reproduction within that cell. I am hoping to adapt this idea into a role play with students playing the parts of various components of the immune system the next time I teach the course.

— Guest Lecturers

After the students had gained a basic understanding of the biomedical basis of AIDS, two guest speakers — from our local PWA Health Group and the American Foundation for AIDS Research (AmFAR) — explained some of the controversies surrounding current efforts and government procedures regarding AIDS drugs.[11]

The representative from our local PWA Health Group shared with the group his criticisms of the current FDA procedures for drug approval in cases of terminal illness. He related how the illness and subsequent death of his lover of nine years had moved him to become involved in smuggling unapproved AIDS drugs into the United States from Japan, Germany, and Israel. No one in the class questioned his right to engage in this activity, despite the fact that it is illegal. The students were impressed with his courage, but they also criticized

178

the Health Group for not putting more effort into reaching lower-income PWAs and PWAs of color.[12]

The speaker from AmFAR discussed the lack of equitable access to experimental AIDS drugs. Most experimental trials are conducted at major research universities; thus, HIV-positive people and PWAs who do not live near urban centers are often excluded, as are those who do not have private physicians to help them fill out the paperwork. In addition, many experimental drug trials blatantly exclude HIV-positive women,[13] and many more subtly discriminate against HIV-positive African Americans and Latino/as.[14] The speaker explored the promise that small, community-based AIDS research clinics, such as the New York Community Research Initiative, hold for improving access to potentially life-saving experimental medications.

— Midterm Exams on Biomedical Section

I gave the students individual take-home exams on the biology of the immune system and HIV infection. The questions included the following:

1. Carefully define AIDS. What do PWAs actually die from?
2. Briefly explain the epidemiology of AIDS in the U.S. and abroad.
3. a) Explain the basic structure and replication of HIV; b) Explain how the major classes of white blood cells function in a normal immune system; c) Explain some of the ways in which HIV infection is thought to interfere with normal immune response.

In general, the students did fairly well on this section of the midterm. Understandably, those with more background in the natural sciences did better; in fact, one biology major's answers were so concise and beautifully illustrated that I plan to use her answers as a handout next year. But the vast majority of students made it clear that they had absorbed enough information about the immune system and HIV infection to comprehend discussions of treatment modalities, vaccine strategies, and so on.

I also asked the students to divide into groups of approximately six people, and gave each team a copy of a "group exam" that was to be discussed, answered, and turned in as a team. The primary purpose of these group exams was to encourage discussions about issues raised in the initial "awareness" section of the course. Questions in this section of the midterm included the following:

1. Your best friend from high school tells you that he or she just tested HIV-positive. Explain in detail what information, including referrals, you would give him or her.
2. Discuss some of the obstacles to negotiating and practicing safer sex.
3. Discuss some of the changes which would have to be made to effectively deal with the AIDS epidemic here on campus, in New York City, and in the U.S. (for extra credit, discuss global policies).

I was pleased with the answers to these group exam questions, many of which displayed creativity and a great deal of thought. In response to Question 1, several teams produced detailed plans of action for the imaginary friend, which included phone numbers for the local HIV-positive support groups and local physicians specializing in AIDS, and other practical data. The answers to Question 3 were also especially impressive; one team even created a detailed proposal for AIDS education on campus, complete with budget estimates. Another team's suggestions for a "flashy, humorous" AIDS education pamphlet for the campus has been adopted by the AIDS Task Force.

Social and Political Context

During the final section of the course, I emphasized five factors that have created fertile ground for the spread of AIDS:

Homophobia/Heterosexism   From the beginning of the AIDS crisis, the reactions of the media and government have been decisively influenced by the fact that the first patients identified with AIDS in the United States were gay. (In fact, AIDS was first, erroneously, called "Gay Related Immune Deficiency," or GRID.) The apathy of the heterosexual public over the fate of gay men and the relative political powerlessness of the gay/lesbian/bisexual community allowed the media and government officials to virtually ignore the disease during the first critical years. As Shilts pointed out, over 21,000 Americans were already dead from AIDS before President Reagan uttered the word in public, in May of 1987. It is simply inconceivable that an infectious disease could have killed 21,000 White, middle-class, *heterosexual* Americans without becoming a major national priority for education and research.

Racism   The continued virulence of racial discrimination in the labor market, the political sphere, and elsewhere has greatly exacerbated the spread of AIDS. The consequent higher levels of poverty among people of color have often limited their access to timely, high-quality health care and, hence, to early AIDS diagnosis and treatment. Racism and insensitivity have resulted in a lack of culturally sensitive and language-appropriate AIDS education materials. For example, although Latino/as are disproportionately represented among the HIV infected, much crucial AIDS prevention and treatment information is simply not available in Spanish. Most of the information available has been translated from English, rather than written in the idioms of the Puerto Rican, Chicano, and other Latino/a communities. The situation is even worse for Asians and other language minorities. Finally, given the large percentage of current PWAs in the United States who are gay and/or people of color, racism has greatly contributed to the relative indifference with which this crisis has been treated by virtually all levels of government.

The Drug Epidemic   The federal government's War on Drugs has overemphasized interrupting the supply of drugs, while giving too little attention to addressing the conditions that give rise to drug use in the first place. For instance, over two-thirds of the monies allocated recently to fight the War on Drugs were earmarked for interdiction and imprisonment, with only one-third allocated to education and treatment. Conditions such as joblessness and homelessness, which contribute to drug use, are rarely addressed at all.

The Crisis in Health Care   The United States and the Republic of South Africa are the only industrialized countries in the world without some form of national health care. Thirty-eight million Americans, a disproportionate number of them people of color, have no health insurance whatsoever and rely upon the emergency rooms of public hospitals for their medical care. An additional fifty-six million are seriously underinsured (V. Navarro, cited in Morris, 1990). This lack of access to health care and health education greatly exacerbates the spread of HIV in these populations.

Male Bias   The medical research establishment in this country has traditionally viewed White males as the norm for clinical drug trials and other forms of medical research. In the case of AIDS, this focus on White males has rendered women largely invisible, except as "vectors" of transmission to men and to "innocent" children. The current medical definition of AIDS, formulated by the Centers for Disease Control (CDC), is based largely upon symptomology in males and ignores pelvic inflammatory disease and other gynecological opportunistic infections.[15] For women, this has led to serious under-diagnosis of AIDS, a consequent lack of proper medical care, and an inability to qualify for necessary social services (ACT UP/New York Women and AIDS Book Group, 1990).

— Required Readings

Readings for this section were rather extensive, and were divided into topic areas.[16] Readings for the subsection on racism included: Renee Sabatier's *Blaming Others: Prejudice, Race, and Worldwide AIDS* (1988); "People of Color and AIDS" (1989) and "Media Network's AIDS/HIV Media Screenings" (1990) by Ray Navarro; and "Fighting HIV in Communities of Color" by Michael Slocum (1989).[17] *Blaming Others,* which explores the dynamics of blame and misunderstanding in the discussions of the origins of HIV, and also the myth of fundamental "differentness" of African AIDS, was well received by the students. They gave it the highest ratings of any text, 4.6 on a 5-point scale, and made comments such as, "Good info! Helps put things into perspective!" and "I wish we could have spent more time on this one. It helps people confront their prejudices and fears." All but one student recommended its use in the next class.

Required readings for the subsection on women and AIDS included selections from *AIDS: The Women* (Rieder & Ruppelt, 1988); "Reproductive Freedom: An Urgent Issue for Lesbians, Gay Men, and People Affected by AIDS" (Wheatley et al., 1989); and "Women: The Missing Persons in the AIDS Epidemic" (Anastos & Marte, 1991).[18] The students found *AIDS: The Women,* a compilation of personal accounts by women PWAs and women caretakers of PWAs, moving, and rated it 4.5 on a 5-point scale. Comments such as "Excellent!" and "Very emotionally moving!" were typical.

The readings for the final section of the course, "AIDS Activism," included David Leavitt's "The Way I Live Now" (1989) from *The New York Times Magazine,* a debate on needle-exchange programs from *The Amsterdam News* (Curtis et al., 1988; Joseph, 1988), a *New York Times* article on the use of theater in AIDS education efforts (Rich, 1988), Sue Rochman's piece on AIDS education in a woman's prison (1989), and Larry Kramer's *Reports from the holocaust* (1989).[19]

Kramer's book, a scathing attack on the lack of media and government response to the AIDS crisis, elicited strong and mixed reactions from the students. One student said:

> Some of the writing in *Reports* was outrageous — but then Larry Kramer is outrageous! . . . I'm very glad you put this book in the reading list. I'm positive I would never have bought such a book on my own — I would have missed out on a great deal of information and never gotten to appreciate a fine writer and a sensitive (if abrasive) human being.

And another wrote:

> Again, very informative. . . . It went into depth about how people, as a whole, can just sit by and do nothing. How this country does not respond — to this day. . . . How when he went to Washington how each one passes the buck — no one's responsible. . . . People (with AIDS) must see large bureacracys [*sic*] as monsters. Larry Kramer sounds totally frustrated with these people — and justifiably so.

Others were not so enthusiastic about Kramer's perspective:

> Why doesn't he address the AIDS problem: women and children and people of color in his book? Why doesn't he address the surrounding areas of racism and classism in this book? Aren't they, along with homophobia, the real things perpetuating AIDS . . . in NYC? . . . Larry Kramer is doing just what we need not to do — we mustn't distance ourselves from the mutual struggles. All minorities must fight for freedom to live the way we choose, freedom to love the way we want, freedom to earn a living and maintain a reasonable personal lifestyle. Larry is doing just what he does not want others to do — he is dividing us.

The numerical evaluations of Kramer's book were similarly divided. Many rated it 5.0, a fair number 1.0, with an average around 4.0. Six students recommended against using this book again — more than for any other assigned book — but more also strongly supported its use, with comments such as "Crucial!" and "Vital!"

— Pedagogy for the Social/Political Context Section
Some lectures were necessary in this section, such as my lectures on the percentage of Americans covered by health insurance, and on the relative merits of the U.S. health insurance system versus the health coverage plans of other industrialized countries.[20] However, most of the social and political material was covered by assigning questions for small group discussion. These questions included the following:

1. Why are the participants in AIDS clinical drug trials overwhelmingly White and male, even in areas where PWAs are disproportionately Black and Latino? Is this a problem? Why? What could be done to change this situation?

2. Why has the War on Drugs not been terribly effective? What kinds of changes would have to occur to truly end the drug epidemic?

3. Discuss the strengths and weaknesses of a national health care plan, such as Canada's, compared with the current U.S. system.

Two videos were also valuable in this section. First we viewed *Bleach, Teach, and Outreach,* a short film on intravenous drug use and AIDS, which provoked a lively discussion on the pros and cons of needle-exchange programs for AIDS prevention.[21]

Next we screened a video by the New York City Human Rights Commission's AIDS Discrimination Unit, *The Second Epidemic,* which dramatized how the stigma against PWAs actually exacerbates the spread of AIDS.[22] In addition, a speaker from the Commission described her work on behalf of PWAs who are victims of AIDS-related discrimination.

The primary point I hoped to make in the social/political section was that the AIDS crisis did not arrive full-blown as a scourge from above, but, rather, that social, political, and economic inequality provided the conditions under which HIV infection could reach epidemic proportions. To address the AIDS crisis successfully in all communities, we must also address the stigmatization and institutionalized inequalities that have allowed this epidemic to occur.

At the end of this section, I gave a take-home final exam, which included questions such as the following:

1. Carefully define racism. Discuss the impact which racism has had on the course of the AIDS epidemic.

2. What changes do you believe would need to be made in the U.S. health care system (and health care financing system) to effectively deal with the AIDS epidemic?

3. Do you believe that pregnant women with AIDS should be permitted to enroll in experimental AIDS drug trials? What about asymptomatic HIV-positive women? Explain your position.

I was generally pleased with the quality of students' answers in the final. The question about racism, for example, elicited several thoughtful answers. For example, one woman explored in detail the impact that educational funding derived primarily from property taxes has on the quality of education in White communities versus communities of color. She concluded her essay with this:

> Only when people in low-income communities of colour [*sic*] have the educational tools and supportive services to really become part of the economic mainstream in this country will they be able to turn away from the hopeless oppressions of the ignorance, poverty, and drugs, which leads to AIDS. Only when the entrenched governmental institutions address their racist policies regarding equality in educational and economic opportunities, will people in these communities be able to respond effectively to the AIDS crisis.

Another woman simply wrote:

> Re: Racism and AIDS: It really pisses me off that:
> — access to health care is dependent upon ability to pay;
> — people of color don't have the same access to clinical trials as White, middle-class men;
> — we buy their theories of the origins of HIV because they agree with what we want to believe (e.g., HIV came from Africa) without ever examining the evidence;

— we assume that people of color invariable contracted HIV through IV drug
use, as if there are not gay people of color (and as if heterosexual transmission
were non-existent.)

The answers to the remaining questions also indicated that the students had
taken these issues seriously, and had a basic understanding of the sociopolitical
forces that have exacerbated the spread of AIDS.

Closure

During the final class session, students volunteered to give reports on their service projects. Two students showed an AIDS education videotape they had made.
The two women, Carla and Anne, took a video camera to a local shopping mall
on several successive Saturdays, and randomly interviewed young people there
about their knowledge of AIDS. Carla and Anne then presented the interviewees
with correct information on AIDS transmission and prevention, including pamphlets produced by a local AIDS service agency, and continued to film while the
shoppers began to assimilate and react to this information.

The state of knowledge of the young people reflected in the video was even
worse than we had expected. The majority of these young people, in 1990 suburban New York, said that AIDS was a "gay disease," and that, being heterosexual,
they were at no risk. Several of the young men bragged about their unsafe sexual
practices. Others expressed concern about transmission through mosquito bites,
the use of public toilets, and other risk-free behaviors. When confronted with
correct information, many were quite startled. The following reaction, by a
woman in her late teens, was typical: "What! You mean I could still get AIDS
even though my boyfriend and I have been going steady for ten months?"

Obviously the interviewees in the tape gained valuable information about HIV
transmission. Carla and Anne and the students who viewed the video learned a
great deal about the dismal state of AIDS education in suburban New York high
schools.

We then ended the class with two participatory exercises, which were designed
to end the class on a hopeful and action-oriented note:

— Future Action

I wrote on the board, "What am I going to do to end the AIDS crisis after this
course is over?", left plenty of chalk, and left the room for ten minutes. When I
returned, the board was filled with comments, ranging from "Demand that my
boyfriend wear a rubber!" to "Work on my homophobia feelings" to "Write a
letter to my Congressperson demanding more funding for AIDS research" to
"Join the Purchase AIDS Task Force."

— The Names Exercise Revisited

I reproduced the list of "Friends who have died of AIDS" from our first class
meeting, but also added a new list: "Friends who are struggling to live with HIV
infection/AIDS." After their involvement with the service project, the students'
second list was much longer than the first. After the list was seemingly complete
and filled two blackboards, an HIV-positive student walked up to the board and
added his own name. After a collective intake of breath on the part of the

students, he was drowned in hugs and promises of support. It seemed a fitting way to end the semester.

CONCLUSION

Judging from both the student evaluations and informal feedback, this course was a success both in imparting information and getting students seriously to reflect on and change their own risk behaviors. I believe that the primary reason for this success was our ability to create a real sense of community in the classroom. The students' inevitable confrontations with their own mortality, with assessing their own risk, and with the difficult ethical and political questions posed by the AIDS crisis occurred not only in isolated dorm rooms, but also in a supportive classroom setting. The students felt free to express their fears and angers, to ask their embarrassing questions, and to work through their own bigotries and prejudices.

Another important factor in the course's success was its role in helping the students begin to overcome their sense of powerlessness and desperation with respect to AIDS, emotions that are more pervasive among students than might be suspected. The service project, the repeated appearance of open PWAs, and the general action-orientation of the class were crucial elements here.

The realistic fear of HIV infection that we, as educators, bring to our students must be coupled with a sense that they *can* do something about AIDS — in their own lives and in society. This sense of shared purpose allows them to move beyond fear-of-AIDS paralysis — to hear themselves, each other, and HIV-positive people and PWAs — and begin to take action against AIDS. This was perhaps expressed most eloquently in the journal of the man who had lost his lover to AIDS:

> How different now this all is for me. How easily and freely I write now: how social I've become. And how has all this come to pass? I think that this class has had alot to do with these changes. First, because AIDS became something that I could talk about. Not only was the taboo on how it has affected me personally removed, (I've been able to talk about S.'s and my lives with people from class . . .), but now I've also got objective ways of discussing AIDS as a political issue, an ethical issue, etc. with people. And this gives me some power over how AIDS effects [*sic*] my life.
>
> Which is another change: my involvement . . . My face hasn't been hidden behind a book all semester . . . But more [important] than talking and hanging out is making things happen . . . Here I mean particularly the [AIDS education] T-shirts I printed and sold. I amazed myself with that project. I'd never silk-screened before in my life. . . . And then M. got the Students' Union to commit the money to the project, and suddenly I was committed not just to myself and the idea, but to other people who were as enthusiastic as I was . . . What alot of barriers to have broken.
>
> All of these things became meaningful to/for me, and also helped me to define me, become part of my identity on campus: He's the guy who made those AIDS activist T-shirts. I am learning how meaning develops out of usage, action. That's how words derive their meaning, and lives too. I found also that my life was getting meaning from involvement with people, with a community. . . . It wasn't until I started interacting this semester with people here [on campus], and with ACT UP that I found this need for meaning actually satisfied. What a remarkable and wonderful change this is.

Students need supportive spaces in which they can freely discuss their fears and confusions about AIDS, as well as avenues to put their energies to constructive use. It is up to us as educators to create such spaces for them.

NOTES

1. A complete video bibliography can be found in the appendix to *Women, AIDS, and Activism* (ACT UP/NY Women and AIDS Book Group, 1990).
2. See Ronald Sullivan, "Needle Exchangers Had Right to Break Law, Judge Rules" (1991).
3. Heterosexism is the belief that everyone is heterosexual, which is often accompanied by homophobia, the fear and/or hatred of lesbians, gay men, and bisexuals. Heterosexism is embodied in institutions (such as in hospital visiting policies, the IRS code), as well as in the beliefs of individuals, media, and government officials.
4. These included the New York City Department of Health's *AIDS: A Resource Guide for New York City* (1991). Many governments in urban areas now publish similar guides.
5. *Divided We Fall: An AIDS Collective* was created and directed by Arlene Xavier.
6. Another work that would serve these purposes is Carol Maso's *The Art Lover* (1990), which was published since I first taught the class. Maso's book is a touching account of the death of her best friend from AIDS.
7. Erica Carter and Simon Watney's *Taking Liberties: AIDS and Cultural Politics* (1989) explores the cultural perceptions and prejudices that lie behind this inaction. Though too advanced for most undergraduates, it is a helpful resource for the teacher and for upper-division students.
8. For more information on the effectiveness of condoms in preventing HIV transmission, see "Condoms and Spermicides: How much Protection?" in *World Population Reports* (World Health Organization, 1989).
9. Teachers should exercise care in selecting articles from *The Science of AIDS*. Some, such as the introductory piece, "The AIDS Epidemic" by Robert Gallo and Luc Montagnier, are comprehensible by most undergraduates. Others, such as William Haseltine and Flossie Wong-Staal's "The Molecular Biology of AIDS," are very difficult for students without a science background. In addition, Max Essex and Phyllis Kanki's piece on the origins of HIV in Africa is highly controversial (see Sabatier, 1988). And, of course, the epidemiology and treatment information must be updated by the instructor. Eve Nichols's *Mobilizing against AIDS* (1989) is a possible alternative text.
10. Non-technical definitions of these and other terms regarding the basic biology of AIDS can be found in the appendix to ACT UP/NY's *Women, AIDS, and Activism* (1990) and in further detail in Mark Harrington's *Glossary of AIDS Drug Trials, Testing, and Treatment Issues* (1988).
11. See, for example, Harrington's "Anatomy of a Disaster: Why is Federal AIDS Research at a Standstill?" (1990) and his *Critique of the AIDS Clinical Trials Group* (1990).
12. John James's *Treatment News,* a monthly newsletter, is a good source of information on experimental drugs for AIDS.
13. Many trials totally exclude HIV-positive women "for the protection of the fetus," even if the woman is not currently heterosexually active or agrees to use reliable birth control. Some trials have mandated sterilization for women participants, but not for men. This is particularly horrendous, given the history of the U.S. government-sponsored sterilization abuse in communities of color, and the fact that 75 percent of women PWAs are African Americans or Latinas (see Committee for Abortion Rights and against Sterilization Abuse, 1988; Davis, 1983).
14. For instance, for reasons not yet identified, HIV-positive African-American men seem to be less likely than HIV-positive White men to carry "p24 antigen," a sub-component of HIV, in their blood. Clinical trials that use measured p24 antigen levels as a

criterion for entry will therefore *de facto* discriminate against African Americans, even if there is no conscious intent to exclude.

15. An official definition of AIDS requires not only a positive HIV antibody test, but the presence of one or more of a number of "indicator" diseases. In extraordinary cases, the diagnosis may be made when HIV antibody testing is unavailable, inconclusive, or thought to be erroneous. The Centers for Disease Control twice (in 1985 and 1987) expanded the list of such "indicator diseases." But critics charge that those opportunistic infections that will infect women (e.g., cervical cancer and resistant pelvic inflammatory disease) and HIV drug users (e.g., bacterial endocarditis) are still not included in the definition. Some of the most common "indicator diseases" include, but are not limited to: PCP (pneumoncystis carinii pneumonia), Kaposi's Sarcoma, toxoplasmotic encephalitis, cytomegalovirus infection of the eyes or bowels, intestinal cryptosporidiosis, extrapulmonary crytococcosis (including crytococcal meningitis), HIV encephalopathy (dementia), MAI/MAC infection (macrobacterium avium complex), oral or esophogal candidiasis (thrush), and PML (progressive multifocal leukoencephalopathy).

16. Readings relevant to the section on homophobia/heterosexism (Shilts, Monette, etc.) have been covered earlier in the course.

17. An excellent article on racism and AIDS, Harlon Dalton's "AIDS in Blackface," is now available in an anthology edited by Nancy MacKenzie, *The AIDS Reader* (1991). Several other important articles are also collected in this reader, which I intend to assign as a required text the next time I teach the class.

18. Since I taught the class, the ACT UP/NY Women and AIDS Book Group has published *Women, AIDS, and Activism* (1990), which contains analyses of the impact of AIDS on many different groups of women — heterosexual women, lesbians, mothers, prostitutes, prisoners, and women of color, as well as numerous personal testimonies by HIV-positive women. I plan to assign readings from this collection the next time I teach this course.

19. Douglass Crimp and Adam Rolston's recent *AIDS Demographics* (1990) discusses ACT UP's use of visual imagery and other art in the fight against AIDS.

20. David Morris's "America's Health Care System is Ailing" (1990) is a helpful reference on this point.

21. *Bleach, Teach, and Outreach* was filmed and directed by Ray Navarro and Catharine Saalfield. It is available for loan from Gay Men's Health Crisis in New York City.

22. *The Second Epidemic*, produced by Amber Hollinbaugh, is available for distribution from the AIDS Discrimination Unit of the New York City Human Rights Commission.

23.

REFERENCES

ACT UP/NY Women and AIDS Book Group. (1990). *Women, AIDS, and activism.* Boston: South End Press.

Anastos, K., & Marte, C. (1991). Women, the missing persons in the AIDS epidemic. In N. MacKenzie (Ed.), *The AIDS reader.* New York: Meridian Books.

Bohne, J., Cunningham, T., Engbretson, J., Fornatoro, K., & Harrington, M. (1989). *Treatment decisions.* New York: ACT UP/NY.

Carter, E., & Watney, S. (Eds.). (1989). *Taking liberties: AIDS and cultural politics.* Bristol, Eng.: Serpent's Tail.

Committee for Abortion Rights and Against Sterilization Abuse. (1988). *Women under attack: Victories, backlash, and the fight against sterilization abuse.* Boston: South End Press.

Crimp, D., & Rolston, A. (1990). *AIDS demographics.* Seattle: Bay Press.

Curtis, J. L., Rangel, C. B., Flake, F., et al. (1988, October 15). Why it mustn't be tried. *Amsterdam News,* p. 15.

Davis, A. (1983). *Women, race, and class.* New York: Vintage.

Eigo, J., Harrington, M., Long, I., McCarthy, M., Spinella, S., & Sugden, R. (1988). *FDA action handbook.* New York: ACT UP/NY.

Fastje, J. (1990). *The effects of AIDS upon sexual behavior among college students.* Unpublished senior thesis, State University of New York, Purchase.

Harrington, M. (1990, March 13). Anatomy of a disaster: Why is federal AIDS research at a standstill? *Village Voice,* p. 15.

Harrington, M. (1990). *A critique of the AIDS Clinical Trials Group.* New York: ACT UP/NY.

Harrington, M., Eigo, J., Kirschenbaum, D., & Long, I. (1988). *Glossary of AIDS drug trials, testing, and treatment issues.* New York: ACT UP/NY.

James, J. (April 1986–ongoing). *AIDS Treatment News.* (Available from P.O. Box 411256, San Francisco, CA 94141)

Joseph, S. (1988, October 15). Needle exchange experimental program: Why it must be tried. *Amsterdam News,* p. 15.

Kramer, L. (1989). *Reports from the holocaust.* New York: St. Martin's.

Leavitt, D. (1989, July 9). The way I live now. *The New York Times Magazine,* p. 16.

Maso, C. (1990). *The art lover.* San Francisco: North Point Press.

Monette, P. (1988). *Borrowed time: An AIDS memoir.* New York: Harcourt Brace Jovanich.

MacKenzie, N. (Ed.) (1991). *The AIDS reader: Social, political, ethical issues.* New York: Meridian Books.

Morris, D. (1990, March/April). America's health care system is ailing. *Utne Reader,* p. 20.

Navarro, R. (1990). Media Network's AIDS/HIV media screenings [Special issue]. *Media Network News, 3*(1).

Navarro, R. (1989). People of color and AIDS. In L. Chou, R. Elovich, C. Goodman, et al., (Eds.), *Target City Hall: An AIDS activist's guide to New York City in 1989.* New York: ACT UP/NY.

New York City Department of Health. (1991). *AIDS: A resource guide for New York City.* New York: Author.

Nichols, E. (1989). *Mobilizing against AIDS.* Cambridge, MA: Harvard University Press, 1989.

Norwood, C. (1988, July). Alarming rise in deaths: Are women showing new AIDS symptoms? *Ms.,* p. 65.

Nussbaum, B. (1990). *Good intentions: How big business and the medical establishment are corrupting the fight against AIDS.* New York: Atlantic Monthly Press.

Patton, C., & Kelly, J. (1988). *Making it: A woman's guide to sex in the age of AIDS.* Ithaca, NY: Firebrand Books.

Pearson, M. (1990, April). Mother Pearson of "Mother's Love." *The Body Positive,* p. 19.

People With AIDS Coalition. (July 1985–ongoing). *PWA Coalition Newsline.* New York: Author.

Rich, F. (1988, August 1). Actors confront AIDS on stage and off. *New York Times,* p. C1.

Rieder, I., & Ruppelt, P. (Eds.). (1988). *AIDS: The women.* San Francisco: Cleis Press.

Rochman, S. (1989, March 17). In an unlikely place, women offer each other AIDS education and love: The story of ACE (AIDS Counsellors and Educators) in Bedford Hills Prison. *Gay Community News,* p. 7.

Sabatier, R. (1988). *Blaming others: Prejudice, race, and worldwide AIDS.* Washington, DC: Panos Institute.

Slocum, M. (1989, November). Fighting AIDS in communities of color. *The Body Positive,* p. 15.

Staff of *Scientific American.* (1989). *The science of AIDS: Readings from* Scientific American. New York: Freeman Co.

Shilts R. (1987). *And the band played on: Politics, people, and the AIDS epidemic.* New York: St. Martin's.

Sullivan, R. (1991, June 22). Needle exchangers had right to break law, judge rules. *New York Times,* p. B1.

Terson, A. (1989, November). All about Alice. *The Body Positive,* p. 8.

Wheatley, M., McCarthy, M., Karp, M., & Glover, T. (1989, September 17). Reproductive freedom: An urgent issue for lesbians, gay men, and people affected by AIDS. *Gay Community News,* p. 5.

Whitmore, G. (1988, January 31). Bearing witness. *The New York Times Magazine,* p. 14.

World Health Organization. (1989). Condoms and spermicides: How much protection? *World Population Reports* (Series L, No. 8). New York: Author.

Worth, C. (1989, July 9). Handle with care. *The New York Times Magazine,* p. 12.

ORGANIZATIONAL RESOURCES — NATIONAL

ACT UP/New York (AIDS Coalition
  to Unleash Power)
135 West 29th St., 10th Fl.
New York, NY 10001
(212) 564-AIDS (2437)

AIDS Counseling and Education (ACE)
Bedford Hills Correctional Facility
287 Harris Rd.
Bedford Hills, NY 10507
(914) 241-3100, Ext. 260

AIDS Treatment Registry
P.O. Box 30234
New York, NY 10011
(212) 268-4196

American Foundation for AIDS Research
  (AmFAR)
1515 Broadway, Suite 3601
New York, NY 10036
(212) 633-1782

The Body Positive
208 West 13th St.
New York, NY 10011
(212) 633-1782

Community Research Initiative (CRI)
155 West 23rd St.
New York, NY 10011
(212) 481-1050

Gay Men's Health Crisis
129 West 20th St.
New York, NY 10011
(212) 807-6655

Haitian Coalition on AIDS
50 Court St., Room 605
Brooklyn, NY 11201
(718) 855-7275

Hispanic AIDS Forum
121 Ave. of the Americas, Suite 505
New York, NY 10013
(212) 966-6336

Minority AIDS Task Force on AIDS
92 St. Nicholas Ave.
New York, NY 10010
(212) 749-2816

National AIDS Network
2033 M St., NW, 18th Fl.
Washington, DC 20036
(202) 293-2437

National Association of People With AIDS
2025 I St., NW
Washington, DC 10006
(202) 429-2856

Parents and Friends of Lesbians and Gays
  (PFLAG)
201 West 13th St. (Duane Church)
New York, NY 10011
(212) 463-0629

People With AIDS Coalition
31 West 26th St.
New York, NY 10010
(212) 532-0290

Women and AIDS Resource Network
  (WARN)
P.O. Box 020525
Brooklyn, NY 11202
(718) 596-6007

Learning to Teach
against the Grain

MARILYN COCHRAN-SMITH

Can prospective teachers learn to be both educators and activists, to regard themselves as agents for change, and to regard reform as an integral part of the social, intellectual, ethical, and political activity of teaching? In this chapter, Marilyn Cochran-Smith argues that a powerful way for student teachers to learn to reform teaching, or what she refers to as "teaching against the grain," is to work in the company of experienced teachers who are themselves struggling to be reformers in their own classrooms, schools, and communities.

Cochran-Smith analyzes two approaches to preparing pre-service teachers to teach against the grain, proposing that differences between them can be understood as the result of different underlying assumptions about knowledge, power, and language in teaching. By analyzing conversations among student teachers and experienced teachers in four urban schools, the author explores the nature of reformers' intellectual perspectives on teaching and demonstrates that regular school-site discussions are an indispensable resource in the education of reformers.

In an essay condemning political and social indifference in pre-war Italy, Antonio Gramsci (1916/1977) forcefully argued that action was everyone's responsibility and that each individual, no matter how apparently powerless, was accountable for the role he [*sic*] played or failed to play in the larger political struggle. Gramsci particularly condemned those who blamed events on the "failure of ideas" or the "collapse of programmes" but at the same time failed to make their own voices heard and failed to lend their own moral and material resources to promote good and resist evil. If we accept Gramsci's notion that indifference is often a mainspring of history, and if we substitute the word "teacher" for Gramsci's "man" and use the feminine pronoun, we have a powerful statement about the accountability of individual educators for their efforts to reform U.S. schools:

> Every [teacher] must be asked to account for the manner in which [she] has fulfilled the task that life has set [her] and continues to set [her] day by day; [she] must be asked to account for what [she] has done, but especially for what [she] has not done. . . . It is time that events should be seen to be the intelligent work of [teachers] and not the products of chance or fatality. And so it is time to have done with the indifferent among us, the skeptics, the people who profit from the small good procured by the activity of a few, but who refuse to take responsibility for the great evil that is allowed to develop and come to pass because of their absence from the struggle. (p. 18)

Harvard Educational Review   Vol. 61   No. 3   August 1991, 279–310.

I use Gramsci's clarion call for social accountability to reassert that teachers are decisionmakers and collaborators who must reclaim their roles in the shaping of practice by taking a stand as both educators and activists (Aronowitz & Giroux, 1985; Greene, 1986; Zeichner, 1986). I do not wish to suggest that teachers alone have the power or the responsibility to reform education by "teaching better," or that teaching can be understood in isolation from the cultures of schools and communities or the historical and political contexts of school and society. But I do wish to insist that teaching is fundamentally a political activity in which every teacher plays a part by design or by default (Ginsburg, 1988; Willis, 1978).

Prospective teachers need to know from the start that they are part of a larger struggle and that they have a responsibility to reform, not just replicate, standard school practices. I argue in this chapter, however, that working to reform teaching, or what can be thought of as *teaching against the grain,* is not a generic skill that can be learned at the university and then "applied" at the school. Teaching against the grain stems from, but also generates, critical perspectives on the macro-level relationships of power, labor, and ideology — relationships that *are* perhaps best examined at the university, where sustained and systematic study is possible. But teaching against the grain is also deeply embedded in the culture and history of teaching at individual schools and in the biographies of particular teachers and their individual or collaborative efforts to alter curricula, raise questions about common practices, and resist inappropriate decisions. These relationships can only be explored in schools in the company of experienced teachers who are themselves engaged in complex, situation-specific, and sometimes losing struggles to work against the grain. For these reasons, I argue that students of teaching cannot learn how to reform teaching in a general sense during the student-teaching period, but only how to be reformers in one specific classroom or school. Struggling along with experienced teachers to be reformers in particular schools and classrooms is an enterprise that is less glamorous — and less grand-sounding — than challenging the hegemony of the educational and societal status quo. But, as I argue throughout this chapter, it may well be that it is the only way to help students generate, and then sustain over the long haul, teachers' critical perspectives on schooling and teachers' commitments to work against the grain inside schools.

In the pages that follow I briefly analyze two approaches to preparing preservice teachers to teach against the grain, approaches that I refer to as *critical dissonance* and *collaborative resonance.* I propose that differences between these two can be understood as the result of different underlying assumptions about knowledge, power, and language in teaching, and the ways these are played out in school-university relationships. I further argue that reforms built on the collaborative resonance of university and school have the potential to provide student teachers with unusually rich learning opportunities. Next, I take readers into four urban schools in the Philadelphia area where student teachers work and talk with experienced teachers who, in a variety of ways, are working against the grain. Drawing on data from these four schools, I present an analysis of teachers' and student teachers' discourse during weekly school-site meetings, revealing the groups' efforts to pose questions, struggle with uncertainty, and build evidence for their reasoning. These conversations provide vivid descriptive evidence that regular school-site talk among experienced reforming teachers and inexperienced student teachers is an indispensable resource in the education of reformers.[1]

CRITICAL DISSONANCE AND COLLABORATIVE RESONANCE

Student-teaching programs specifically designed to foster critical inquiry and prepare prospective teachers to be reformers are part of a small minority of pre-service programs across the country (Edmundsen, 1990; Goodlad, 1990; Grant & Secada, 1990; Zeichner, Liston, Mahlios, & Gomez, 1988).[2] Within this small group of programs, however, two significant variations in theory and practice can be distinguished as the products of two different sets of assumptions about the power and knowledge relationships of the school and the university. The differences between critical dissonance and collaborative resonance are most evident in the ways the problems of student teaching are conceptualized, the goals of student teaching are articulated, and the strategies of student-teaching programs are designed.

Critical Dissonance

One approach to preparing student teachers to work against the grain is to create *critical dissonance*, or *incongruity based on a critical perspective*, between what students learn about teaching and schooling at the university and what they already know and continue to learn about them in the schools. In student-teaching programs based on critical dissonance, the "problem of student teaching" is generally identified as its tendency to bolster utilitarian perspectives on teaching and ultimately to perpetuate existing instructional and institutional practices (Beyer, 1984; Feiman-Nemser, 1983; Goodman, 1986b, Tabachnick & Zeichner, 1984; Zeichner, Tabachnick, & Densmore, 1987). The goal of these programs is to interrupt the potentially conservative influence of student teachers' school-based experiences and instead to help them develop stronger, more critical perspectives that confront issues of race, class, power, labor, and gender, and to call into question the implications of standard school policy and practice. The strategies of programs intended to foster critical dissonance include: methods courses that emphasize alternative teaching strategies, field experiences coupled with ethnographic studies of schooling, critical theory-based curriculum study, student-teaching seminars and journals in which students reflect critically on their teaching experiences, supervision that emphasizes individual growth, and action research projects carried out in schools (Beyer, 1984; Gitlin & Teitelbaum, 1983; Goodman, 1986b; Zeichner & Liston, 1987).

Programs that aim to create critical dissonance are intended to be transformative, to help students broaden their visions and develop the analytical skills needed to interrogate and reinvent their own perspectives. Unfortunately, these programs have had limited success. Critical reflection is difficult, especially because cooperating teachers who do not have reflective skills themselves often co-opt the effort (Calderhead, 1989). Further, the intentions of programs are not necessarily implemented in practice (Zeichner et al., 1987), particularly in the interactions of students and their university and school-based supervisors

(Zeichner et al., 1988) and in methods and fieldwork courses (Beyer, 1984; Goodman, 1986a,b). Over time, such programs encourage some critique, but actually alter students' outlooks very little (Feiman-Nemser, 1990; Zeichner et al., 1987).

Few educators would disagree that preparing more liberally educated teachers to think critically and to help their students think critically as well is an essential goal for student-teaching programs. However, subtle but troubling messages about power, language, and knowledge are embedded in programs that aim to provoke critical dissonance between university and school: the way to link theory and practice is to bring a critical perspective to bear upon the institutional and instructional arrangements of schooling; people outside of the institutions of schooling are the agents who have developed these critical perspectives and thus can liberalize and reform the people and activities inside; the "wisdom" of teachers' practice is a conservative point of view that has to be gotten around, exposed, or changed; and, the language and conceptual frameworks most useful for describing and critiquing teachers' work lives need not be familiar to teachers or articulated in their own voices.[3] This means that the radical critique prompted by critical dissonance, which argues in the abstract for the knowledge, voices, and power of teachers themselves, may in reality "set up" school-based teachers to be exposed and criticized in university-led courses, and may inadvertently convey the message that teachers' lived experiences are unenlightened and even unimportant. Efforts to connect theory and practice through critical dissonance may thus contribute to the irreconcilability of the two, to what Feiman-Nemser and Buchmann (1985) call the "two worlds pitfall" of separation of the world of practice/school from the world of theory/university.

Collaborative Resonance

A second approach to preparing student teachers to work against the grain is to create *collaborative resonance,* or *intensification based on a co-labor of learning communities,* by linking what student teachers learn from their university-based experiences with what they learn from their school-based experiences. In programs based on resonance, the "problem of student teaching" is thought of as its failure to provide student teachers with not only the analytical skills needed to critique standard procedures and connect theory and practice, but also the resources needed to function as reforming teachers throughout their teaching careers in diverse school contexts. The goal is to prolong and intensify the influences of university *and* school experiences, both of which are viewed as potentially liberalizing. Students and teachers alike critique the cultures of teaching and schooling, research their own practices, articulate their own expertise, and call into question the policies and language of schooling that are taken for granted.

The strategies of programs intended to foster collaborative resonance, some of which are similar to strategies of programs intended to foster dissonance, include: placement of student teachers in sites where school-wide reform and restructuring efforts are underway, or where small groups of teachers are engaged in reform inside larger, more traditional schools; action research and teacher research projects conducted cooperatively by student teachers and experienced teachers; alternative curriculum and methods courses that emphasize critical perspectives but also feature assignments critiqued in both university and school settings; cases of practice and problem situations constructed by experienced teachers as grist for discussion among student teachers; collaborative inquiry at school-site meetings and university-site seminars; and joint program planning and assessment by teachers and teacher educators (Carter, 1988; Clift, Veal, Johnson, & Holland, 1990; Cochran-Smith, 1991; Cochran-Smith, Larkin, & Lytle, 1990; Cochran-Smith & Lytle, 1992; Larkin, 1990; Rochester City Schools/University of Rochester Ford Foundation Report, 1988–1989; Ross, 1988).

Programs based on resonance share with programs intended to stimulate dissonance the view that, in and of themselves, the formal aspects of pre-service preparation are largely incapable of altering students' perspectives (Zeichner, Tabachnick, & Densmore, 1987), while the less formal, experiential aspects of student teaching are potentially more powerful (Feiman-Nemser, 1983). Both recognize that an important part of what happens during the student-teaching period is "occupational socialization" (Corbett, 1980), or learning the culture of the profession (Evertson, 1990; Little, 1987), including how to behave, talk, and think like experienced members, and both aim to interrupt the socialization that normally occurs. But unlike programs intended to provoke dissonance, programs based on resonance simultaneously aim to capitalize on the potency of teaching cultures to alter students' perspectives by creating or tapping into contexts that support ongoing learning by student teachers in the company of experienced teachers, who are themselves actively engaged in efforts to reform, research, or transform teaching (Evertson, 1990; Richardson-Koehler, 1988).

Taken as a whole, the messages embedded in programs based on collaborative resonance are significantly different in several respects from those in many other programs: the way to link theory and practice is through a process of self-critical and systematic inquiry about teaching, learning, and schooling (Cochran-Smith & Lytle, 1990); this kind of inquiry is most effective within a larger occupational culture of collaboration wherein novices and experienced professionals alike work to learn from, interpret, and ultimately alter the day-to-day life of schools; power is shared among participants in the community, and knowledge about teaching is fluid and socially constructed; the wisdom, language, critique, and theoretical frameworks of school-based reforming teachers are as essential to a knowledge base for teaching as are those of university-based teacher educators and researchers (Lytle & Cochran-Smith, 1991); and, in the end, the power to liberalize and reinvent notions of teaching, learning, and schooling is located in neither the university nor the school, but in the collaborative work of the two.

Student-teaching programs that aim for collaborative resonance are rooted in a tradition of participatory democracy. They recognize that there are many people who have developed incisive and articulate critiques of teaching and schooling based on years of professional work *inside* schools. When it comes to reform-minded teaching, these emic perspectives are regarded as different from, but as important as, the etic critiques developed by people who have devoted their professional lives to work about, but *outside of*, schools. Programs based on resonance attempt to bring together people with emic and etic perspectives on teaching against the grain — not to homogenize ideas or create consensus in language and thought, but in order to intensify through co-labor the opportunities student teachers have to learn to teach against the grain.

TEACHING AGAINST THE GRAIN

Teachers who work against the grain are in the minority. Often they must raise their voices against teaching and testing practices that have been "proven" effective by large-scale educational research and delivered to the doorsteps of their schools in slick packages. Often they must demonstrate that they are competent at widely practiced modes of teaching and assessing children's learning, despite the fact that they are battling to develop and use alternative modes. Often they must provide evidence that their students are making sufficient progress according to standard measures of learning, despite the fact that they place little stock in those measures and believe, on the contrary, that they work against the best interests of their children. It is not surprising that teachers who work against the grain are sometimes at odds with their administrators and evaluators. They are not always the teachers selected as teachers of the year, nor the ones pointed out by their colleagues as the cream of the faculty, and they are not necessarily the ones whom school principals judge to be best suited for work with student teachers.

To teach against the grain, teachers have to understand and work both *within* and *around* the culture of teaching and the politics of schooling at their particular schools and within their larger school systems and communities. They cannot simply announce better ways of doing things, as outsiders are likely to do. They have to teach differently without judging the ways others teach or dismissing the ideas others espouse. Unlike researchers who remain outside the schools, teachers who are committed to working against the grain inside their schools are not at liberty to publicly announce brilliant but excoriating critiques of their colleagues and the bureaucracies in which they labor. Their ultimate commitment is to the school lives and futures of the children with whom they live and work. Without condescension or defensiveness, they have to work with parents and other teachers on different ways of seeing and measuring development, connecting and dividing knowledge, and knowing about teaching and schooling. They have to be astute observers of individual learners with the ability to pose and explore questions that transcend cultural attribution, institutional habit, and the alleged certainty of outside experts. They have to see beyond and through the conventional labels and practices that sustain the status quo by raising unanswerable and often uncomfortable questions. Perhaps most importantly, teachers who work against the grain must name and wrestle with their own doubts, must fend off the fatigue of reform and depend on the strength of their individual and collaborative convictions that their work ultimately makes a difference in the fabric of social responsibility.

Teaching against the grain is challenging and sometimes discouraging work, and it is often difficult for experienced teachers to keep on and keep heart, and even more difficult for student teachers — often young and always inexperienced in the politics of schooling — to join the struggle. Some student teachers can learn to describe and critique the macro-level relationships of schools and schooling within university courses and seminars (Beyer, 1986; Goodman, 1986a; Zeichner et al., 1987), and many can write convincingly and sincerely of their desires to change the world of education, to touch the lives of their own students. In most of their student-teaching placements, however, there are few opportunities for either the experienced teachers (Goodlad, 1984; Lieberman & Miller, 1984) or the student teachers (Griffin, 1986; Lanier, 1986) to participate in thoughtful inquiry, reflect on their daily decisions, or collaborate with others (Little, 1987; Su, 1990). In most of their encounters with school and university supervisors, student teachers are encouraged to talk about "relevant" and technical rather than critical or epistemological aspects of teaching (Borko, Livingston, McCaleb, & Mauro, 1988; Hursh, 1988; Zeichner et al., 1988). Finally, in most of their pre-service programs, the role of the teacher as an agent for change is not emphasized, and students are not deliberately socialized into assuming responsibility for school reform and renewal (Edmundsen, 1990; Goodlad, 1990).

As I illustrate in the next section, however, student teachers' relationships and collaborations with teachers who are themselves struggling to teach against the grain make for a different kind of experience. Working and talking regularly with experienced teachers who share the goal of teaching differently allow student teachers to participate in their ways of knowing and reforming teaching. These relationships lead student teachers to see that larger and grander school reform efforts are deeply entangled with their own biographies as educators, the decisions they make and permit others to make about the children in their classrooms, and the discussions that occur (or fail to occur) at their schools. Despite their inexperience, student teachers do learn about teaching against the grain when they talk with experienced teachers within a collaborative context where questions are urged, answers are not expected, and the tentative forays of beginners are supported.

The Students and Their Pre-Service Program

To illustrate how opportunities to work and talk with reformers may provide student teachers with unique opportunities to learn about teaching against the grain, I focus in the remainder of this chapter on data collected in urban elementary schools in the Philadelphia area where student teachers worked actively with both university mentors and school-based teachers engaged in the enterprise of reform. I explore the range and variation of learning opportunities available to student teachers within the weekly teacher-researcher school-site meeting — one of the major contexts of this student-teaching program, which is intended to build on the collaborative resonance of university and school experiences.

Participants in the school-site meetings were student teachers, cooperating teachers, and university supervisors in Project START, a fifth-year pre-service program in elementary education at the University of Pennsylvania.[4] In Project START, all participants (students, as well as cooperating teachers, university supervisors, and course instructors) are encouraged to view themselves as researchers, reformers, and reflective professionals responsible for critiquing and creating curriculum, instruction, forms of assessment, and the institutional arrangements of schooling. The combination of several instructional and supervisory structures makes the student-teaching portion of the program somewhat unusual. Twenty to twenty-five students progress through the twelve-month program as a cohort, participating together in study groups, seminars, courses, and teacher-research groups. Each student teacher simultaneously completes university course work and a full year of student teaching in the same classroom with the same teacher (five months of student teaching two days per week, three months of student teaching five days per week). Sub-cohorts of three or four student teachers are placed at specially selected elementary school sites with cooperating teachers who, in a variety of ways, are working against the grain. They are involved, for instance, in curricular redesign projects, teacher research and publication, alternative schools and programs, grass-roots parent-teacher community groups, teacher networks and collaboratives, or other teaching- and school-reform efforts. Alternative methods courses emphasize critical issues in theory and practice and require projects that are implemented in student-teaching classrooms and critiqued in both university and school settings. All participants in the program are teachers, learners, and researchers They have opportunities to participate in many varieties of teacher research through course assignments, school and university-site activities, in-house and regional publications and professional forums, and the larger professional community.[5] Each sub-cohort of student teachers, cooperating teachers, and university supervisor meets weekly in a school-site, teacher-researcher group meeting to reflect on their work. All cohorts meet together monthly for a university-site seminar on teaching, learning, and learning to teach. University supervisors and program organizers meet biweekly in a teacher-educator-as-researcher group to inquire about their own theories and practices of teacher education. Supervisors, program organizers, and cooperating teachers meet twice yearly to assess and revise the program (Cochran-Smith, 1991).

The Teachers and Their Schools

In this chapter I draw on examples from school-site meetings that occurred over the course of one student teaching year (September–May) at four schools: Charles A. Beard, a small desegregated Philadelphia public school; Stephen R. Morris, a large Philadelphia public school; Edgeview Elementary, a public school in a small urban area on the edge of Philadelphia; and Community Central Lower School, a small central Philadelphia independent school (see Table 1).[6] These four schools were selected to demonstrate the range of variety in urban school-site discussions. The small groups of student teachers assigned to these schools met weekly as teacher-researcher groups with their cooperating teachers and university supervisors to raise questions and reflect on issues of theory and practice. Over the course of the year, the four schools hosted more than seventy teacher-researcher meetings, ranging in length from 30 to 90 minutes.

In the pages that follow, I use observational data to reveal some of the "intellectual work" of teaching against the grain, as well as some detail about the ways this work is accomplished in small collaborative discussion groups. I use the term "intellectual work" to refer to the particular interpretive tasks that are taken on, and the particular ways of talking about teaching that are common to the conversations of reforming teachers. In other words, intellectual work refers to the patterns of thinking, talking, and knowing about teaching that are characteristic of teachers engaged in the enterprise of reform: the problems they pose about children, the dilemmas they find impossible to answer, the knowledge they make problematic, the evidence they seek in order to document and explore particular issues, the bodies of knowledge they bring to bear on particular situations, the ways they connect diverse experiences, and the themes they explore as central to understanding teaching (Cochran-Smith, 1990b). I present excerpts from four conversations, each focusing on a different topic and each from a different school with its own culture of teaching and history of reform.[7] Each reveals something about the ways teachers work together to challenge ideas and confront problems in their own schools and classrooms. Each also reveals something about the personal passion and cost of this work. Most importantly, the conversations demonstrate why student teachers need opportunities to live and work with reformers if they themselves are to embrace a reformer's stance toward teaching and schooling.

COLLABORATION, INTELLECTUAL WORK, AND THE CULTURE OF REFORM

Rethinking the Language of Teaching

At Community Central Lower School, the threads of progressive philosophy are woven tightly into long-standing traditions of peaceful Quaker education. At the core of the culture is a deep commitment to community, diversity, and self-criti-

TABLE I
School Sites by Size, Population, Type, and Teachers

	Charles A. Beard Elementary	Stephen R. Morris Elementary	Edgeview Elementary School	Community Central Lower School
Size of School	300 K–4	1,200 K–4	400 K–5	180 K–4
Population Served	Black (74%) White (25%) Other (1%)	Black (98%) Other (2%)	White (64%) Asian (30%) Black (6%)	White (60%) Black (30%) Asian, Hispanic (10%)
Type/ Location	Public/ Large urban area	Public/ Large urban area	Public/ Small urban area	Private/ Large urban area
Student Teachers (ST)	3	3	3	4
Cooperating Teachers (CT)	4	3	3	4
University Supervisors (US)	1	1	1	1

cal inquiry. Teachers strive to educate the mind, body, and spirit of all students and to prepare them to live more fully in the present as well as the future. In an important sense, daily school life at Community Central itself represents a transformative vision of what is possible in education. An emergent curriculum, alternative forms of assessment, and a stable student body of more than 30 percent minority students (by far the highest proportion of non-White students in an independent school in the area) make for a visible culture of reform and serve as an ongoing critique of standard public and private school practice and principle. But the habit at Community Central is also to question the school's own practices: one teacher commented that she had chosen to work at the school because it was never "self-satisfied."

At Community Central, teachers and student teachers alike are encouraged to question assumptions and to ask questions of themselves and others. One experienced teacher pointed this out to the student teachers:

> Don't ever apologize for being a teacher and always talk about it in an intellectual way to really show that as a responsibility, you have to keep learning. . . . As a model for your peers and colleagues, there is a way to say that there aren't any easy answers. . . . Especially as a new teacher, in a way you are given permission to ask *why* as a new teacher. And as a colleague it's your responsibility to constantly say, "Well, that's *an* answer," or, "That's an easy answer and what we need to do is to take some time to *really* think about the issue, talk about all the ways we can get information to illuminate what's going on, and then talk about all the strategies we can use to strengthen the situation." And that's much more complicated. But you're still modeling being a thinking individual, which is what you want to do. And some principals don't like that, you know, but then some principals are in a very isolated position too. . . . So the thought of having some faculty people who are really alive and asking good probing questions also could liberate a whole faculty.

Within a culture of reform and reflection, the teacher-researcher group at Community Central raised questions about the assumptions underlying school policies and the consequences of their labeling practices. Borrowing from Giroux's (1984) article, "Rethinking the Language of Schooling," I regard this form of intellectual work as *rethinking the language of teaching* — a collaborative process of uncovering the values and assumptions implicit in language and then thinking through the nature of the relationships it legitimates.

In one teacher-researcher meeting at Community Central, for example, the group discussed the consequences of the school's long-standing practice of labeling some students "transition children"; that is, children who complete kindergarten but are "not ready" for first grade, and hence spend two years in either first or second grade. An excerpt from their conversation demonstrates what it means to do the intellectual work of rethinking the language of teaching.[8]

> *Sherry Watson-Gage (CT 3/4):* I do not believe in a transition class, or having it — period! As a parent [in this school], last January I got a letter from my child's teacher, actually in November, when she had spent a month and a half with him. She said to me, "He may be a candidate for transition." I said, "Why?" And she said, "It's not academic, it's emotional." . . . I think all of those discussions are very fuzzy and [I know] they have to be in November, but what it said to me was, "He's not all right" — not that he's not perfect because, goodness, I know that, but it was, "He's not all right. There is something wrong with him. And we're now going to

lower our expectations for the amount of growth that he is going to go through because we're not thinking probably that he will go to first grade — he'll go to transition."

Sheila Jules-James (CT 3/4): What would you do then with a child who was not ready?

Sherry Watson-Gage (CT 3/4): See, that to me is a hard thing. What does it mean not to be ready? Because last year, I had children who were "not ready" for third grade, and they are great in fourth grade. Now how do you predict? And what does it mean? I have fourth-grade children who have been transition children [years ago], and it's still an issue for them. They still say, "I was a transition child." And so they are still carrying something around [with them]. And nobody ever said it with glee, "I was a transition child!"

[The problem is, when a teacher makes] a judgment that a child may not be ready for first grade, knowing the immense amount of development that a kid can go through in one year . . . the school, I think, has a lot of talking to do. And I think we should talk among ourselves, but I think we should also talk to parents who have gone through the experience, because it doesn't serve the school well. It may serve certain children really well, and those children we should pay attention to. But what is the experience? [What can we see by] following a transition kid through to see if it really does help?

[*The conversation continued during the meeting the following week.*]

Sheila Jules-James (CT 3/4): I think it's a way of giving children more options, of expanding options, rather than saying, "OK, you're in kindergarten so you're now on this track that goes this way." I think it's a way of broadening the base and saying to a family, . . . "This is a child who may need three years in primary." And do you take that first year early? Do you take that extra year early, or do you take it at the end? . . . I think transition is . . . not a situation that has any easy solution. And I think what works for one family may not work for another child or another family. I see there being children who need more attention or more time in some way and they need it for a wide variety of reasons, and how do we give it to them without damaging their self-esteem or damaging their families' self-esteem or the way their families feel about them?

Over the course of two lengthy school-site conversations, members of the teacher-researcher group helped one another begin to do the intellectual work of rethinking the language of learning and development. Specifically, they worked to make the labels, language, and practices of children's early growth problematic, an activity that Tom (1985) emphasizes is a "conscious attempt on the part of the teacher to suspend judgment about some aspect of the teaching situation and, instead, to consider alternatives to established practice" (p. 37). The conversation was dominated by the experienced teachers, but it really began at the start of the school year (and several weeks prior to the conversation actually quoted above) when one student teacher commented, "I'm just not really sure what those [transition] classes are about and how they came to be set up like that and whose decision it was and which kids get placed in those classrooms and that kind of thing." Her question prompted an experienced teacher to express dissatisfaction with the practice of establishing transition classes, which eventually led to the group's exploration of the issue and to repeated admissions that the question had no ready answer.

Tom has argued that critical theorists have sometimes failed to provide an adequate enough account of individual intention and human agency in the development and evolution of culture, so that teachers can move beyond "deterministic thinking" and toward "intentionality" (1985, p. 38). What is especially important about the intellectual work accomplished in the excerpt above is that participants regard the teacher herself as one of the agents who has the right, and indeed the obligation, to make certain aspects of teaching problematic. In the discourse of teacher-researcher meetings, the underlying image of the teacher as an active agent poses a sharp contrast to the image of the teacher as a pawn pushed around by the fingers of habit, standard procedure, and expert outsider knowledge. Instead, the teacher is put forward as one who is centrally responsible for raising questions, interrogating her own knowledge and experiences, and then beginning to take responsible and reasoned action.

Posing Problems of Practice

The Charles A. Beard School, part of the large city school system, provides two educational alternatives to parents — "the open classroom track" and "the traditional track." The hallmark of the culture of teaching in the open classrooms is an ongoing effort to learn from children's language and work, to draw from observations of single cases teaching strategies that can be used in other cases, and to construct curriculum that strengthens children's abilities by building on their own resources. The existence of two distinct traditions of teaching provides ongoing grist for comparison and an informal culture of critique. In addition, the city system's intensifying uniformity and standardization of curriculum and testing make it increasingly difficult for teachers to teach to children's strengths and to maintain a long view of their development. As one teacher talked to the student teachers about her teaching history, she described the culture of reform of which she and others in the group had been part for many years:

> It was the beginning for me of seeing how much what we do affects what the children produce and how much we limit them with unspoken messages when we give them worksheets and when we give them dittos and fill-ins. . . . When I was put back into a second-third grade, I immediately wanted to change the class around and do a lot of art. . . . Of course the principal that I had then thought it was outrageous. But that began a tradition, and it was very, very hard to be in a place where you knew that you could do something for children that would be meaningful and relevant for them, but the powers-that-be had other ideas about what school was all about. And it really became an ongoing theme in my life, and I think in many people's lives, that whatever culture the kids are from, the school culture becomes yet another piece that is overlaid on them. And when it doesn't have any fit with their own culture, with what they've brought, it really becomes very hard for them to see school as relevant and to be able to feel themselves as valuable people. And I finally had to leave that place because I just felt I was so stymied in what I wanted to do. . . . I realized that we had to take hard looks at the kids and do the kind of work that they were already showing us was important to them. So that's what I tried to do.

Charles A. Beard is a small desegregated school with a strong history of parent-teacher cooperation and a commitment to community involvement. Although as a school Beard does not have a commitment to open education, the teachers who are members of the teacher-researcher group are heavily involved in a teacher-initiated, long-term, and primarily outside-of-school culture of activism, reflection, and progressive education. They are founding members of a twelve-year-old teachers' cooperative group that meets weekly in members' homes to reflect on their work, and they are participants in many local and national forums on teaching, learning, and evaluation. In these groups, teachers labor together to construct knowledge for teaching and resist intellectual dependence on expert wisdom alone, which, they believe, can limit children's possibilities.

Within a culture of commitment to public education and to the social and democratic construction of knowledge for teaching, the Beard teacher-researcher group frequently uses guidelines from "Descriptive Review of a Child" and other documentary processes described in Carini (1986). These begin with a teacher's focusing question about a specific child or issue to be explored through systematic observation and oral inquiry. In site meetings over the course of a year, a frequent focus of the group's intellectual work was the development of questions, or what Schön (1983) describes as "problem setting." Schön reminds us that problems of professional practice do not present themselves ready-made, but rather that "the [practice] situation is complex and uncertain, and there is a problem in finding the problem" (p. 129).

In one teacher-researcher conversation, for example, student teachers were struggling to choose individual children whom, as an assignment for one of their courses, they would observe over time in the classroom and then present to the school-site group. Their cooperating teachers emphasized posing problems from which they could learn how to teach the individual child, as well as other children. Their emphasis was consistently on understanding the generalities of teaching by exploring its particulars:

Sharon Bates (CT 4): The key thing is to pick a child you have a question about and that you honestly want to describe and get feedback on. . . . You have to think of a question for the child. This is the hardest part. It has to be with you and the child. It can't just be centered on you.

Karen Johnston (CT 3): There might be a third grader [about] whom you feel, "Am I going to know that child any better when I leave here?" Or, "How am I going to work with this child when I feel some of these barriers?" That would be one kind of question. It's not just, "How am I going to work with this child?"

Rita Greenberger (CT 1): Another kind of question might be, "How am I going to get this child to know I mean business?" or "How can I get this child to be a functioning part of the group — to improve his reading or improve the way he relates to other children?"

Sharon Bates (CT 4): It also could be a question about reading and writing, like "How can I help someone to read?" Those questions seem to be the ones that you seem to be more comfortable with through what you have already learned in the [university] classroom. And some of these other questions about social relationships and management are the harder ones.

Jenny Gold (ST 3/4): Does it have to be a question, or can it be an analyzation [*sic*] of somebody?

203

Rita Greenberger (CT 1): It can be an issue.

Karen Johnston (CT 3): What is *your* question? [*addressing Sharon Bates, who has mentioned earlier that she will make a presentation about a child at a teacher-researcher conference the following week.*]

Sharon Bates (CT 4): It's about how to help Anwar. He's a person who with reading checks things out a lot with adults when it doesn't make sense. When he has a question, it's not like he reads a whole book and then wonders about it. He reads and then he really needs to ask a question right away if it is something he doesn't understand. I think you, Jenny, experience him as very disruptive a lot of the time. He's always up and down.

Jenny Gold (ST 3/4): With activities on the rug I do.

Sharon Bates (CT 4): My question is how to support him in his reading to keep the questioning that he does, because it is really very valuable to him, but to become more independent, so that he won't be frustrated when he gets into a classroom situation in which he might not get his questions answered. . . . When he read the autobiography of Jackie Robinson, he got stuck after reading the first forty pages. "This is all about Negro this and that and isn't about baseball." That's just how he put it and that's not what he wanted to know right then about Jackie Robinson. It wasn't that he didn't want to know about Blacks, it was just that he wanted to get to the baseball part. . . . I got the sense that if I hadn't been there to talk about it right then it would have been, "I can't do that because I can't answer that question." He's captured into reading now, but you have to hold him still, . . . so my question is how to support him in this path.

In this and other conversations, members of the group explored together the process of finding questions/setting problems about individual children. The teachers described and demonstrated the ways they constructed questions out of close observations of children, from multiple perspectives. The problem Sharon Bates posed was not simply a version of how to teach reading or how to apply theories of reading in her classroom. Rather, she posed a problem about how to understand Anwar as reader, learner, and asker of questions, and how over time to connect with his resources in order to strengthen them.

The cooperating teachers at Charles A. Beard helped student teachers frame and reframe questions, repeatedly directing them to return to observations from the classroom, uncover the prior questions that were embedded in present ones, and develop generative structures of inquiry. Their process of mentoring was not unlike Schön's (1983, 1987) description of the ways supervisors in architecture and psychotherapy work with students — by reframing their ways of looking at the problems of design and counseling, and by both implicitly criticizing the students' own ways of framing the problems and also suggesting new ways to think about solutions. Teachers at Charles A. Beard were not certain about how to solve every problem, nor did they think that every problem had a solution. Nevertheless, their conversations with student teachers over a year clearly indicate that they were certain both that teaching was primarily an activity of intellectual problem-setting and that the best sources of information about how to set problems were the children themselves. One of the most striking aspects of problem-setting is the image it conveys to student teachers about the teacher's relationship to knowledge. The "teacher" implicit in the conversations at Charles

A. Beard was not separated from the knowledge of teaching, nor was the teacher simply the practitioner or applier of others' theoretical principles. Rather, she was a builder of knowledge and theory, which, as Smyth (1987) reminds us, is no mere academic distinction:

> What is at issue is the right of practitioners to be emancipated from the stifling effects of unquestioned habits, routines and precedents, and in their stead to develop ways of analysis and enquiry that enable the exposure of values, beliefs and assumptions held and embodied in the way practitioners experience and lead their lives. Implicit in what is being discussed is the distinction between two competing sociological views or ways of knowing about teaching; on the one hand a "scientist" approach to teaching involving the collection of facts to be used to predict and control teaching, and on the other, a "critical" approach committed to the notion of practitioners developing theories of their own which help them to interpret, understand and eventually to transform the social life of schools. (p. 12)

In their discussion, teacher researchers collaboratively built theory and knowledge frameworks out of the experience of specific cases that cut across classrooms, age levels of children, and cultural backgrounds (Cochran-Smith, 1989). In this way, they were intimately involved in a process of transforming the social life of the school and doing what Knoblauch and Brannon (1988) call "knowing their own knowledge."

Constructing Curriculum

Edgeview Elementary School serves a diverse working-class community of mostly White families, a small number of Black families, some recent immigrants from Korea and Greece, and families of other cultures who have lived in the community for a number of years. There is a strong culture in the school of positive community involvement; friendly relations among children, teachers, principal, and parents; and an ecumenical tolerance for various teaching "styles."

Although there is a comfortable sense of congeniality at Edgeview, teachers work largely by themselves, and as is the case in many schools (Little, 1987; Lytle & Fecho, 1989), there is a culture of isolation. The three experienced teachers who were part of the teacher-researcher group were united more by their belief in alternative reading/language arts programs that utilize literature and children's writing instead of basal reading instructional materials than by actual collaborative work.

However, the curriculum and assessment policies of the school district are traditional, and a few years ago, the district began to place increased emphasis on standard procedures and curriculum uniformity. The culture of reform of Edgeview's teacher-researcher group was bound up with the construction of an alternative curriculum and with demonstrating that children could learn to read from real literature rather than from texts constructed specifically for the purpose of instruction. During the year prior to the school-site meetings mentioned here, the teachers struggled with administrators over whether or not literature could be used at the second-grade level. One of the teachers described the struggle to her student teacher:

> They fought us about novels last year [because some people think] our children's backgrounds are lacking and they haven't got support from home and experience

in reading. . . . [They think] they need things simpler. They need the "See Dick run. See Jane run," and the novel isn't written in that form. It's not simplified. And [they think] they're not ready except for the smart kids. . . . So our principal finally said to us, "You can use novels, but you have to test the children in the tests for the reading series, and you have to teach the same skills that are in the reading series." . . . So I do it. And we showed him. I mean, I have folders full of stuff . . . where the kids are learning short *a* and long — all the things that he thinks they need to learn. . . . So he told us we could try it . . . and review it. . . . [And then later he said no, but] we presented our case anyway, and basically we said, "Show us where it hasn't worked. Show us that our kids aren't reading. Show us . . .". We got the parents, too, . . . and the kids to say they liked novels. It was very risky. . . . We cheered when he told us we could stay in novels. . . . This year I never even went and discussed it with him. I'm just assuming that I am going to do it. . . . If we hadn't won that battle, I probably wouldn't have come back.

As part of a group effort aimed at curriculum reform working within a larger school-system culture of standardized teaching and assessment, the teacher-researcher group at Edgeview raised questions about teaching, planning, and understanding curriculum, in particular reading, writing, and language. This form of intellectual work, which can be thought of as *constructing curriculum,* is more than deciding how to teach the material predetermined in a teacher's guide or a pupil's text. It requires that teachers consider the long-range consequences of what and why they teach, as well as the daily decisions about how they teach it. In conversations over the course of the year, the Edgeview teacher-researcher group discussed the underlying differences between teaching with basal texts and teaching with trade books. They compared curricula that emphasized isolated skills with those that concentrated on broader understanding. In the conversation below, they reflected on a district in-service session designed to get them to think of literature as a supplement to, but not an alternative to, the "real" curriculum of basal reading materials:

Charlie Dougherty (CT 5): One of the points that was being made to us was the possibility to use novels as a supplement. Now that is what I think is ludicrous to do.

Leslie Franks (CT 5): For us.

Charlie Dougherty (CT 5): You can't do it. *Either* you are going to use the basals *or* the novels.

Leslie Franks (CT 5): You can't go back and forth . . . because it squashes the enthusiasm. And what happens is the kids tend to moan and groan through the whole basal unit that you are doing, and you're ruining their growth. And when you go back to the novels, they know it is for a one-night stand. A one-night stand! And then they are back again to basals, which is like suicide.

Charlie Dougherty (CT 5): It's a silly idea.

Leslie Franks (CT 5): And actually that *is* what it is. You commit suicide by doing novels *and* basals . . .

Charlie Dougherty (CT 5): The [basal] books we have are sinful! So we have a different situation with [fifth graders], . . . at least to an extent. . . . Mary [the second-grade teacher who had to fight to convince others that literature was appropriate for younger children as well as older children] has things to consider that we don't. She has to work with the [decoding] skills and we can focus more on comprehension.

Leslie Franks (CT 5): And also as they progress in years, when you talk about standardized testing, that is one of the big things that you find. . . . It's the little paragraph that you have to read now [on the tests] — What is the main idea? Now what do you want to do first? What were the supporting details? And if you can do that with the novel, you are so much more in tune to detect these [on the test]. Case in point — our kids have done beautifully on [standardized comprehension] testing.

Charlie Dougherty (CT 5): They blew the top off!

Phyllis Kim (ST 5): I don't think I understand basals well enough, but I really don't understand why you can't go back and forth using basals and novels if you were using the same approach — an inferential [approach]?

Mary Thailing (CT 2): Yes, if you were just giving a child a book [and not using the teacher's manuals and workbook exercises], you could do whatever you wanted with it.

Phyllis Kim (ST 5): I was thinking that if I were in a school district next year where I have basals and I could only use novels when I could afford to buy them, could I do something like that?

Mary Thailing (CT 2): [You could do with] a basal story everything that you do with a novel . . .

Charlie Dougherty (CT 5): I don't know if you can.

Mary Thailing (CT 2): Yes you can. If it's a story that is a *real* story. I mean that's in there [in the basal] . . .

In this conversation the group struggled with the problem of combining two kinds of materials for reading instruction that are grounded in basically incompatible perspectives on language learning — conflicting perspectives on language as a system, language learning as a process, and children as language learners and users. Zumwalt (1989) argues that a "curricular vision of teaching" is essential for all beginning teachers if they are going to be prepared to function as professional decisionmakers in their field. Without it, she cautions, the beginning teacher tends to settle for "what works" in the classroom rather than what could be:

> If prospective teachers do not understand that questions of "what" and "why" are as central to teaching as the understandably pressing questions of "how," not only is the range and quality of their decisionmaking drastically limited, but teaching can easily drift into a meaningless activity, for students as well as for teachers. (p. 174)

Also underlying this discussion was the conflict among teachers and administrators (and among teachers themselves) about their roles as curriculum implementors and tinkers on the one hand, or critics and creators on the other. Finally, their discussion implicitly touched on sorting out possible meanings of "curriculum" itself, which, as Zumwalt points out, is essential to the understandings of beginning teachers, lest they operate according to a notion of curriculum as a particular set of textbooks, tests, and curriculum guides.

Confronting the Dilemmas of Teaching

At Stephen R. Morris Elementary, the slender threads of the open classroom tradition are knotted and entangled with the broader strands of the history of segregation and desegregation in the city. Morris offers a small "open" track, a "traditional" track, and a "midway" track from which parents can choose options for their children. The culture of teaching in the open track is built on a commitment to closely observing children, providing a rich environment out of which children's own curiosities can drive the curriculum, and continuously reflecting on practice in the company of other committed professionals. But Morris serves more than 1,200 children who, for complex historical reasons, are from poor Black homes, while the middle-class Black and White parents in the immediate and immediately adjacent neighborhoods choose to have their children bused to other desegregated city schools or sent to private schools. Conditions at Morris are difficult, special programs are limited, and the culture of teaching in the school at large is traditional. Teachers in the Morris teacher-researcher group had a transformative vision of education, but they worked within a context of poverty, increasing school district testing and curriculum strictures, and few opportunities for collaboration. One teacher noted to the student teachers:

> At the end of the year, I look over the year and I always feel there's more I could have done. And there are parts of the year I really feel good about and parts of the year I don't feel good about. But you're still only one human being. You can't do everything. I feel that what I offer children is very rich, and if children just get a little bit of that or if they get the idea that not everything has to be the same all the time [then it's worth it]. And there's this thing called thinking. I felt that what I did was important for those children [and their thinking]. It gave them a little experience that maybe will stick with them, and maybe they'll be lucky and have an echoing of that experience so it'll be, "Aha!" and maybe it will be, "I remember that!" Maybe that'll happen. I hope it will. I try to tell the children that they might not have a chance to do the things that they're doing in this classroom the rest of their time in school. I tell them that I feel very sad that I have to tell that to them.
> . . .
> One of the thoughts I have is that I'm sixty-three. Technically, you can teach until you're seventy. At this point I would like to teach forever. I can't imagine doing anything other than teach. But it's not as enjoyable as it used to be. I mean . . . just being in an environment where I feel I'm unappreciated makes it very, very hard. It's okay once the door is closed, and I'm in here, but it's very hard to walk out of the door.

As a school community, Morris does not have a commitment to the principles of progressive education or teacher empowerment. But the Morris teachers who were members of the school-site group were actively involved in a long-standing culture of teacher inquiry and British primary school traditions and, like the Beard teachers, were founding members of a teacher collaborative that met weekly. One of the teachers in the group had published her teaching journal, another wrote articles on urban teaching, and yet another was instrumental in the founding and shaping of early childhood education in the area. In teacher-researcher meetings at Morris, teachers struggled with many questions that had no answers, and many problems that had no solutions. Borrowing language from Lampert (1985) and Berlak and Berlak (1981), I refer to this form of intellectual work as *confronting the dilemmas of teaching*, a process of identifying and wrestling with educational issues that are characterized by equally strong but incompatible and competing claims to justice.

In one teacher-researcher meeting at Morris, for example, the group had talked about recent court decisions that affected girls' and boys' schools in the area. They also discussed the negative consequences and the possible advantages for minority children of *segregated* schooling situations. The fact that one of the student teachers in the group was a Black woman who had attended mostly White schools throughout her educational history, and that all three experienced teachers in the group were White women who had made enormous personal and professional commitments to teaching in mostly Black public schools, were critical factors in the discussion:

Ellen Freeman (CT 1/2): One question I have is about middle-class teachers who don't have the experiences of the children they teach. . . . I have noticed something about . . . a few of the Black boys that I've taught, and I came to some conclusions about them and what would be the place for them — what kinds of teachers would be best for them to have. And I don't know, I mean, I don't know if this is racist or not. There were some very bright Black children in that class. They were in a desegregated class. They were learning to read and write and spell and all that, but there was also a group of extremely bright White boys in the class, . . . and the White boys were well-behaved. . . . They always did the "right thing." And the Black kids often misbehaved, and they often baited me in some ways.

Later in fourth grade . . . [one of them] was [taken out of the desegregated class] and put into the class of a Black teacher with all Black kids. . . . At the end of year, [he] won a behavior award in the school. What it made me think was that . . . we need to have all boys' high schools *de*segregated because it's important for boys to be in schools with girls. But we [also] need girls' high schools for girls to excel without men, without boys — I wonder, sometimes, if . . . some Black children need to be in schools that are not desegregated where they see themselves as leaders within their community — I don't know — I mean it really is a question, and I've thought a lot about it. . . . It's just a question, because I think we need girls' high schools *and* I think we need all boys' schools to be *de*segregated. . . .

Teresa Green (ST K): I think that the point Ellen brought up is important. Your awareness of those boys in the classroom, and what you might have done differently, or what transformation you saw happen to them when they were in a different situation impresses me. . . . I mean, it does make a difference. . . . I know from previous experience that an integrated situation versus a segregated situation can do positive or negative things for you. . . . I've been a minority in predominantly all-White situations from the time that I was six or seven. And it does make a difference. And some of the differences are negative. And it's important to find out that sometimes people can be stronger when they are with people that they need to be with — when they are in supportive environments. . . .

Polly Spellman (CT K): But I don't think you learn how to be strong in the abstract. Just as I don't think you learn how to use freedom unless you have freedom. Freedom isn't something you read about and then follow directions. It's something you have to experience. Well, I feel it's the same thing about kids in schools. Though I could see some positive things to girls' schools, the big banner is that everybody should be able to function to their fullest in any school. . . . Schools that are putting all the children under the same umbrella, I don't think you learn how to be part of the real world when you get into that kind of school. . . . I just don't think that we get any closer to learning how to operate by having exclusions. . . .

Teresa Green (ST K): But you're talking the ideal! The reality is of the world. The reality of the situation is that Black kids cannot go into predominantly White situations and come out with the same kind of security, the same kind of support that they would get in a different environment. Those are the facts. It's not the ideal but those are the facts. . . .

Polly Spellman (CT K): So, let's go back to segregated schools?

Ellen Freeman (CT 1/2): It's not really a segregated school, Polly. That's not what I'm talking about either. I am talking about choices. I think that's a good term for it. I think that is important. But I guess I'm *not* talking about choices for everybody. I have to say that. I don't agree with Karen about boys' high schools. I do not think that the people who have traditionally been in power should be allowed — *allowed* — to have choices. . . .

Teresa Green (ST K): But that's contradictory —

Ellen Freeman (CT 1/2): I know it is —

Karen Garfield (CT K-5): What Ellen is saying is that the heavy power [that] has always been a certain way needs to skew the other way. . . .

In this discussion, teachers worked together to confront the dilemmas created by race, class, and gender segregation of educational opportunities. They wrestled to reconcile the irreconcilable issues of the possible advantages for minority children of going to school with children of their own race or gender groups versus the clear disadvantages of being segregated from the culture of power. It is significant that there was no consensus in this conversation, especially in the comments of Ellen Freeman, who knew full well that what she was saying was, in a certain sense, both contradictory and critical.

A key aspect of this conversation is that members of the group named one of the dilemmas of teaching and wrestled with the fact that there was no answer to it within the current structures of schooling and society. Their conversation makes it clear that there is a distinction between a dilemma of teaching and a problem of teaching. A problem is a question posed for solution or at least action, a situation that may be perplexing and difficult, but *not* one that is ultimately unapproachable. The Morris teachers (and the teacher-research groups at other schools) demonstrated clear ways of thinking, talking, and knowing about the problems of teaching. A dilemma, on the other hand, is a situation of teaching that presents two or more logical alternatives, the loss of *either* of which is equally unfavorable and disagreeable. A dilemma poses two or more competing claims to justice, fairness, and morality. The dilemma confronted above probed the means-ends relationships of schooling and raised critical questions about the interests served by the current structures of schooling.

Fenstermacher (1990) points out that in current controversies over the professionalization of schooling, the moral dimensions of teaching, although primary, are often either ignored or forgotten:

> The rhetoric of the professionalization of teaching is grounded primarily in the knowledge base of teaching, not the moral base. Therefore, it is a rhetoric that clusters around notions pertinent to knowledge, such as expertise, skill, competence, objectivity, validity, and assessment. Yet . . . these are not the concepts that capture the essential meaning of teaching. Without the specification of the moral principles and purposes of teaching, the concept amounts to little more than a technical performance to no particular point. Just as a physician who has no idea of why or to what end he or she practices medicine or a lawyer who lacks any sense of the rule of law in the just society, a teacher without moral purpose is aimless, as open to incivility and harm as to good. (pp. 132–133)

At Stephen R. Morris, the group identified and confronted one of the moral dilemmas of teaching. Their intellectual work did not "solve" the problem nor adjudicate which side of the scale should be more heavily weighted in matters of race, gender, and educational opportunity. But their work clearly announced that there *is* a moral base to teaching, not just a knowledge base, and that prospective teachers must confront that moral base in order to reclaim their responsibility in the classroom.

Student Teachers as Reformers

It is clear in the conversations excerpted in this chapter that student teachers did not dominate, and in many instances did not take equal part in, teacher-researcher school-site meetings. In most instances, cooperating teachers rather than university-based supervisors or student teachers themselves took the lead. Across contexts in the program, however, we have mounting anecdotal as well as empirical evidence that student teachers' emerging theories of practice are deeply embedded in their observations and conversations with experienced mentors who work against the grain, as well as in their readings of and writings about a rich and diverse collection of theoretical and pedagogical literature.[9] In this final section, I present several excerpts from one student teachers's journals, essays, and post-program interviews in order to shed light on the link between student teachers' opportunities to work with reformers and their interpretations and perspectives on their own work as teachers.

Maggie Schmidt was one of the four student teachers placed at Community Central Lower School, an independent center-city Philadelphia school with its roots in progressive philosophy and Quaker education (see Table 1). As mentioned earlier in this chapter, Community Central's emergent curriculum, diverse student population, and strong commitment to community created a culture of collaboration and developed a tradition of reform and critique of much of public and private school practice. In an interview at the end of her student-teaching program, Maggie talked about the influence on her of the culture of collaboration that exists in the school as well as in meetings with cooperating teachers:

I was at Community Central. It's a place that's almost too good to be true, really. Of course it's a private school so it's not part of a school system. Everyone there collaborates, everyone talks about everything, specialists work hand in hand with the teachers, the principal is wonderful. It's really an ideal environment. In some ways I think that's [been] a detriment to me because in some ways it makes me unprepared to deal with the reality, but on the other hand I think it was really good for me to see. Now I have a vision of what can happen in a school between people as opposed to going out there and just saying, "Well forget it, it's a pipe dream to want this type of collaboration, this type of work." It's really a very ideal place as far as those types of relationships go. . . . I feel like I have a sense of direction, I know what to look for. I don't think I had that before. I think I was very fortunate to have been at Central at the time I was — to be able to participate in all this thinking, collaboration, discussion.

As her words indicate, it was critical for Maggie and for many other student teachers not simply to read about, but also to participate in, a reformed professional culture. Their experiences demonstrated that alternative ways of teaching and teachers working collaboratively were not just the "pipe dreams" of university-based teacher educators, but were instead a possible reality.

One of the central themes that emerges from Maggie's journals and essays during her student-teaching year is the tension between respecting and controlling children. Working and talking regularly with experienced teachers allowed her to observe, reflect on, and question their ways of working with children, and also prompted her to interrogate these in relation to her own school experiences and what she had come to think of as the "normal" school relationships of teachers and children.

In her first journal entry about Community Central, for example, Maggie wrote about the cooperating teachers' attitudes toward children, as well as their attitudes toward the school and their own work as teachers, attitudes that struck her as quite different from that of other teachers:

There are many things about the staff here which I find quite striking, but foremost among these are their high regard for the school and their high regard for the children. . . . I have spoken to many many teachers in my life — from friends of my parents to day camp co-workers, to my own former teachers — and while many of them have expressed deeply felt feelings of love/commitment toward their students, I cannot recall any who had anything particularly complimentary to say about the school or school district in which they worked. At Community Central, however, I have heard many teachers express their considerable pleasure about working in an environment which they consider exciting, fair, supportive, and respectful of their professionalism. . . . We (the student teachers) have been made to feel so welcome here! I felt very comfortable at the faculty and [teacher-research] team meetings — not like an outsider at all.

Maggie continued in a number of journal entries to reflect on teachers' ways of respecting and working with children. She commented in detail about their approach to "controlling" children after she had attended back-to-school night several weeks later and heard the principal's address to the parents:

[The principal's] speech dealt with the themes of two of my previous journals and thus was of great interest to me — the themes of how different "discipline" at

Community Central is from that of other places in my experience, and of the degree to which one's knowledge of a child's personal life comes into play in dealing with him/her. Certainly the two issues have a lot to do with each other, although I didn't deal with them that way in my journals. I'm very curious as to how much these two issues interact, and also where one draws the line between them — for example, how many violent incidents does one accept from the child mentioned above before some type of stricter disciplinary action is taken? Or if two children are consistently getting into fights (not with each other), and one has a more difficult home situation that the other, is it fair to treat that child more leniently than the other?

Maggie wrote about the tensions between discipline and respect for children throughout much of the school year, especially when the behavior of her experienced teacher colleagues seemed to her to be most against the grain, or most unlike that which she took for granted. As she talked about these issues with her cooperating teacher, her university supervisor, and in weekly group meetings, she raised a number of questions about the interrelationships of culture, community, and ways of raising children. She began to wrestle with questions about how to have respectful relationships with children in more traditional kinds of school settings and about the conflict that sometimes arises between teachers' views of what's best for children and what their own parents and community may believe.

It is becoming more and more clear to me how much the Quaker ideas of responsibility and cooperation influence the tone of Community Central. In particular, I witnessed two "disciplinary" actions last week, which I found striking in contrast to my own experience of school "discipline" and what it entails. The first situation involved a castle, which two of the children had built together. The two [first-grade] boys involved became embroiled in a furious battle over who should get to take the castle home. Susan [the cooperating teacher] tried to get the two to talk through their problem, even at one point suggesting the possibility of leaving the castle at school so that they both could use it (an idea which they angrily rejected), but to no avail. Neither child would compromise, except in a very angry/bitter manner, which Susan did not allow because she felt that it wouldn't truly be a mutually agreed upon compromise. When all of Susan's attempts had failed, she sought out "Teacher Rachel," the director of the school, to talk to the children. The boys were told that Teacher Rachel would help them sort out their problem, which indeed she did. (They agreed, after all, to leave the castle at school, and signed a contract to that effect. Both children seemed pleased with this arrangement, and in fact, were inseparable pals for the rest of the day.)

The whole incident was, to me, quite antithetical to my conception of being "sent to the principal's office." The children were not scolded, either by Susan or Rachel, and no attempt was made to make them feel ashamed of what many might call their "bad" behavior. The principal was portrayed not as someone in authority who was going to discipline them or solve the problem for them in her own way, but rather as an outside party coming in to facilitate their negotiations. The scenario bore more resemblance to the calling in of a federal mediator than it did to "going to the principal."

In the next section of her journal, Maggie described her cooperating teachers' handling of a day when the children were unusually rowdy. The teacher canceled one favorite activity, and instead gave the children an extra recess to allow them to let off steam.

The children were thus given a clear message about acceptable classroom behavior and were given a sense of empowerment — "This only happens if you make it happen" — both without yelling or putting down the children.

I found both of these situations fascinating and quite indicative of the atmosphere of the school. However, as someone who in all likelihood will not end up working in a private Quaker school, I wonder how I could handle a similar situation in a public-school setting.

On and off throughout her student-teaching year, Maggie wrote about the importance of the "vision" she was gaining from the cooperating teachers group at Community Central, but also struggled with what she anticipated would be the problems of living by that vision in another community and another school culture. She repeatedly played off what she observed and talked about with her cooperating teachers on the one hand, and her own experiences as a school child and what she had come to expect of most schools on the other.

Maggie did end up teaching at a private school for her first year, but a private school as different from Community Central as it could possibly have been. Riverstreet Academy was a small and very ill-equipped nursery and elementary school located in the heart of a crowded urban area in New Jersey. A tiny storefront school, the Academy served the children of welfare mothers involved in a state work program. Maggie's kindergarten class was composed of three Hispanic and twenty-four Black children from the immediate inner-city area, for whom the state provided all-day tuition so their mothers could work. Maggie had almost no resources, very little assistance, and none of the professional collaboration and colleagueship she had learned to value at Community Central. There is a great deal to say about Maggie's struggle to survive in this very difficult setting and, almost against all odds, to teach a progressive curriculum and respond to the needs of the children. But Maggie's own words, written in an essay at the end of her first year of teaching, are probably the most effective way to substantiate the point that the issues and questions she had a chance to consider in the company of experienced teachers during her student teaching time helped her construct the meanings of her own later teaching experiences.

As part of our follow-up study of their program, the student teachers in Maggie's cohort were interviewed three times and wrote two essays during their first year as teachers. For one of the essays, we invited the group to read Herbert Kohl's review of *Among Schoolchildren* by Tracy Kidder, which appeared in *The Nation* (1989), and then write about some of their own first-year experiences. In his review, Kohl was critical of Kidder, and also of the teacher, Chris Zajac, particularly for her unquestioning adherence to the textbook curriculum and her compulsion to maintain control. In her essay, Maggie reflected on Zajac's teaching, Kohl's critique, and her own year-long struggle at Riverstreet Academy. The threads of her earlier student-teaching journal entries — especially her comments about discipline, respect, and community — are quite visible in the fabric of her first year essay, part of which appears below:

> While I agree with Kohl's assertion that "empowerment" is preferable to "control," I cannot help but feel that his views present a gross oversimplification, particularly when it comes to interacting with children from an urban population.
>
> To begin with, socioeconomic issues are not the only factors at work in a city classroom. As I reflect on the control problems in my own classroom this past year

— and yes, "control" was an issue for me, as it was for Chris Zajac — sorry, Mr. Kohl — I have to conclude that the relatively low socioeconomic status of my students was less of a factor than the cultural differences which come into play when a middle-class White teacher enters a primarily Black urban classroom. . . .

[Here is] my dilemma, or rather, dilemmas. Do I continue trying to maintain control using means with which I am . . . familiar/comfortable (offering choices, keeping my voice down, etc.), but which are often ineffective? Do I remain true to my beliefs at the expense of my classroom time and my personal sanity? Do I compromise my beliefs and do what is "practical" in order to have the day run more smoothly? . . .

I am still negotiating my way through these issues, trying to find a compromise that I can live with and that my students can learn with. . . .

It would be nice to think, as Kohl clearly does, that my efforts to empower my kindergartners will eventually eradicate the need for classroom discipline — but I certainly do not see that as being the case. While my gut reaction to that word, "control," is a negative one, the reality of the matter is that a teacher *does* need to maintain control in the classroom. The issue, then, is not one of "to control or not to control" but rather how to maintain a level of control that is not invasive of my students' right to empowerment and their development of *self*-discipline.

I am still not sure what the proper course of action is in my case. I continue to struggle with conflicting ideas, values, feelings, and realities. What I *am* sure of is that this is not an easy issue in any case.

Maggie's reflections are reminiscent of the intellectual work accomplished in the school-site group meetings described earlier in this article. As did the small groups of cooperating teachers and student teachers, Maggie makes problematic the interrelationships of culture, class, school-community relationships, democratic education, and classroom control. And she concludes, as the school-site groups often did, that although the moral and ethical dimensions of their dilemmas have no clear-cut solutions, they must be confronted and grappled with.

CONCLUSION

Though a deep intellectual discourse among student teachers and their school and university mentors is essential in light of the larger reform agenda for U.S. education (Lanier, 1986), it is uncommon and difficult to sustain during the student-teaching period (Calderhead, 1989; Zeichner et al., 1988).[10] And yet, as the excerpts throughout this chapter demonstrate, it *is* essential and possible. Indeed, the conversations that occurred in school-site meetings over the course of a year provide a "proof of possibility" of rich and complex discourse among experienced teachers and student teachers. This discourse is more provocative than the exchanges common in clinical supervision and wider ranging than the feedback usually given in response to particular lessons or teaching techniques. It is clear in the literature, however, that conventional supervisory structures are unlikely to generate this kind of discourse (Zeichner et al., 1988; Zeichner & Liston, 1985).

Teaching against the Grain: Alternative Roles and Structures

What made this kind of discourse possible was the combination of several program structures. Most importantly, the foundation for all the structures was a deep commitment to the development of "collaborative resonance," or intensification of opportunities to learn from teaching through the co-labor of communities. These communities were composed of school-based cooperating teachers, university-based program directors and course instructors, and student teachers and supervisors who straddled the ground between them. Underlying the work of the community was respect for the knowledge and expertise of those who had invested their professional lives in work inside schools, as well as those who had developed their knowledge of teaching through work about, but primarily outside of, schools. Student teachers were invited, and indeed expected, to raise questions and pose problems in the language of both school and university. They were expected to weave their emerging critiques with the threads of both insider and outsider knowledge. In contrast to programs based on critical dissonance, then, where the intention is to interrupt the effects of student teachers' school-based experiences, programs based on collaborative resonance aim to capitalize on these. They do so by teaching critical perspectives and alternative interpretations at the university, but also placing students within a culture of reform for their student-teaching experiences.

The commitment to building collaborative resonance was instantiated in several key social and organizational structures: university-site monthly seminars where teacher-researcher teams from all school sites met together over the course of a year to consider teaching and learning across grades, schools, and school systems; three publications, distributed locally, featuring news, opinion, and essays by past and present project participants; dissemination and discussion of common readings in the various sites; co-planning by teacher educators and school-based teachers of seminar topics, student teachers' assignments, and program strategies; and participation by project members (including students) in local, regional, and national networks of teacher researchers.

Second, as part of a community of co-learners, the roles of all project participants were redefined. Student teachers were expected to construct their own emerging theories of teaching and learning, call into question conventional practices, write about their work, and participate with their experienced mentors as inquiring professionals. It was understood that the primary role of students was *not* to imitate the instructional styles of their mentors. Concurrently, it became clear that the role of cooperating teachers was much more extensive than the demonstration and evaluation of teaching strategies. Some cooperating teachers had been active for many years in teacher organizations that promoted collaborative inquiry, social responsibility, progressive education, and curriculum reconstruction. They brought an inquiry-centered perspective to their roles and worked to articulate their perspectives to student teachers and support students' initial forays into inquiry. In addition, the role of the university supervisor was redefined to include research on practice and co-inquiry. Supervision-as-inquiry meant that in addition to their regular meetings with students and cooperating teachers, supervisors also met regularly with project leaders to reflect on their work as teacher educators and compare the nature of their interactions with students and teachers to the goals and intentions of the program. This provided a connection between supervisor and pre-service curriculum that is sometimes missing in student-teaching programs.

Finally, the very existence of weekly school-site meetings helped to make possible an intellectually based student teacher/experienced teacher discourse on teaching and learning. Site meetings of at least forty-five minutes per week were built into the requirements of the program, allowing enough time for the beginnings of substantive discussion. Students' teaching placements for a full year permitted continuity of discussions and supported the development of each teacher-researcher group as a community, across grade levels and experiences. This was possible in part because group members came to know one another's contexts of reference and to see one another's growth from the long view. Finally, and perhaps most importantly, school-site meetings were *not* set up according to the conventional model of clinical supervision, which more or less necessitates that the topic of discussion is feedback and evaluation of individual lessons. To the contrary, in the site-meeting context, individual lessons could not be the topic of conversation since the seven to nine participants in each group worked in different classrooms. Together these critical features of the program — the larger collaborative community, the redefinition of roles, and the weekly, year-long inquiry sessions — created participation structures (Erickson & Schultz, 1981) for school-site conversations that had built into them the expectation of serious talk about teaching and reforming teaching, and made it possible for these kinds of conversations to occur (Cochran-Smith, 1989).

Teaching against the Grain: Alternative Themes and Visions

One of the most important things that happened at school-site meetings was that student teachers were exposed to certain visions of teaching that are not necessarily in keeping with the norms of the profession. "Vision" is generally taken to mean the physical sense of sight or the act of seeing with the eye. However, additional definitions of the word include "that which is seen by other than normal sight" and "the ability to perceive something not actually visible." These meanings of vision help to clarify why it is critical that student teachers have opportunities to talk and work with teachers who are actively engaged in school reform from inside schools. Braided into the social and intellectual relationships of student teachers and experienced reforming teachers is exploration of alternative ways to think about and talk about teaching, ways perhaps not normally seen by teachers and administrators who work *with* the grain but also not normally seen by university-based teachers and researchers who work *outside* of schools. Working with experienced school-based reformers exposes student teachers to alternative visions of teaching that enrich, but also alter, the perspectives they learn in their university courses, as well as the perspectives they learn from the larger culture of teaching.

Reformers' visions of teaching include alternative ways of interpreting classroom events, thinking through conflicts with parents or administrators, and interpreting children's strengths and vulnerabilities. They include alternative ways of documenting and measuring learning, transforming and constructing curriculum, and thinking through issues of race, class, and culture. Table 2 summarizes five of the themes of teaching against the grain that were explored in the school-site conversations I have reported in this chapter and in the program more generally.

217

TABLE 2
Teaching against the Grain: Five Themes

1. *Problematics*
   a. The language, practices, and policies of teaching and schooling are socially constructed and evolving, not given and static.
   b. Teachers raise questions, challenge assumptions, and examine both the long- and short-term consequences of standard practice.

2. *Knowledge for Teaching*
   a. Teachers are knowledge-makers and theory-generators, as well as knowledge-users and theory-translators.
   b. Teachers have expertise based on their inside-school perspectives that is different from, and as valuable as, the expertise of outside researchers, administrators, and specialists.
   c. Teachers draw on outsiders' and insiders' expertise as well as on their own knowledge of the politics of schooling to make decisions and, when necessary, challenge others' decisions in order to protect and support their students.

3. *Curriculum and Instruction*
   a. Teachers are the creators and interpreters of curriculum, not just its implementors.
   b. Teachers adjust, adapt, discard, and construct the curriculum so that it builds on the resources of their students, exposes them to a multicultural world, and prepares them to participate in a democracy.
   c. To teach effectively, teachers are continuously involved in a process of theory-building and theory-using, based on close observations of children, collaborative reflections on experience, and wide reading and writing in content and pedagogy, as well as many other areas — there is no empirical warrant for the most effective teaching techniques.

4. *Students*
   a. Students are individual learners, who bring their own resources to the learning context and construct their own meanings from it.
   b. Students' vulnerabilities are best addressed by adjusting the learning context to tap into those resources and build on students' strengths.
   c. Close observations from multiple perspectives help teachers learn how to teach the individual child, as well as all other children.

5. *Teaching, Learning, and Reforming*
   a. Learning to teach is a process that begins before the pre-service period and continues throughout the lifetime
   b. Learning to teach is a process of collaborating with school-based, community-based, and university-based colleagues in order to examine assumptions, generalize to and from individual cases, and know one's own knowledge
   c. Teachers sustain their commitments and enhance their expertise through a process of self-critical and systematic inquiry about their work
   d. Reforming is an integral part of the social, intellectual, ethical, and political activity of teaching
   e. Teachers' most visible work as reformers is inside-out and bottom-up, but they also collaborate on reforms spear-headed outside of schools and from the top down within schools

Struggling with experienced teachers who are working to reform teaching within complicated and highly specific situations inside of schools is the only context within which student teachers can have theory- and practice-based conversations that deal with the extraordinary complexity of teaching and reforming teaching. There is a paradox, then, in learning to teach against the grain — it is only in the apparent "narrowness" of work in particular classrooms and in the "boundedness" of discussions of highly contextualized instances of practice that student teachers actually have opportunities to confront the broadest themes of reform. Essentially this means that the only way for beginners to learn to be both educators and activists is to struggle over time in the company of experienced teachers who are themselves committed to collaboration and reform in their own classrooms, schools, and communities.

There are many people who are involved in the struggle for educational reform — teachers, administrators, parents, teacher educators, researchers, consultants, and supervisors. In some instances, reformers are located in small pockets within much larger institutions; in other instances, whole faculties or large sub-groups of faculties are working together to reinvent school and institutional structures, alter roles and responsibilities, and recreate curricula. One significant way to expand and build on reform efforts is to link student teachers with experienced and new educational reformers. As communities of school- and university-based teachers develop, they become known outside of their own groups, and others come to join them in their work. Experienced reformers share their strategies as well as their questions with colleagues who are newer to the enterprise of teaching against the grain. In a community based on co-labor, each individual's opportunity to learn from teaching is intensified and enriched by the questions, struggles, and triumphs of every other individual.

NOTES

1. This analysis draws on my experiences as teacher and teacher educator over the last nineteen years, as well as on data collected from one innovative student teaching program over a three-year period. Materials considered include: dialogue journals, essays on teaching and learning, audio-recorded weekly school-site meetings and monthly university seminars, small-scale classroom studies, and program documents. Research methods are described in Cochran-Smith (1989).
2. In a review of alternatives in pre-service education, Feiman-Nemser (1990) points out that programs with a "critical/social orientation" combine a radical critique of schooling with a progressive social vision. These are clearly in the minority of teacher-education programs. She cites only two examples — the "New College" experiment at Teachers College from 1932–1936, and the current University of Wisconsin-Madison program in elementary education. Similarly, in Goodlad's (1990) recent survey of pre-service programs nationwide, only 5 percent of student and faculty respondents, when questioned about the role of teachers in schools, alluded to the idea that the teacher could be an agent for change, and no program respondents indicated that they intentionally placed student teachers in centers of school renewal or reform (Edmundsen, 1990). See also Stallings and Kowalski (1990) for a review of research on professional development schools, portal schools, and laboratory schools, and Wilbur, Lambert, and Young (1988) for an overview of models of school-university partnerships.
3. This list of assumptions is based on a more elaborated conceptual analysis of innovative student-teaching programs in Cochran-Smith (1990, p. 183), wherein programs based on critical dissonance, collaborative resonance, and consonance (a third approach that is not aimed at preparing student teachers to challenge the status quo,

and which I do not describe in this chapter) are analyzed; the analysis includes examples of programs.

4. Project START is supported by grants from the Fund for the Improvement of Post-secondary Education (FIPSE), the Milken Family Foundation, and the National Council of Teachers of English Research Foundation. Underlying the program is a "theory of practice," which unites particular views of teaching, knowledge in teaching, and learning to teach. These are described in Cochran-Smith (1989).

5. We have argued elsewhere (Cochran-Smith & Lytle, 1990; Lytle & Cochran-Smith, 1990) that teacher research enfranchises the teacher as a contributor to the knowledge base about teaching and learning. A working typology of teacher research — essay, journals, oral inquiry processes, and classroom studies — acknowledges the array of writing by teachers that may properly be regarded as research. In Project START, student teachers have the opportunity to engage in all four types of research.

6. Names of participants and schools are pseudonyms; excerpts from school-site conversations have been edited for length and clarity.

7. Research Assistants Alisa Belzer and Delia Turner read, organized, and marked transcriptions of more than seventy school-site discussions. Working with them has enriched the interpretations in this chapter.

8. Notations following names indicate whether the speaker is a Cooperating Teacher (CT) or a Student Teacher (ST) and what grade level he or she teaches; for example, CT 3 indicates that the speaker is a Cooperating Teacher in a third-grade classroom.

9. The accumulating data are part of a ten-year, two-part study to document the developmental course, kinds of learning, and eventual consequences of the curriculum. The first traces the progress of one cohort of student teachers throughout the pre-service program and into the first year of teaching, exploring students' opportunities to learn to be teachers and reformers within the social and organizational contexts of the program. The second is a longitudinal study of the intellectual lives and professional careers of a smaller group of the same student teachers that follows them through the early career years, a time when new teachers often redefine their knowledge and make major career decisions. Both draw on essays, studies, and commentaries by teacher researchers analyzing their own learning experiences as student teachers, cooperating teachers, and supervisors in Project START, as well as in-depth interviews, teacher-researcher group meetings, and program documents (see Cochran-Smith, 1989, 1990, 1991, and other work in progress).

10. Each and every school-site conversation was *not* provocative and deeply intellectual. In fact, a number of conversations, especially early in the year, centered on practical matters, and some of the conversations at every school site were superficial or truncated. However, as the above examples show, many conversations were rich and probing, and through them participants accomplished a great deal of intellectual work.

REFERENCES

Aronowitz, S., & Giroux, H. (1985). *Education under siege.* New York: New World Foundation.

Berlak, A., & Berlak, H. (1981). *Dilemmas of schooling: Teaching and social change.* London: Methuen.

Beyer, L. (1984). Field experience, ideology and the development of critical reflectivity. *Journal of Teacher Education, 35*(3), 36–41.

Beyer, L. (1986). Critical theory and the art of teaching. *Journal of Curriculum and Supervision, 1*(3), 221–232.

Borko, H., Livingston, C., McCaleb, J., & Mauro, L. (1988). Student teachers' planning and post-lesson reflections: Patterns and implications for teacher preparation. In J. Calderhead (Ed.), *Teachers' professional learning* (pp. 55–83). London: Falmer Press.

Calderhead, J. (1989). Reflective teaching and teacher education. *Teaching and Teacher Education, 5*(1), 43–52.

Carini, P. (1986). *Prospect's documentary processes.* Bennington, VT: Prospect Center and School.

Carter, K. (1988). Using cases to frame mentor-novice conversations about teaching. *Theory into Practice, 27*(3), 214–222.

Clift, R., Veal, M. L., Johnson, M., & Holland, P. (1990). Restructuring teacher education through collaborative action research. *Journal of Teacher Education, 41*(2), 52–62.

Cochran-Smith, M. (1989). *Of questions not answers: The discourse of student teachers and their school and university mentors.* Paper presented at annual meeting of American Educational Research Association, San Francisco.

Cochran-Smith, M. (1990). *Student teachers and teacher research: Learning to think like a teacher.* Paper presented at annual meeting of American Educational Research Association, Boston.

Cochran-Smith, M. (1991). Reinventing student teaching. *Journal of Teacher Education, 42*(2), 104–118.

Cochran-Smith, M., Larkin, J., & Lytle, S. (1990). *Network of new and experienced urban teachers.* Unpublished yearly report to the Fund for the Improvement of Post-Secondary Education, Washington, DC.

Cochran-Smith, M., & Lytle, S. L. (1990). Research on teaching and teacher research: The issues that divide. *Educational Researcher, 19*(2), 2–11.

Cochran-Smith, M., & Lytle, S. (1992). Communities for teacher research: Fringe or forefront? *American Journal of Education, 100,* 298–324.

Corbett, H. D. (1980). Using occupational socialization research to explain patterns of influence during student teaching. *Journal of Teacher Education, 31*(6), 11–13.

Edmundsen, P. J. (1990). A normative look at the curriculum in teacher education. *Phi Delta Kappan, 71,* 717–722.

Erickson, F., & Schultz, J. (1981). When is a context? Some issues and methods in the analysis of social competence. In J. Green & C. Wallat (Eds.), *Ethnography and language in educational settings* (pp. 147–159). Norwood, NJ: Ablex.

Evertson, C. M. (1990). Bridging knowledge and action through clinical experiences. In David D. Dill and Associates (Ed.), *What teachers need to know* (pp. 94–109). San Francisco: Jossey-Bass.

Feiman-Nemser, S. (1983). Learning to teach. In L. S. Shulman & G. Sykes (Eds.), *Handbook of teaching and policy* (pp. 150–170). New York: Longman.

Feiman-Nemser, S. (1990). Teacher preparation: Structural and conceptual alternatives. In W. R. Houston (Ed.), *Handbook of research on teacher education* (pp. 212–233). New York: Macmillan.

Feiman-Nemser, S., & Buchmann, M. (1985). Pitfalls of experience in teacher preparation. *Teachers College Record, 87,* 53–65.

Fenstermacher, G. (1990). Some moral considerations on teaching as a profession. In J. Goodlad, R. Soder, & K. A. Sirotnik (Eds.), *The moral dimensions of teaching* (pp. 130–151). San Francisco: Jossey-Bass.

Ginsburg, M. (1988). *Contradictions in teacher education and society: A critical analysis.* Philadelphia: Falmer Press.

Giroux, H. (1984). Rethinking the language of schooling. *Language Arts, 61*(1), 33–40.

Gitlin, A., & Teitelbaum, K. (1983). Linking theory and practice: The use of ethnographic methodology by prospective teachers. *Journal of Education for Teaching, 9,* 225–234.

Goodlad, J. I. (1984). *A place called school.* New York: McGraw-Hill.

Goodlad, J. I. (1990). Studying the education of educators: From conception to findings. *Phi Delta Kappan, 71,* 698–701.

Goodman, J. (1986a). Making early field experience meaningful: A critical approach. *Journal of Teacher Education, 12*(2), 109–125.

Goodman, J. (1986b). University education courses and the professional preparation of teachers: A descriptive analysis. *Teaching and Teacher Education, 2,* 341–353.

Gramsci, A. (1916/1977). Indifference. In Q. Hoare (Ed.), *Antonio Gramsci: Selections from political writings 1910–1920* (pp. 17–18). London: Lawrence & Wishart.

Grant, C. A., & Secada, W. G. (1990). Preparing teachers for diversity. In W. R. Houston (Ed.), *Handbook of research on teacher education* (pp. 403–422). New York: Macmillan.

Greene, M. (1986). Reflections and passion in teaching. *Journal of Curriculum and Supervision, 2*, 68–81.

Griffin, G. (1986). Clinical teacher education. In J. Hoffman & S. Edwards (Eds.), *Reality and reform of teacher education.* New York: Random House.

Hursh, D. (1988). *Liberal discourse and organizational structure as barriers to reflective teaching: An ethnographic study.* Unpublished manuscript, Swarthmore College.

Knoblauch, C. H., & Brannon, L. (1988). Knowing our knowledge: A phenomenological basis for teacher research. In L. Z. Smith (Ed.), *Audits of meaning: A festschrift in honor of Ann E. Berthoff* (pp. 17–28). Portsmouth, NH: Boynton/Cook.

Kohl, H. (1989, November 6). Teach by number schools. *The Nation,* pp. 537–538.

Lampert, M. (1985). How do teachers manage to teach? Perspectives on problems in practice. *Harvard Educational Review, 55,* 178–194.

Lanier, J. E. (1986). Research on teacher education. In M. C. Wittrock (Ed.), *Handbook of research on teaching* (3rd ed.) (pp. 527–569). New York: Macmillan.

Larkin, J. M. (1990). *Reinventing urban teacher education.* Paper presented at annual meeting of American Association of Colleges of Teacher Education, Chicago.

Lieberman, A., & Miller, L. (1984). *Teachers, their world and their work.* Washington, DC: Association for Supervision and Curriculum Development.

Little, J. W. (1987). Teachers as colleagues. In V. Richardson-Koehler (Ed.), *Educators' handbook: A research perspective* (pp. 194–218). New York: Longman.

Lytle, S. L., & Cochran-Smith, M. (1990). Learning from teacher research. *Teachers College Record, 92,* 83–103.

Lytle, S. L., & Cochran-Smith, M. (1991). *Teacher research as a way of knowing.* Paper presented at annual meeting of American Educational Research Association, Chicago.

Lytle, S. L., & Fecho, R. (1989). *Meeting strangers in familiar places: Teacher collaboration by cross-visitation.* Paper presented at annual meeting of American Educational Research Association, San Francisco.

Richardson-Koehler, V. (1988). Barriers to the effective supervision of student teachers: A field study. *Journal of Teacher Education, 39*(2), 28–34.

Rochester City Schools/University of Rochester Ford Foundation Report. (1988–1989). *Professional development site: A community of learners. Part A.* Rochester, NY.

Ross, D. (1988). Action research for preservice teachers: A description of why and how. *Peabody Journal of Education, 64,* 131–150.

Schön, D. A. (1983). *The reflective practitioner.* San Francisco: Jossey-Bass.

Schön, D. A. (1987). *Educating the reflective practitioner.* San Francisco: Jossey-Bass.

Smyth, W. J. (1987). *A rationale for teachers' critical pedagogy: A handbook.* Victoria, Australia: Deakin University Press.

Stallings, J. A., & Kowalski, T. (1990). Research on professional development schools. In W. R. Houston (Ed.), *Handbook of research on teacher education* (pp. 251–263). New York: Macmillan.

Su, Z. (1990). The function of the peer group in teacher socialization. *Phi Delta Kappan, 71,* 723–727.

Tabachnick, B. R., & Zeichner, K. (1984). The impact of the student teaching experience on the development of teacher perspectives. *Journal of Teacher Education, 35,* 28–36.

Tom, A. R. (1985). Inquiring into inquiry-oriented teacher education. *Journal of Teacher Education, 36*(5), 35–44.

Wilbur, T. P., Lambert, L. M., & Young, M. J. (1988). *School college partnerships: A look at the major national models.* Washington, DC: National Association of Secondary School Principals.

Willis, P. E. (1978). *Learning to labour.* Hampshire, Eng.: Gower.

Zeichner, K. (1986). Preparing reflective teachers: An overview of instructional strategies which have been employed in preservice teacher education. *International Journal of Educational Research, 7,* 565–575.

Zeichner, K., & Liston, D. (1985). Varieties of discourse in supervisory conferences. *Teaching and Teacher Education, 1,* 155–174.

Zeichner, K., & Liston, D. (1987). Teaching student teachers to reflect. *Harvard Educational Review, 57,* 1–22.

Zeichner, K., Liston, D., Mahlios, M., & Gomez, M. (1988). The structure and goals of a student teaching program and the character and quality of supervisory discourse. *Teaching and Teacher Education, 4,* 349–362.

Zeichner, K., Tabachnick, B., & Densmore, K. (1987). Individual, institutional and cultural influences on the development of teachers' craft knowledge. In J. Calderhead (Ed.), *Exploring teachers' thinking* (pp. 21–59). London: Cassell.

Zumwalt, K. I. (1989). Beginning professional teachers: The need for a curricular vision of teaching. In M. Reynolds (Ed.), *Knowledge base for the beginning teacher* (pp. 173–184). New York: Pergamon Press, for the American Association of Colleges for Teacher Education.

About the Contributors

NICHOLAS C. BURBULES, Associate Professor in the Department of Educational Policy Studies at the University of Illinois, Urbana-Champaign, is interested in the philosophy of education. He is also the editor of *Educational Theory*. His publications include *Dialogue in Teaching: Theory and Practice* (1993) and "Communicative Virtues and Educational Relations" in H. Alexander, Ed., *Philosophy of Education 1992: Proceedings of the Forty-Eighth Annual Meeting of the Philosophy of Education Society* (with S. Rice, 1993).

KIMBERLY CHRISTENSEN is Associate Professor of Economics and Women's Studies at the State University of New York at Purchase. Her professional interests focus on the economics of race, class, and gender. She is a member of ACT UP/New York, an AIDS activism/education organization, and has received the Statewide Chancellor's Award for Teaching Excellence. She is a contributor to *Women, AIDS, and Activism*, edited by the ACT UP/NY Women and AIDS Book Group (1990), and is author of "Political Determinants of Income Changes for African American Women and Men" in *Review of Radical Political Economics* (1992).

MARILYN COCHRAN-SMITH is Associate Professor of Education at the University of Pennsylvania Graduate School of Education. She is also Director of Project START, a fifth-year pre-service program in elementary education at the University. Her major professional interests are teacher research, teacher education, and early literacy. Her publications include *The Making of a Reader* (1984), *Learning to Write Differently* (with C. L. Paris and J. L. Kahn, 1991), and *Inside/Outside: Teacher Research and Knowledge* (with S. L. Lytle, 1993).

MARCIA CURTIS, Deputy Director of the Writing Program at the University of Massachusetts at Amherst, is interested in basic writing and multicultural education, as well as composing and computers. Her recent articles include "The Virtual Context: Ethnography with Computer-Equipped Writing Classrooms" in G. Hawisher and P. LeBlanc, Eds., *Re-Imagining Computers and Composition: Teaching and Research in the Virtual Age* (1992), and "Diversity in Required Writing Courses" in M. Adams, Ed., *Promoting Diversity in College Classrooms: Innovative Responses for the Curriculum, Faculty, and Institutions* (with A. Herrington, 1992).

ELIZABETH ELLSWORTH is Associate Professor in the Department of Curriculum and Instruction at the University of Wisconsin-Madison. Her work focuses on the intersections and collisions of cultural studies, media studies, and pedagogy. Her recent publications include "AIDS: Cultural Analysis/Cultural Activism" in *Educational Studies* (in press), and "Representation, Self-Representation, and the Meanings of Difference: Questions for Educators" in R. Martusewicz and W. Reynolds, Eds., *Critical Perspectives in the Social Foundations* (in press).

ANNE J. HERRINGTON is Director of the Writing Program and Professor of English at the University of Massachusetts at Amherst. Her professional interests include basic writing, writing and learning across the disciplines, and multicultural education. She is coeditor of *Writing, Teaching, and Learning in the Disciplines* (with C. Moran, 1992), and coauthor of "Diversity in Required Writing Courses" in M. Adams, Ed., *Promoting Diversity*

225

in College Classrooms: Innovative Responses for the Curriculum, Faculty, and Institutions (with M. Curtis, 1992).

JUNE JORDAN, a poet and political writer, is Professor of African-American Studies and Women's Studies at the University of California at Berkeley. She was born in Harlem and raised in the Bedford-Stuyvesant neighborhood of Brooklyn, New York. She is a political columnist for *The Progressive* and a contributing editor to the *San Francisco Bay Guardian.* Her most recent books are *Technical Difficulties,* a collection of political essays, and *The Haruko/Love Poetry,* her collection of new and selected love poems.

MARY S. LEACH is Associate Professor at Ohio State University, Columbus. Gender, educational theory, and theories of difference are her major fields of interest. Her articles include "Toward Writing Feminist Scholarship into History of Education" (1990) and "Mothers of In(ter)vention: Women's Writing in Philosophy of Education" (1991), both in *Educational Theory.*

MAGDA LEWIS is a Queen's National Scholar and Assistant Professor of Sociology in the Faculty of Education at Queen's University, Kingston, Canada. Her research work investigates the possibilities and conditions for transformative pedagogy through the application of feminist politics in the classroom. She has published widely on the experiences of women in the academy; her most recent book is *Without a Word: Teaching beyond Women's Silence* (1993).

SUZANNE RICE is Assistant Professor of Educational Policy and Leadership at the University of Kansas. Her research focuses on critical theory, feminist theory, and moral education. She is coauthor of "Communicative Virtues and Educational Relations" in H. Alexander, Ed., *Philosophy of Education 1992: Proceedings of the Forty-Eighth Annual Meeting of the Philosophy of Education Society* (with N. Burbules, 1993), and author of "Teaching and Learning through Story and Dialogue" in *Educational Theory* (1993).

BEVERLY DANIEL TATUM is Associate Professor in the Department of Psychology and Education at Mount Holyoke College, South Hadley, Massachusetts. Her research interests include racial identity development theory, identity development of African-American adolescents raised in predominantly White communities, and pedagogical issues involved in teaching about oppression. She is author of *Assimilation Blues: Black Families in a White Community* (1987).

KATHLEEN WEILER is Assistant Professor of Education at Tufts University. Her major research interests include feminist pedagogy and the history of women teachers. She is author of *Women Teaching for Change* (1988), and coeditor of *Feminism and Social Justice in Education: International Perspectives* (with M. Arnot, 1993).

About the Editors

KATHRYN GEISMAR is a developmental psychologist and doctoral student at the Harvard Graduate School of Education. She has worked with Carol Gilligan and Annie Rogers on their pioneering work with adolescent girls, focusing on fostering girls' resiliency and courage through artistic expression. A former elementary school teacher, Geismar is currently focused in her research on the topic of recovery from sexual abuse, and on the development of violence prevention and intervention programs within the Cambridge (Massachusetts) public schools.

GUITELE NICOLEAU is a doctoral candidate in Administration, Planning, and Social Policy at the Harvard Graduate School of Education. The focus of her research is community education and lifelong learning, with a particular interest in educational practices that enhance the participation of marginalized voices in framing the discourse of educational policies. A native of Haiti who grew up in the United States, Nicoleau is currently writing her dissertation on the implementation of a community-based AIDS education program with Haitian adolescents in an urban community in Massachusetts.